DISTRIBUTED AND PARALLEL EMBEDDED SYSTEMS

IFIP - The International Federation for Information Processing

IFIP was founded in 1960 under the auspices of UNESCO, following the First World Computer Congress held in Paris the previous year. An umbrella organization for societies working in information processing, IFIP's aim is two-fold: to support information processing within its member countries and to encourage technology transfer to developing nations. As its mission statement clearly states,

IFIP's mission is to be the leading, truly international, apolitical organization which encourages and assists in the development, exploitation and application of information technology for the benefit of all people.

IFIP is a non-profitmaking organization, run almost solely by 2500 volunteers. It operates through a number of technical committees, which organize events and publications. IFIP's events range from an international congress to local seminars, but the most important are:

- The IFIP World Computer Congress, held every second year;
- open conferences;
- working conferences.

The flagship event is the IFIP World Computer Congress, at which both invited and contributed papers are presented. Contributed papers are rigorously refereed and the rejection rate is high.

As with the Congress, participation in the open conferences is open to all and papers may be invited or submitted. Again, submitted papers are stringently refereed.

The working conferences are structured differently. They are usually run by a working group and attendance is small and by invitation only. Their purpose is to create an atmosphere conducive to innovation and development. Refereeing is less rigorous and papers are subjected to extensive group discussion.

Publications arising from IFIP events vary. The papers presented at the IFIP World Computer Congress and at open conferences are published as conference proceedings, while the results of the working conferences are often published as collections of selected and edited papers.

Any national society whose primary activity is in information may apply to become a full member of IFIP, although full membership is restricted to one society per country. Full members are entitled to vote at the annual General Assembly, National societies preferring a less committed involvement may apply for associate or corresponding membership. Associate members enjoy the same benefits as full members, but without voting rights. Corresponding members are not represented in IFIP bodies. Affiliated membership is open to non-national societies, and individual and honorary membership schemes are also offered.

DISTRIBUTED AND PARALLEL EMBEDDED SYSTEMS

IFIP WG10.3/WG10.5 International Workshop on Distributed and Parallel Embedded Systems (DIPES'98) October 5-6, 1998, Schloß Eringerfeld, Germany

Edited by

Franz J. Rammig
University of Paderborn
Germany

SPRINGER SCIENCE+BUSINESS MEDIA, LLC

Library of Congress Cataloging-in-Publication Data

IFIP WG10.3/WG10.5 International Workshop on Distributed and Parallel Embedded Systems (1998 : Schloß Eringerfeld, Germany)
Distributed and parallel embedded systems : IFIP WG10.3/WG10.5 International Workshop on Distributed and Parallel Embedded Systems (DIPES'98), October 5-6, 1998, Schloß Eringerfeld, Germany / edited by Franz J. Rammig.

Includes bibliographical references (p.).
ISBN 978-1-4757-5006-5 ISBN 978-0-387-35570-2 (eBook)
DOI 10.1007/978-0-387-35570-2

1. Electronic data processing—Distributed processing Congresses. 2. Parallel processing (Electronic computers) Congresses. 3. Embedded computer systems Congresses. I. Rammig, F.J. II. Title.

QA76.9.D5I3477 1998
004'.36—dc21 99-37323
CIP

Printed on acid-free paper.

Contents

Preface

Embedded systems are becoming one of the major driving forces in computer science. There are studies that predict in 2010 10 times as many computer scientists to work in this area as in the traditional ones. On the other hand it is the impact of embedded information technology that dictates the pace in most engineering domains. Nearly all technical products above a certain level of complexity are not only controlled but more and more even dominated by their embedded computer system. Such systems range from telecommunications devices and any kind of consumer products to automobiles, aircrafts and even complete production lines.

Traditionally such embedded control systems have been implemented in a monolithic, centralised way. Recently distributed solutions are gaining increasing importance. In this approach the control task is carried out by a number of controllers distributed over the entire system and connected by some interconnect network, like fieldbusses. Such a distributed embedded system may consist of a few controllers, up to some hundred ones as in today's top range automobiles, or even thousands of them in the case of production lines. The individual nodes of such a network usually consist of a processor (micro controller) together with some sensors and actuators. For more demanding control applications more powerful local controllers are neccessary based on parallel architectures such as VLIW or processors with dedicated coprocessors. Distribution and parallelism in embedded systems design increase the engineering challenges and require new development methods and tools.

This book is the result of the international workshop DIPES'98 (Distributed and Parallel Embedded Systems), organised by IFIP WG 10.3 (Concurrent Systems) and WG 10.5 (Design and Engineering of Electronic Systems). The workshop took place in October 5th + 6th, 1998 in Schloss Eringerfeld near Paderborn, Germany. The authors of the contributions had the opportunity to include the results of the lively discussions during the workshop into their papers. So this book reflects the most recent point of view of experts from Brazil, Finland, France, Germany, Italy, Portugal, USA.

The book is organised in six chapters, reflecting recent trends in the field of distributed embedded systems.

- **Chapter 1** *(Formalisms for Embedded System Design)* deals with IP-based system design and various approaches to multi-language formalisms.
- **Chapter 2** *(Synthesis from Synchronous/Asynchronous Specification)* discusses alternative synthesis techniques based on Message Sequence Charts (MSC), StateCharts, and Predicate/Transition Nets.
- **Chapter 3** *(Partitioning and Load-Balancing)* contains contributions that discuss this important issue from various points of view.
- **Chapter 4** *(Verification and Validation)* includes both, formal techniques for precise verification and more pragmatic approaches to validation.

- **Chapter** *5 (Design Environments)* collects a variety of yet academic design environments for distributed embedded systems. It can be expected that these approaches will influence the industrial state of the art.
- **Chapter 6** *(Object Oriented Approaches)* finally discusses various impacts of this software engineering technique on distributed embedded systems.

Franz J. Rammig

IFIP Workshop on Distributed and Parallel Embedded Systems - DIPES'98

General Chairman

Franz J. Rammig

Program Chairman

Franz J. Rammig

Local Arrangements

Carsten Böke

Co-sponsoring Institutions

IFIP WG 10.3 (Concurrent Systems)
IFIP WG 10.5 (Design and Engineering of Electronic Systems)

Program Committee

Makoto Amamiya (Japan)
Arndt Bode (Germany)
Michel Cosnard (France)
Erik Dirkx (Belgium)
Daniel D. Gajski (USA)
Guang R. Gao (USA)
Jean-Luc Gaudiot (USA)
Morven Gentleman (Canada)
Ulrich Kiffmeier (Germany)
Ahmed Jerraya (France)
Chris Jesshope (New Zealand)
Erik Maehle (Germany)
Carlos E. Pereira (Brazil)
Franz J. Rammig (Germany)
Jean-Luc Roux (France)
Bernd-Heinrich Schmitfranz (Germany)

Acknowledgements

We thank the organisations that by their donations helped us to obtain this scientific result:

DaimlerChrysler AG Research
dSPACE GmbH
Paderborn University, Heinz Nixdorf Institut

1 FORMALISMS FOR EMBEDDED SYSTEM DESIGN

IP-CENTRIC METHODOLOGY AND SPECIFICATION LANGUAGE

System Level Design of Embedded Systems

Daniel D. Gajski, Rainer Dömer and Jianwen Zhu
Department of Information and Computer Science
University of California, Irvine
Irvine, California, USA

In this paper, we demonstrate the application of the specify-explore-refine (SER) paradigm for an IP-centric codesign of embedded systems. We describe the necessary design tasks required to map an abstract executable specification of the system to the architectural implementation model. We also describe the final and intermediate models generated as a result of these design tasks. The executable specification and its refinements should support easy insertion and reuse of IPs.

Although several languages are currently used for system design, none of them completely meets the unique requirements of system modelling with support for IP reuse. This paper discusses the requirements and objectives for system languages and describes a C-based language called SpecC, which precisely covers these requirements in an orthogonal manner.

Finally, we describe the design environment which is based on our codesign methodology.

1. Introduction

New technologies allow designers to generate chips with more than 10 million transistors on a single chip. The main problem at this complexity is designer productivity. Although the chip complexity measured in number of transistors per chip has increased at the rate of 60 percent per year in the past, the productivity measured in number of transistors designed per day by a single designer has increased only at the rate of 20 percent. This growing gap between the complexity and productivity rates may have the catastrophic effect of slowing down semiconductor industry.

One of the main solutions for solving this problem is increasing the level of abstraction in design of complex chips. The abstraction level increase should be reflected in descriptions, components, tools, and design methodology.

First, modelling or describing designs on the gate or RT level is not sufficient. Moving to executable specifications (behavior) and architectural descriptions (structure) is necessary to improve design productivity.

In order to explore different architectural solutions, we must use higher-level components beyond RTL components, such as registers, counters, ALUs, multipliers, etc. These higher-level components, frequently called IPs, are changing the business and design models. In order to use IPs, we need a methodology that will allow easy insertion of IPs in designs. This new methodology must have well-defined models of design representation, so that IP can be easily inserted or replaced when supplies disappear or IPs get discontinued. In order to achieve easy insertion and replacement, the design models must separate computation from communication, in addition to abstracting those two functions. This way, IP can be inserted by changing only the communication interface to the rest of the design.

Finally, the above IP-centric design methodology must be supported by CAD tools that will allow easy capture of executable specification, architecture exploration with IPs, and RTL hand-off to semiconductor fabs.

In this paper, we present such an IP-centric methodology, starting with an executable specification, define the abstract models used for architectural exploration, synthesis, and hand-off, and describe the necessary tools to support this methodology.

We also describe a C based language, called SpecC, for describing all the models in the methodology, and the SpecC Design Environment which supports all the transformations and explorations indicated in the methodology.

2. Related Work

For system-level synthesis, in particular codesign and coverification, academia, as well as industry, has developed a set of promising approaches and methodologies. Important university projects include Chinook [5], Cosmos [13], Cosyma [8], CoWare [23], Lycos [19], Polis [2], Ptolemy [14], Scenic [17], SpecCharts [22], Statecharts [7], and Weld [3].

Looking at this list, several systems already exist that assist designers with the design of embedded systems. However, none of todays systems covers the whole spectrum of codesign tasks. Instead, most systems focus on a subset of these problems.

3. System Design Methodology

A methodology is a set of models and transformations, possibly implemented by CAD tools, that refines the abstract, functional or behavioral specification into a detailed implementation description ready for manufacturing. The system methodology [10] starts with an *executable specification* as shown in Figure 1. This specification describes the functionality as well as the performance, power, cost and other constraints of the intended design. It does not make any premature allusions to implementation details. The specification is captured directly in a

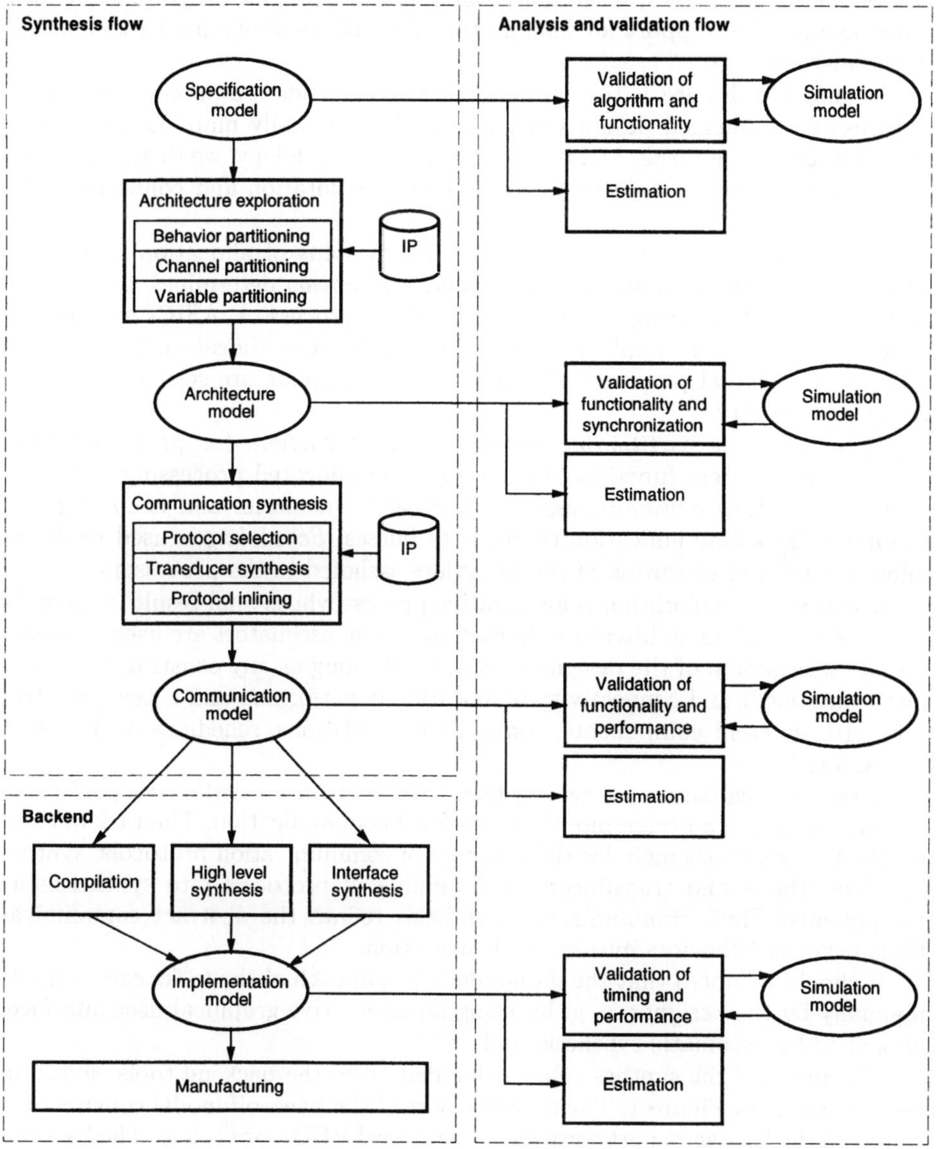

Figure 1. The codesign methodology in the SpecC Design Environment

formal specification language such as SpecC (see Section 4.3), that supports different models in the methodology.

Since designers do not like to learn the syntax and semantics of a new language, the executable specification can be captured with a graphical editor that generates the specification from well-known graphical forms, such as block diagrams, connectivity tables, communication channels, timing diagrams, bubble charts, hierarchical trees, scheduling charts, and others. Such a graphical editor must also provide support for manual transformations of one model to another in the methodology.

As shown in Figure 1, the synthesis flow of the codesign process consists of a series of well-defined design steps which will eventually map the executable specification to the target architecture. In this methodology, we distinguish two major system level tasks, namely architecture exploration and communication synthesis.

Architecture exploration includes the design steps of allocation and partitioning of behaviors, channels and variables. *Allocation* determines the number and the types of the system components, such as processors, ASICs and busses, which will be used to implement the system behavior. Allocation includes the reuse of intellectual property (IP), when IP components are selected from the component library.

Then, *behavior partitioning* distributes the behaviors (or processes) that comprise the system functionality amongst the allocated processing elements, whereas *variable partitioning* assigns variables to memories and *channel partitioning* assigns communication channels to busses. *Scheduling* is used to determine the order of execution of the behaviors assigned to the processors.

Architecture exploration is an iterative process whose final result is the definition of the system architecture. In each iteration, estimators are used to evaluate the satisfaction of the design constraints. As long as any constraints are not met, component and connectivity reallocation is performed and a new architecture with different components, connectivity, partitions, schedules or protocols is evaluated.

After the architecture model is defined, *communication synthesis* is performed in order to obtain a design model with refined communication. The task of communication synthesis includes the selection of communication protocols, synthesis of interfaces and transducers, and inlining of protocols into synthesizable components. Thus, communication synthesis refines the abstract communications between behaviors into an implementation.

It should be noted that the design decisions in each of the tasks can be made manually by the designer, e. g. by using an interactive graphical user interface, as well as by automatic synthesis tools.

The result of the synthesis flow is handed-off to the backend tools, shown in the lower part of Figure 1. The software part of the hand-off model consists of C code and the hardware part consists of behavioral VHDL or C code. The backend tools include compilers, a high-level synthesis tool and an interface synthesizer. The compilers are used to compile the software C code for the processor on which the code is mapped. The high-level synthesis tool is used to synthesize the functionality mapped to custom hardware. The interface synthesizer is used to implement the functionality of interfaces needed to connect different processors, memories and IPs.

During each design step, the design model is statically analyzed to estimate certain quality metrics such as performance, cost and power consumption. This design model is also used in simulation to verify the correctness of the design at the corresponding step. For example, at the specification stage, the simulation model is used to verify the functional correctness of the intended design. After architecture exploration, the simulation model will verify the synchronization between behaviors on different processing elements (PEs). After communication synthesis, the simulation model is used to verify the performance of the system including computation and communication.

At any stage, if the verification fails, a debugger can be used to locate and fix the errors. Usually, standard software debuggers can be used which provide the ability to set break points anywhere in the source code and allow detailed state inspection at any time.

3.1. IP Requirements

The use of Intellectual Property introduces additional requirements on the system design methodology. In order to identify the specification segments that can be implemented by an IP, or to replace one IP by another one, the system specification and its refined models must clearly identify the specific IP segment or the IP functionality must be deduced from the description. On the other hand, if the meaning of a model or one of its parts is difficult to discover, it is also difficult to see whether an IP can be used for its implementation.

This situation is well demonstrated in a much broader problem of design methodologies: simulatable vs. synthesizable languages. We know that almost any language (C, C++, Java, VHDL, Verilog, etc.) can be used for writing simulatable models. However, each design can be described in many different ways, all of them producing correct simulation results. Therefore, an IP function can be described in many different ways inside the system specification without being recognized as an IP description. In such a case, IP insertion is not possible. Similarly, replacing one IP with another with slightly different functionality or descriptions is not possible.

For example, a controller, whose computational model is a finite state machine, can be easily described by a `case` statement in which the cases represent the states. Similarly, an array of coefficients can be described with a `case` statement in which the cases represent the coefficient indices. In order to synthesize the description with these two case statements, we have to realize that the first statement should be implemented as a controller and the second as a look-up ROM. If the designer or a synthesis tool cannot distinguish between these two meanings, there is no possibility that a correct implementation can be obtained from that description although it will produce correct simulation results.

Therefore, in order to synthesize a proper architecture, we need a specification or a model that clearly identifies synthesizable functions including IP functions. In order to allow easy insertion and replacement of IPs, a model must also separate computation from communication, because different IPs have different communication protocols and busses connecting IPs may not match either of the IP protocols. The solution is to encapsulate different IPs and busses within virtual components and channels by introducing wrappers to hide detailed protocols and allow virtual objects to communicate via shared variables and complex data structures. In the methodology presented in Figure 1, the executable specification is written using shared variables for communication between behaviors or processes, while models used for architecture exploration use virtual components and channels for easy insertion and replacement of IPs. The final communication model exposes the protocols and uses again shared variables to describe individual wires and busses used in communication. Thus, the architecture exploration is performed on the model that clearly separates computations (behaviors) from communication (channels) and allows a *plug-and-play* approach for IPs.

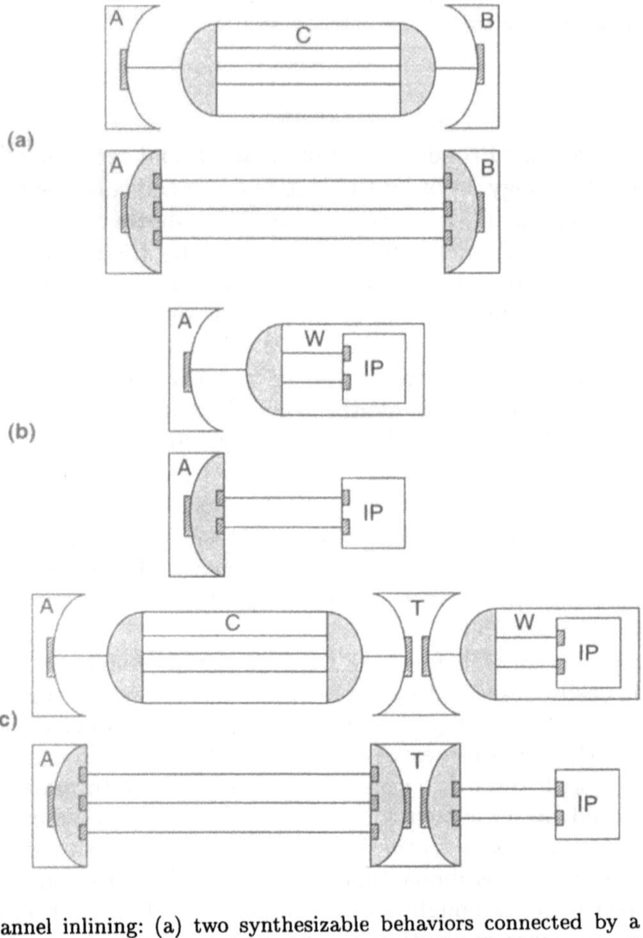

Figure 2. Channel inlining: (a) two synthesizable behaviors connected by a channel, (b) synthesizable behavior connected to an IP, (c) a synthesizable behavior connected to an IP through an incompatible channel.

However, there is a difference between functions defined in a channel and functions in a behavior. While the functions of a behavior specify its own functionality, the functions of a channel specify the functionality of the caller, in other words, when the system is implemented, they will get *inlined* into the connected behaviors or into transducers between the behaviors. When a channel is inlined, the encapsulated variables are exposed serving as communication media, and the functions become part of the caller. This is shown in Figure 2(a) where the channel C connecting behaviors A and B is inlined, assuming that A and B will be implemented as custom hardware parts. In such custom parts, the computation and communication will be realized by the same datapath and controlled by one controller.

The situation is different when a behavior is not synthesizable, such as in a processor core with a fixed protocol. This can be modelled using a *wrapper* which is a channel encapsulating a fixed behavior while providing higher-level communication functions that deal with the specific protocol of the internal component. For example, a MPEG decoder component with a wrapper can be used by other behaviors simply by calling the decode function provided by the wrapper. Figure 2(b) shows the inlining of the wrapper in component A allowing the communication between A and IP to use the IP protocol. On the other hand, whenever two channels (or wrappers) encapsulating incompatible protocols need to be connected, as shown in Figure 2(c), an interface component or transducer has to be inserted into which the channel functions will be inlined during communication refinement.

4. The Language

With this generic methodology in mind, Section 4.1 discusses the requirements and goals for system description languages and Section 4.2 compares traditional languages with these requirements. Since none of the languages supports all concepts a new modelling language called SpecC is proposed and presented in Section 4.3.

4.1. Modelling Language Requirements

For the codesign methodology presented above, it is desirable that *one* language is used for all models at all stages. Such a methodology is called ***homogeneous*** in contrast to heterogeneous approaches [14, 23], where a system is specified in one language and then is transformed into another, or is represented by a mixture of several languages at the same time.

This homogeneous methodology does not suffer from simulator interfacing problems or cumbersome translations between languages with different semantics. Instead one set of tools can be used for all models and synthesis tasks are merely transformations from one program into a more detailed one using the same language. This is also important for *reuse*, because design models in the library can be used in the system without modification (*"plug-and-play"*) and a new design can be used directly as a library component.

System design places unique requirements on the specification and modelling language being used. In particular the language must be

1. executable,
2. modular and
3. complete.

1. Executability of the language is of crucial importance for simulation. The system specification must be validated to assure that exactly the intended

functionality is captured. Simulation is also necessary for the intermediate design models whose functionality must be equivalent to the behavior of the model before the refinement.

2. Modularity is required to clearly separate functionality from communication, which is necessary in a model at a high level of abstraction. It also enables the decomposition of a system into a hierarchical network of components. *Behavioral hierarchy* is used to decompose a system's behavior into sequential or concurrent subbehaviors, whereas *structural hierarchy* decomposes a system into a set of interconnected components.
   Modularity is also required to support design reuse and the incorporation of intellectual property. During refinement, modularity helps to keep changes in the system description local so that other parts of the design are not affected. For example, communication refinement should only replace abstract channels with more detailed ones without modifying the components using these channels. The locality of changes makes refinement tools simpler and the generated results more understandable.
3. Completeness is obviously a requirement. A system language must cover all concepts commonly found in embedded systems. In addition to (a) behavioral and (b) structural hierarchy this includes (c) concurrency, (d) synchronization, (e) exception handling and (f) timing, as discussed in detail in [9]. For explicit modelling of Mealy and Moore type finite state machines, (g) state transitions have to be supported.
   Furthermore, it is desirable that these concepts are organized orthogonally (independent from each other) so that the language can be minimal. In addition to these requirements, the language should be easy to understand and easy to learn.

4.2. Traditional languages

Most traditional languages lack one or more of the requirements discussed in Section 4.1 and therefore cannot be used for system modelling without problems. Figure 3 lists examples of current languages [25, 12, 7, 22, 27, 1, 29] and shows which requirements they support and which are missing.

Because the traditional languages are not sufficient, a new language must be developed, either from scratch or as an extension of an existing language. The SpecC language [6] represents the latter approach as it is built on top of C.

4.3. The SpecC language

This section introduces the SpecC language and shows how SpecC covers all the requirements discussed before. SpecC is a superset of ANSI-C. C was selected because of its high acceptance in software development and its large library of already existing code.

A SpecC program can be executed after compilation with the SpecC compiler which first generates an intermediate C++ model of the program that is then compiled by a standard compiler for execution on the host machine.

	Verilog	VHDL	Statecharts	SpecCharts	C	Java	SpecC
Behavioral Hierarchy	○	○	●	●	○	○	●
Structural Hierarchy	●	●	○	○	○	○	●
Concurrency	●	●	●	●	○	◑	●
Synchronization	●	●	●	●	○	●	●
Exception Handling	●	○	◑	●	◑	●	●
Timing	●	●	◑	◑	○	○	●
State Transitions	○	○	●	●	○	○	●

○ not supported ◑ partly supported ● fully supported

Figure 3. Language Comparison

Modularity, providing structural and behavioral hierarchy, and the special constructs making SpecC complete are described next.

4.4. Structural Hierarchy

Semantically, the functionality of a system is captured as a a hierarchical network of behaviors interconnected by hierarchical channels. Syntactically, a SpecC program consists of a set of *behavior*, *channel* and *interface* declarations.

A *behavior* is a class consisting of a set of ports, a set of component instantiations, a set of private variables and functions, and a public `main` function. Through its ports, a behavior can be connected to other behaviors or channels in order to communicate. A behavior is called a composite behavior if it contains instantiations of child behaviors. Otherwise it is called a leaf behavior. The functionality of a behavior is specified by its functions starting with the `main` function.

A *channel* is a class that encapsulates communication. It consists of a set of variables and functions, called methods, which define a communication protocol. A channel can be hierarchical, for example subchannels can be used to specify lower level communication.

An *interface* represents a flexible link between behaviors and channels. It consists of declarations of communication methods which will be defined in a channel.

For example, the following SpecC description specifies the system shown in Figure 4:

```
interface L { void Write(int x); };
interface R { int  Read (void);  };
```

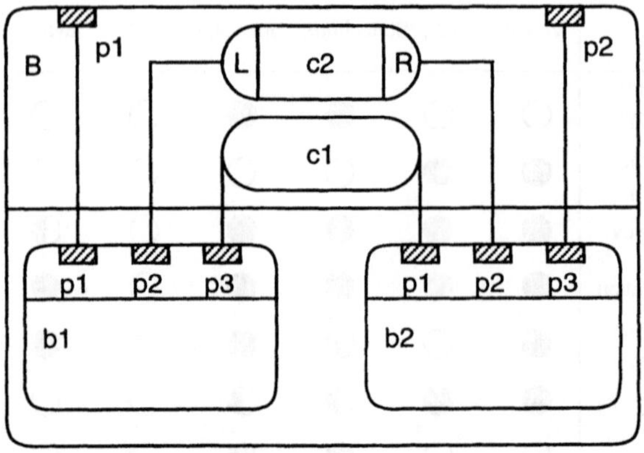

Figure 4. Basic Structure of a SpecC Model

```
channel C implements L, R
{
int Data; bool Valid;

void Write(int x)
   { Data = x; Valid = true; }
int Read(void)
   { while(! Valid) waitfor(10);
     return(Data); }
};

behavior B1(in int p1, L p2, in int p3)
{
void main(void)
   { /* ... */ p2.Write(p1); }
};

behavior B2(out int p1, R p2, out int p3)
{
void main(void)
   { /* ... */ p3 = p2.Read(); }
};

behavior B(in int p1, out int p2)
{
int c1;
C   c2;
B1  b1(p1, c2, c1);
B2  b2(c1, c2, p2);

void main(void)
   { par { b1.main(); b2.main(); } }
};
```

The example system specifies a behavior B consisting of two subbehaviors b1

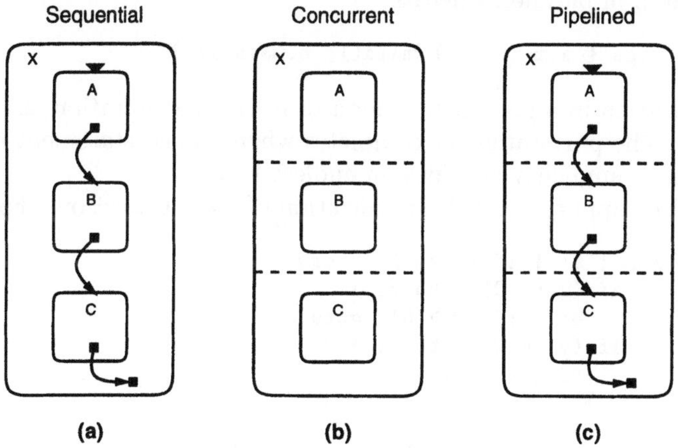

Figure 5. Behavioral Hierarchy

and b2 which execute in parallel and communicate via integer c1 and channel c2. Thus structural hierarchy is specified by the tree of child behavior instantiations and the interconnection of their ports via variables and channels. Behaviors define functionality, and the time of communication, whereas channels define how the communication is performed.

4.5. Behavioral Hierarchy

The composition of child behaviors in time is called behavioral hierarchy. Child behaviors can either be executed sequentially or concurrently. Sequential execution can be specified by standard imperative statements or as a finite state machine with explicit state transitions. Concurrent execution is either parallel or pipelined.

For example, we can specify a behavior being the sequential composition of the child behaviors using sequential statements, as shown in Figure 5(a), where `X` finishes when the last behavior `C` finishes. Second, we can use the parallel composition using the `par` construct, as shown in Figure 5(b), where `X` finishes when all its child behaviors `A`, `B` and `C` are finished. Also, pipelined composition is supported using the `pipe` construct, as shown in Figure 5(c), where `X` starts again when the slowest behavior finishes.

Syntactically, behavioral hierarchy is specified in the `main` function of a composite behavior. For example, with `a`, `b`, and `c` being instantiated child behaviors, the sequence of calls

```
a.main(); b.main(); c.main();
```

simply specifies sequential execution of `a`, `b`, `c`. The `par` and `pipe` statements specify concurrent execution. For example,

```
par { a.main(); b.main(); c.main(); }
```

executes a, b, c in parallel, whereas

```
pipe { a.main(); b.main(); c.main(); }
```

specifies execution in a pipelined fashion (a in the first iteration, a and b in the second, ...). The par statement completes when its last statement finishes, the pipe statement implicitly specifies an endless loop.

SpecC also supports explicit specification of state transitions. For example

```
fsm { a: { if (x > 0)  break;
   if (x <= 0) goto b; }
      b: { if (y > 0)  goto a;
   if (y == 0) goto b; }
      c: { break; }
    }
```

specifies the state transitions of a finite state machine model with three behaviors a, b, c. Implicitly the first label in the fsm statement specifies the initial state (a). The FSM exits when a break statement is executed.

In summary, behavioral hierarchy is captured by the tree of function calls to the behavior main methods.

4.6. *Synchronization*

Concurrent behaviors usually must be synchronized in order to be cooperative. In SpecC, a built-in type *event* serves as the basic unit of synchronization. Events can only be used as arguments to wait and notify statements (or with exceptions as explained in Section 4.7). A wait statement suspends the current behavior from execution until one of the specified events is notified by another behavior. The notify statement triggers all specified events so that all behaviors waiting on one of these events can resume their execution.

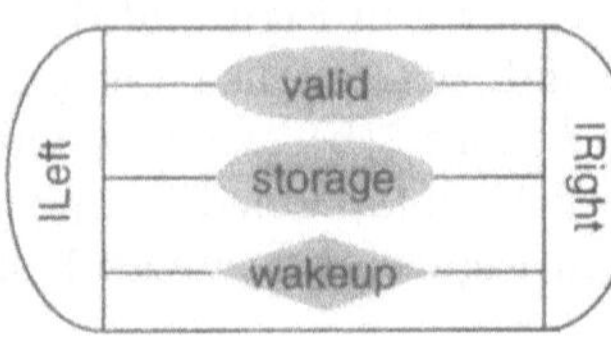


```
interface ILeft {
    void write( int val );
    };
interface IRight {
    int   read( void );
    };
```

(a)

```
channel CShared( void )
   implements ILeft, IRight {
   int     storage;
   bool    valid;
   event  wakeup;
   void write( int val ) {
          storage = val;
          valid = true;
          notify( wakeup ); }
   int    read( void ) {
          while ( !valid )
             wait( wakeup );
          valid = false;
          return storage; } };
```

(b)

Figure 6. Example for simple Shared Memory Channel

For example, Figure 6 shows a simple shared memory channel CShared that, in addition to a valid bit, uses the event wakeup to allow only synchronized

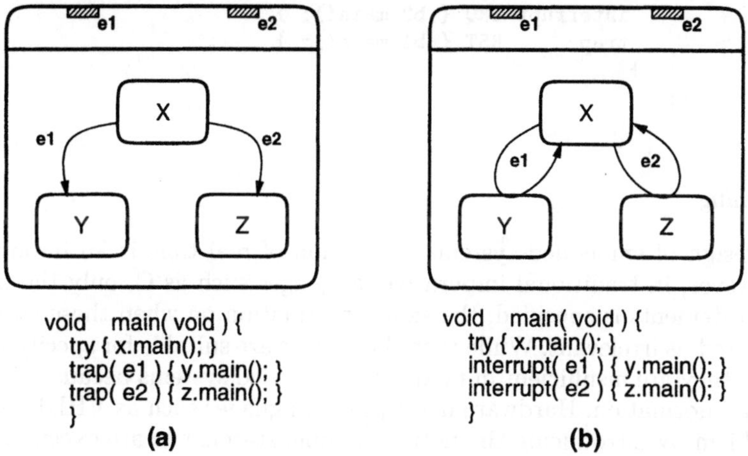

Figure 7. Exception handling: (a) abortion, (b) interrupt.

accesses to its `storage`. With this channel, it is assured that a consumer will always get valid data.

4.7. Exception Handling

SpecC provides support for two types of exceptions, namely ***abortion*** (or trap) and ***interrupt***, as shown in Figure 7.

The `try-trap` construct, illustrated in Figure 7(a), aborts behavior `x` immediately when one of the events `e1`, `e2` occurs. The execution of behavior `x` (and all its child behaviors) is terminated without completing its computation and control is transferred to behavior `y` in case of `e1`, to behavior `z` in case of `e2`. This type of exception usually is used to model the reset of a system.

On the other hand, the `try-interrupt` construct, as shown in Figure 7(b), can be used to model interrupts. Here again, execution of behavior `x` is stopped immediately for events `e1` and `e2`, and behavior `y` or `z`, respectively, is started to service the interrupt. After completion of interrupt handlers `y` and `z` control is transferred back to behavior `x` and execution is resumed right at the point where it was stopped.

For both types of exceptions, in case two or more events happen at the same time, priority is given to the first listed event.

It should be noted that interrupt and abortion type exceptions can be mixed in SpecC. For example, the following code specifies a behavior `B` with a resetable child behavior `b1` and an interrupt handler `b2`.

```
behavior B (in event IRQ, in event RST)
{
B_sub b1, b2;

void main(void)
   { try { b1.main(); }
```

```
            interrupt IRQ { b2.main(); }
            trap      RST { b1.main(); }
        }
    };
```

4.8. Timing

In the design of embedded systems the notion of real time is an important issue. However, in traditional imperative languages such as C, only the ordering among statements is specified, the exact information on when these statements are executed, is irrelevant. While these languages are suitable for specifying functionality, they are insufficient in modeling embedded systems because of the lack of timing information. Hardware description languages such as VHDL overcome this problem by introducing the notion of time: statements are executed at discrete points in time and their execution delay is zero. While VHDL gives an exact definition of timing for each statement, such a treatment often leads to *over-specification.*

One obvious over-specification is the case when VHDL is used to specify functional behavior. The timing of functional behaviors is unknown until they are synthesized. The assumption of zero execution time is too optimistic and there are chances to miss design errors during specification validation. Other cases of over-specification are timing constraints and timing delays, where events have to happen, or, are guaranteed to happen in a *time range*, instead of at a fixed point in time, as restricted by VHDL.

SpecC overcomes this problem by differentiating between two types of timing information, *exact timing* and *timing ranges.* Exact timing is used when the timing is known, for example the execution delay of an already synthesized component. This is specified with a `waitfor` statement which suspends the execution of the current behavior for a specified time. The time is measured in real time units such as nanoseconds. Simulation time is only increased by `waitfor` statements, other statements are always executed in zero time.

Timing ranges are used to specify timing constraints at the specification level. SpecC supports timing information in terms of *timing diagrams* with minimum and maximum time constraints. Timing ranges are specified as 4-tuples $T = \langle l1, l2, min, max \rangle$ with the `range` statement. For example,

```
range(l1; l2; 10; 20);
```

specifies at least 10 but not more than 20 time units spent between labels `l1` and `l2`.

Consider, for example, the timing diagram of the read protocol for a static RAM, as shown in Figure 8(a). In order to read a word from the SRAM, the address of the data is supplied at the `address` port and the read operation is selected by assigning 1 to the `read` and 0 to the `write` port. The selected word then can be accessed at the `data` port. The diagram in Figure 8(a) explicitly specifies all timing constraints that have to be satisfied during this read access. These constraints are specified as arcs between pairs of events annotated with

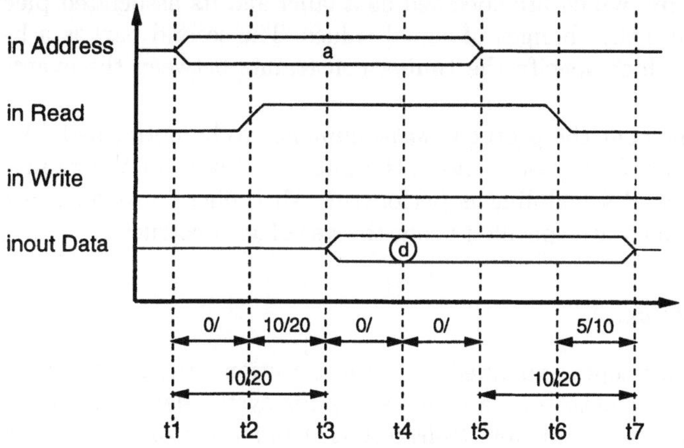

(a)

```
interface I_SRAM {
  void read_word(bit[15:0] a,
                 bit[15:0] *d);
};

behavior B_SRAM(
    in bit[15:0] addr,
    inout bit[15:0] data,
    in bool rd,
    in bool wr ) {
  void main( void ) { ... }
};

channel C_SRAM( void )
  implements I_SRAM {
   bit[15:0]  Address, Data;
   bool       Read, Write;
   B_SRAM sram(
               Address, Data,
               Read, Write );

   void read_word(bit[15:0] a,
               bit[15:0] *d ) { ... }
};
```

(b)

```
void read_word(
      bit[15:0] a, bit[15:0] *d ) {
  do {
     t1 : { Address = a; }
     t2 : { Read = 1; }
     t3 : { }
     t4 : { *d = Data; }
     t5 : { Address = 0; }
     t6 : { Read = 0; }
     t7 : { }
     }
  timing {
     range( t1; t2; 0; );
     range( t1; t3; 10; 20 );
     range( t2; t3; 10; 20 );
     range( t3; t4; 0; );
     range( t4; t5; 0; );
     range( t5; t7; 10; 20 );
     range( t6; t7; 5; 10 );
     }
}
```

(c)

```
void read_word(
      bit[15:0] a, bit[15:0] *d ) {
  Address = a;
  Read = 1;
  waitfor(10);
  *d = Data;
  Address = 0;
  Read = 0;
  waitfor(10);
  }
```

(d)

Figure 8. Timing Example: SRAM Read Protocol: (a) timing diagram, (b) SRAM channel, (c) specification level timing, (d) implementation level timing.

x/y, where x specifies the minimum and y the maximum time between the value changes of the signals.

Figure 8(b) shows the SpecC source code of a SRAM channel C_SRAM, which instantiates the behavior B_SRAM, and the signals, which are mapped to the ports of the SRAM. Access to the memory is provided by the read_word method, which encapsulates the read protocol explained above (due to space constraints write access is ignored).

Figure 8(c) shows the source code of the read_word method at the specification level. The do-timing construct used here effectively describes all information contained in the timing diagram. The first part of the construct lists all the events of the diagram, which are specified as a label and its associated piece of code, which describes the changes of signal values. The second part is a list of `range` statements, which specify the timing constraints between the events, as explained above.

In order to implement the protocol, *scheduling* has to be performed for each `do-timing` statement. Figure 8(d) shows the implementation of the `read_word` method after an ASAP scheduling is performed. All timing constraints are replaced by delays, which are specified using the `waitfor` construct.

4.9. Additional features

In addition to the concepts explained in the last sections, the SpecC language supports further constructs that are necessary for system-level design. First, SpecC provides explicit support for *Boolean* (`bool`) and *bitvector* (`bit[:]`) types, in addition to all types provided by ANSI-C.

Also, constructs for binary import of pre-compiled SpecC code and support of persistent annotation for objects in the language are provided. Since these constructs are beyond the scope of this paper, please refer to [6] for further details.

In conclusion, the Sections 4.4 to 4.8 show that the SpecC language satisfies the requirements of executability, modularity and completeness, as discussed in Section 4.1.

It has to be emphasized, that the advantage of SpecC lies in its *orthogonal constructs* which implement *orthogonal concepts*. All SpecC constructs are independent of each other, unlike for example signals in VHDL, which are used for synchronization, communication and timing. The SpecC language covers the complete set of system concepts with a minimal set of constructs. Therefore it is easy to learn and easy to understand.

5. The System

We have developed the SpecC Environment as shown in Figure 9. The design is specified with the help of the *SpecC Editor* which provides a graphical user interface (GUI). The SpecC Editor is also used for displaying the system models at different design stages and allows the designer to execute transformations on the models in an interactive or automatic manner. Different aspects of the design model are displayed in separate windows. For example, the structural hierarchy of the system under design is displayed in a hierarchy browser, whereas the mapping of ports and variables is shown in a connectivity window. All windows support interactive modification of the design.

In analogy to the methodology described in Section 3, the SpecC synthesis system consists of a set of tools, such as the *Estimator*, the *Allocator* and *Partitioner*, the *Scheduler*, and the *Communication Synthesizer*, which operate on the *SIR*, the SpecC Intermediate Representation. A SIR file can be obtained initially by compiling SpecC source code using the *SpecC Compiler*. It contains the symbol table and the abstract syntax tree of the corresponding SpecC code.

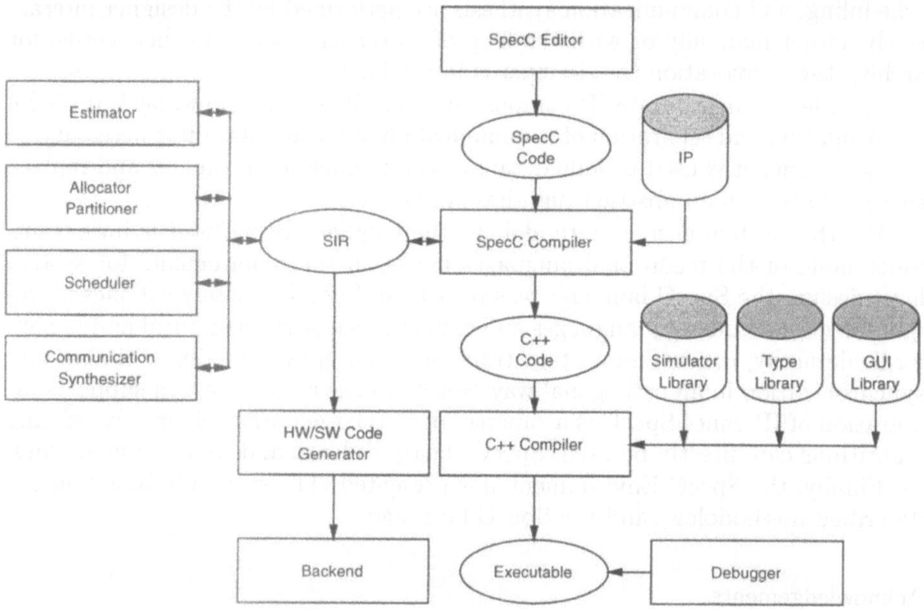

Figure 9. The SpecC Environment (SCE)

It also contains explicit information such as the type of each expression which is implicit in the source.

The SpecC compiler can also automatically generate simulation code in the form of C++, which can then be compiled and linked with a set of predefined libraries in order to generate an executable.

The *Simulation Library* implements a discrete event simulator by maintaining a time wheel which schedules concurrent threads. The *Type Library* provides an implementation of data types such as bitvector and multi-valued logic. The *GUI Library* helps to visualize signal waveforms and supports graphical entry of stimuli.

A standard source-level debugger can be used to debug the executable. The *HW/SW Code Generator* exports the implementation level SIR into C or HDL code.

6. Conclusion

With the background of a specify-explore-refine paradigm, an IP-centric methodology for the codesign of embedded systems was presented. The methodology consists of a set of well-defined tasks and design models which allow the easy insertion and reuse of intellectual property.

In particular, the design methodology starts with an executable specification of the system under design and eventually creates an implementation architecture ready for manufacturing. The intermediate tasks of allocation, partitioning, scheduling, and communication synthesis are performed by the designer interactively, either manually or with the help of automatic tools. In other words, for architecture exploration the designer is in the loop.

In order to incorporate IP components and allow "plug-and-play", protocol encapsulation and separation of communication and computation is necessary. A wrapper concept is used to hide details of communication protocols and replace these details with an abstract high-level interface.

For this system design methodology, the language being used is important. Since none of the traditional languages meets all the requirements for system level design, the SpecC language was presented. SpecC precisely satisfies all requirements for codesign languages and explicitly supports structural and behavioral hierarchy, concurrency, state transitions, exception handling, timing and synchronization in an orthogonal way. SpecC encourages reuse and supports integration of IP. Since SpecC is a superset of C, a large library of already existing algorithms can directly be used. SpecC is easy to learn and easy to understand.

Finally, the SpecC Environment was presented. The system is based on the described methodology and the SpecC language.

Acknowledgements

We would like to acknowledge the support of the various granting agencies who have contributed research funding, without which this work would not have been possible. This work was supported in part by grants from: Hitachi, Grant #-H22003; Toshiba, Grant #-TC-20881; SRC, Grant #-97-DJ-146; and Rockwell, Grant #-RSS-24141.

References

1. K. Arnold, J. Gosling; *The Java Programming Language*; Addison-Wesley, 1996.
2. F. Balarin, P. Giusto, A. Jurecska, C. Passerone, E. Sentovich, B. Tabbara, M. Chiodo, H. Hsieh, L. Lavagno, A. Sangiovanni-Vincentelli, K. Suzuki. *Hardware-Software Co-Design of Embedded Systems, The POLIS approach.* Kluwer Academic Publishers, April 1997.
3. F. Chan, M. Spiller, R. Newton. "WELD – An Environment for Web-Based Electronic Design". In *Proceedings of the Design Automation Conference*, San Francisco, 1998.
4. M. Chiodo, P. Giusto, H. Hsieh, A. Jurecska, L. Lavagno, A. Sangiovanni-Vincentelli. "A Formal Specification Model for Hardware/Software Codesign". In *Proceedings of International Workshop on Hardware-Software Codesign*, Oct. 1993.
5. P. Chou, R. Ortega, G. Borriello. "The Chinook Hardware/Software Co-Synthesis System". In *International Symposium on System Synthesis*, Cannes, France, Sept. 1995.
6. R. Dömer, J. Zhu, D. Gajski. *The SpecC Language Reference Manual.* University of California, Irvine, Technical Report ICS-TR-98-13, March 1998.
7. D. Drusinsky and D. Harel. "Using Statecharts for hardware description and synthesis". In *IEEE Transactions on Computer Aided Design*, 1989.
8. R. Ernst, et. al. "The COSYMA Environment for Hardware-Software Cosynthesis of Small Embedded Systems". In *Microprocessors and Microsystems*, Vol. 20, No. 3, May 1996.
9. D. Gajski, F. Vahid, S. Narayan, J. Gong. *Specification and Design of Embedded Systems.* Prentice Hall, New Jersey, 1994.
10. D. Gajski, J. Zhu, R. Dömer. "Essential Issues in Codesign". In *Hardware/Software Co-Design: Principles and Practice*, edited by J. Staunstrup, W. Wolf. Kluwer Academic Publishers, 1997.

11. R. Gupta, C. Coelho., G. De Micheli. "Synthesis and simulation of digital systems containing interacting hardware and software components". In *Proceedings of the 29th ACM, IEEE Design Automation Conference*, 1992.
12. IEEE Inc., N.Y. *IEEE Standard VHDL Language Reference Manual*, 1998.
13. T. Ismail, M. Abid, A. Jerraya. "COSMOS: A Codesign Approach for Communicating Systems". In *Proceedings of the International Workshop on Hardware- Software Codesign*. IEEE CS Press, 1994.
14. A. Kalavade, E. Lee. "A Hardware/Software Codesign Methodology for DSP Applications". In *IEEE Design and Test*, Sept. 1993.
15. G. Koch, U. Kebschull, W. Rosenstiel. "A prototyping architecture for hardware/software codesign in the COBRA project". In *Proceedings of the third International Workshop on Hardware/Software Codesign*, IEEE Computer Society Press, 1994.
16. D. Ku, G. De Micheli. "HardwareC – A Language for Hardware Design, Version 2.0". Tech. Rep. CSL-TR-90-419, Stanford University, April 1990.
17. S. Liao, S. Tjiang, R. Gupta. "An Efficient Implementation of Reactivity for Modeling Hardware in the Scenic Design Environment". In *Proceedings of the 34th Design Automation Conference*, Anaheim, California, USA, 1997.
18. C. Liem, F. Nacabal, C. Valderrama, P. Paulin, A. Jerraya. "System-on-a-chip cosimulation and compilation". In *IEEE Design & Test of Computers*, 1997.
19. J. Madsen, J. Grode, P. Knudsen. "Hardware/Software Partitioning using the LYCOS System". In *Hardware/Software Co-Design: Principles and Practice*, edited by J. Staunstrup, W. Wolf. Kluwer Academic Publishers, 1997.
20. P. Marwedel, G. Goossens. *Code Generation for Embedded Processors*. Kluwer Academic Publishers, 1995.
21. G. De Micheli. *Synthesis and Optimization of Digital Circuits*. McGraw Hill, 1994.
22. S. Narayan, F. Vahid, D. Gajski. "System Specification and Synthesis with the SpecCharts Language". In *Proceedings of the International Conference on Computer Aided Design*, 1991.
23. K. Rompaey, D. Verkest, I. Bolsens, H. De Man. "CoWare – A design environment for heterogeneous hardware/software systems". In *Proceedings of the European Design Automation Conference*, 1996.
24. B. Stroustrup. *The C++ Programming Language*, third edition. Addison-Wesley, 1997.
25. D. Thomas, P. Moorby. *The Verilog Hardware Description Language*. Kluwer Academic Publishers, 1991.
26. J. Staunstrup, W. Wolf, et. al. *Hardware/Software Co-Design: Principles and Practice*, Kluwer Academic Publishers, 1997.
27. X3 Secretariat. *The C Language*. X3J11/90-013, ISO Standard ISO/IEC 9899. Computer and Business Equipment Manufacturers Association, Washington, DC, USA, 1990.
28. T. Yen, W. Wolf. *Hardware-software Co-synthesis of Distributed Embedded Systems*. Kluwer Academic Publishers, 1997.
29. J. Zhu, R. Dömer, D. Gajski. "Syntax and Semantics of the SpecC Language". In *Proceedings of the Synthesis and System Integration of Mixed Technologies*, Osaka, Japan, Dec. 1997.

MULTILANGUAGE DESIGN

Bernd Kleinjohann[1]

1. Introduction

During the last years the production costs for IT systems have steadily decreased with regard to their complexity. IT applications that had to be realized as expensive PCBs in earlier times can now be realized on a single chip, which is, of course, much cheaper. Furthermore, low cost broad band communication media are available. Typically, the market requires IT systems that realize a set of specific features for the end user in a given environment, so called embedded systems. Some examples for such embedded systems are interfaces of mobile phones, or more generally end user interfaces for communication products, set top boxes for digital TV, or control modules in cars, airplanes or buildings. For these different application domains a variety of modeling languages with domain specific features was developed in the past. C/C++ / VHDL , for instance, as used in hardware/software codesign, do not fulfil the designers requirements for modeling of embedded systems. In order to cover the entire functionality of an embedded system, subsystems have to be specified in different languages that support the modeling of application domain specific features. As an example the control system of a car may serve: The body electronic is usually specified using discrete state based languages, whereas for the specification of control subsystems for window lifts, power train, or ABS continuous data flow based languages are used. At higher levels the car itself may be seen as a system that is embedded in a network of telematic services, that will be specified in typical languages of the telecommunication domain.

In this tutorial we will present how different languages can be used together during design of embedded systems. Figure 1 describes this in principle. Starting with a specification in several language (A, B), an integration model has to be defined that allows to realize a design process that generates an implementation for the specified modules consisting of some realization parts (V, W, X, Y) and their communication. Section 2 will summarize current practice in design of embedded systems and investigate some problems arising during such multilanguage design processes. Section 3 will especially encounter semantic problems at the interfaces of system parts specified

[1] C-LAB, Fürstenalle 11, 33094 Paderborn, Germany, Email: bernd@c-lab.de

in different languages. In Sections 4 and 5 we will introduce the concepts of *language coupling* and *language integration*, that are based on two different types of integration models. For *language coupling* mechanisms for the connection of inputs and outputs of subsystems modelled in different languages have to be provided without changing the original subsystem models. For *language integration* models specified in different languages have to be transformed into a common model.

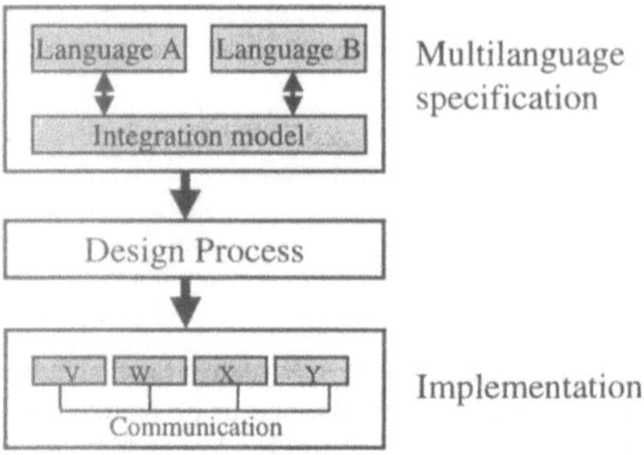

Figure 1: Multilanguage design

2. The Design Process

The design process has to consider three independent aspects: *applications, architectures*, and *design methods*. The first aspect, we will consider, are the *applications*. They usually rise various requirements and constraints, typical for the specific application domain. Embedded systems often have to fulfil a specific task in a dedicated environment like the above mentioned control system of a car or a mobile phone. Typically an embedded system has to fulfil real time constraints. Here we distinguish soft real time requirements, for instance for the transmission of audio and video data, and hard real time requirements that apply for vehicle control systems, for instance. Furthermore, many applications are extremely security critical, but nevertheless obey a strong cost pressure. Non predictable reactions of such applications cannot be tolerated due to serious damage they may cause.As an example how to cope with these conflicting requirements, the X-by-wire technology may serve, that will be introduced to mass products like cars.

The second aspect in the design of embedded systems is the *target architecture* typically consisting of a software and a hardware part. The hardware architecture, for instance in automotive applications, is usually given by a set of electronic control units (ECU) connected by a communication module (see Figure 2). In this domain the topology of the hardware architecture is often determined by the mechanical construction, having in mind that the cable tree in a vehicle is a main cost factor. In contrast, for private TV sets with video camera and stereo equipment, the topology may change during their run time, if for instance the portable video camera is (dis)connected to (from) the equipment.

Each node (ECU, see Figure 2) in the often predetermined topology may contain several computing kernels, memory units, and application specific periphery. The target hardware for the computing kernels (micro controller, digital signal processor, programmable gate array, or application specific hardware) has to be determined for each node. Furthermore, size and type of the memory units (RAM, ROM, FLASH) and the set of periphery components (e. g. AD-/DA transmitters, serial and parallel ports, or communication interfaces) have to be defined. These realization decisions have to be taken for each node considering its performance and cost requirements. Whenever possible, existing architecture families, that can be parameterized appropriately, should be chosen for cost reduction reasons.

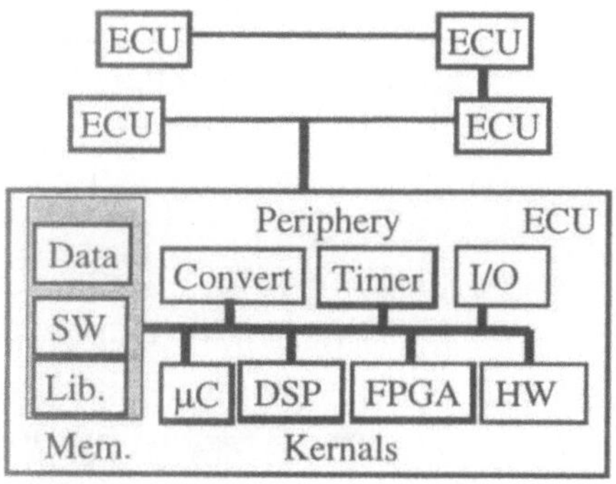

Figure 2: Hardware architecture

The dimensioning of the memory elements has to be done with regard to the expected data traffic and software size. The software to be stored consists of two parts: the *basic services* that have to be configured for the application and the actual *application software*. The *basic services* usually comprise operating system and communication functions as well as interface functions for interaction with the periphery, application specific hardware, or hardware programmable components (FPGA). For real time applications standard operating system interfaces like OSEK (OSEK, 1997) are available. However, recent trends show that even such basic services are realized for a specific application (degradable operating system). The actual *application software* is given by those functions realizing the top level specification, usually provided in different languages, with its constraints.

Figure 3 represents the principle *design method* for embedded systems. The basis for the depicted design steps is an initial specification of the system and its constraints. Embedded systems and thus also their specifications contain various types of functions or tasks. Discrete control tasks are usually specified using state based notations, whereas for the specification of analogue control tasks differential equations or in the discretized case data flow notations are frequently used. The structure of such a multiparadigm specification should follow the functional grouping of system tasks, in order to support an independent development of different system parts

The initial specification has to be split into independently executable tasks. Then, the run time and performance requirements for these tasks are estimated and the tasks are allocated to the specific nodes in the hardware architecture considering the specified constraints. Afterwards the scheduling is done in order to estimate whether the timing constraints can be fulfilled. In the subsequent step the tasks allocated to the various nodes have to be realized. If a given controller (selected from a set of existing hardware controllers) shall be used, the software for this controller has to be generated. Otherwise, classical hardware/software codesign methods can be used. In this case, it has to be decided which parts of the task are implemented in software and which ones in hardware. Afterwards the required hardware and software have to be realized.

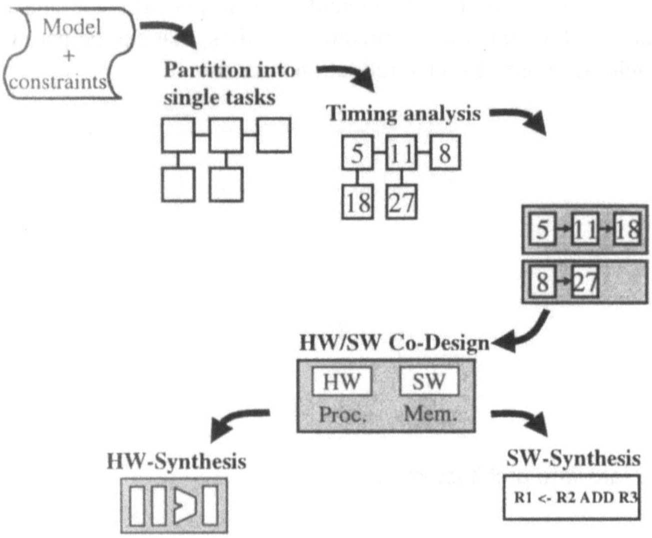

Figure 3: Simplified design flow for embedded systems

The above design process has been presented in a rather simplified manner. Usually many iteration steps are necessary to reach a satisfying result. For multilanguage design, however the specification phase plays a crucial role, since it influences the entire design process, especially if the specification consists of different languages. Only by the integration of different specification languages a well defined basis for subsequent design steps can be reached. In order to preserve existing libraries and know how in industrial design processes, also the integration of specification languages following the same paradigm is reasonable. Therefore, we will concentrate on this phase and its impact in the rest of this tutorial.

3. The Semantics of Systems

This section will investigate the problem of interfacing different system specifications in order to have a serious basis for the integration of languages. The role of interfaces and their semantics for system specification and realization will be explained.

The specification of a system part in a specific language can be regarded as the specification of an open subsystem that communicates with its environment. Even if only the behavior of the system part under design is explicitly specified, the expected behavior of the environment is at least implicitly given.

The observable behavior at an interface between a system part and its environment is indirectly given by their specifications (system part and environment). For the specification of interfaces at an open system part (no explicit environment specification is given) different notations are in use. Interfaces of continuous systems can be represented by trajectories, i. e. a curve of vectors from a continuous domain over the continuous time axis. Discrete interfaces can be characterized by streams or traces (van de Snepsheut, 1985).

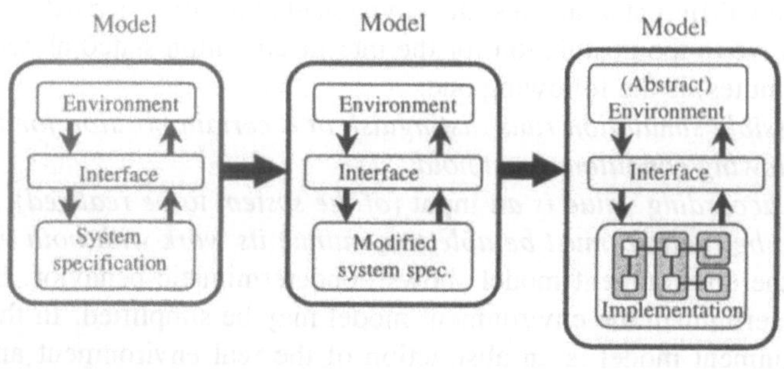

Figure 4: Interfaces between subsystems

In this context the goal of the design process can be characterized as depicted in Figure 4: The specification of a (sub)system to be realized should be transformed in such a way that it consists merely of models of easily realizable or already realized system components. This process is usually carried out in multiple steps as already mentioned in Section 2. During this process also the original environment model may be substituted by a more abstract model in order to simplify it (see below). For each step it is expected that the interface between the (sub)system and its environment remains the same or is in a well defined relation to the original interface definition (see Figure 5).

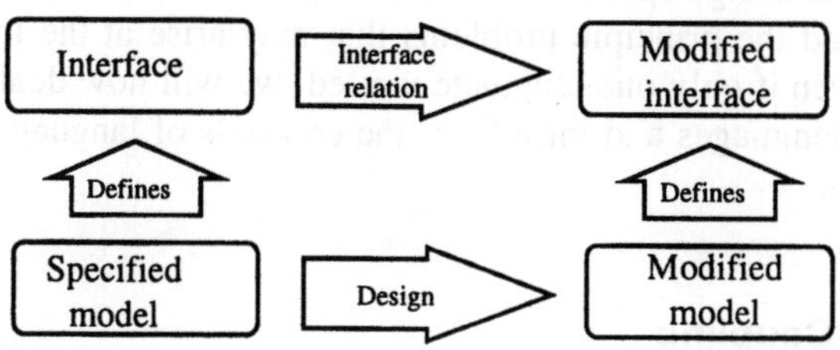

Figure 5: Specification and interface relation

Usually it is expected that the diagram presented in Figure 5 commutes. However, for continuous interfaces described by trajectories tolerable deviations from the original one may be defined. Consequently, all realizations whose trajectories are within the allowable deviation range are correct realizations.

For systems with discrete interfaces the realization is expected to show exactly the originally specified interface behavior. However, this expectation leads to surprising results, since several specification languages like, for instance, Statecharts contain inherently nondeterministic behavior. By nondeterministic behavior we mean that a possible simulation run is not exactly predetermined by the specification.

In practice this inherent nondeterminism is resolved by the simulation tools in a specific design environment, or it is at least restricted by so called 'don't care' values. Thus, depending on the applied simulation tool different realizations may be postulated for the same specification. If a system realization should behave exactly as predicted by a simulation run, the simulation semantics must at least partially be considered. In cases where such a simulator and the real time operating system of the target hardware follow different strategies, the envisioned realization is partly impossible.

An alternative to the postulation for the interface relation stated above (diagram in Figure 5 commutes) is the following one.

If two possible simulation runs distinguish at a certain position for the first time, one of the following conditions must hold:

1. *If the according value is an* input *(of the system to be realized), then the system to be realized must be able to continue its work with both values.* In this case the environment model shows nondeterministic behavior. By the use of nondeterminism the environment model may be simplified. In these cases the environment model is an abstraction of the real environment and may show behavior that cannot occur in reality. Vice versa, it may happen that the environment model does not completely specify the behavior of the real environment. For these omitted environment behavior the realized system will show no reaction or incorrect reactions.
2. *If the simulation runs distinguish first in an* output *value, only one alternative reaction must be implemented by the system to be realized.* In this case the system to be realized shows nondeterministic behavior, that can be used to optimize the system realization, since only one alternative reaction must be realized. The knowledge about this nondeterministic behavior is also needed for defining an integration semantics. However, classical simulators do not suffice for detecting such cases, but a tool would be needed that can navigate through the design space characterized by that nondeterminism.

Having in mind the principle problems that may arise at the interfaces of system specifications, even if only one language is used, we will now deal with the composition of multiple languages and introduce the concepts of language coupling and language integration.

4. Language Coupling

One way of composing several specification languages is *language coupling*. For language coupling the interfaces of subsystems specified in different languages have to be connected. This can be reached by explicitly describing the connections between the subsystems with a corresponding tool or implicitly by naming conventions for identifiers (using the same identifiers in different subsystem specifications). The subsystem models are not changed at all and follow the paradigms of those languages used for their specification. Hence, assertions regarding the entire system are restricted to the subsystem interfaces. The design process works independently on the model parts as depicted in Figure 6.

The following example shows some problems that may arise during language coupling. In this example Statecharts and discretized differential equations will be coupled.

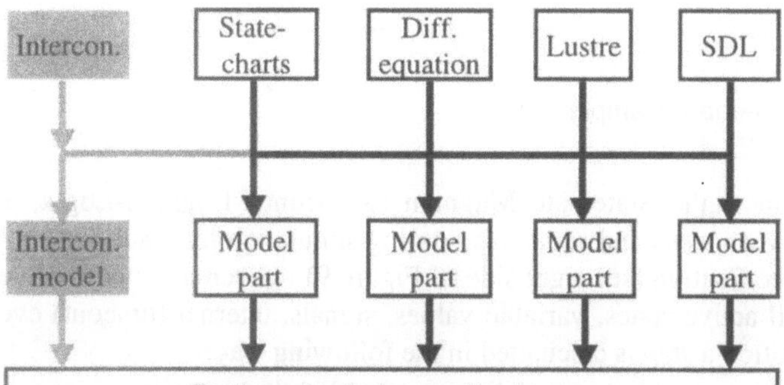

Figure 6: Language coupling

Statecharts (Harel, 1977) are a state based formalism. Figure 7 shows an example modelling a remote TV controller. Hierarchical and orthogonal states are supported. The state *TV* has the parallel substates *Standby* and *On*. *On* is divided into two orthogonal states separated by a dashed line, which again have two substates each. A broadcast mechanism is used for inter state communication. State transitions can be annotated with events (*On, Off, TXT, Sound, Mute*) and actions, and signal values. Arrows starting at a dot denote default states. For example, *Standby* is the substate of TV which is entered by default, if a state transition to TV occurs. Value changes (events) and variable values can be checked in conditions. Signal values can be changed in actions. Longer lasting activities may be controlled by start, stop or activate. The timing model is causal, the definition of timers is possible (events). The synchronous simulation of Statecharts is based on the so called *synchrony hypothesis*:

- All actions are executed in zero time and
- the system reacts quicker than its environment.

Input/output for Statechart models is realized by the change/reading of external signals. The interface behavior of Statecharts can be described by interpreting changes of input or output signals (including the new value) as symbols in a trace. Such a trace corresponds to a simulation run of a Statechart. However, when interpreting these simulation runs, one should be aware, that the simulation semantics may differ between different Statechart simulators.

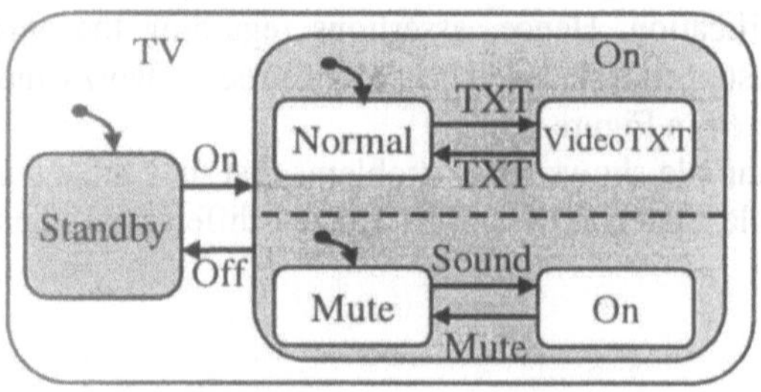

Figure 7: Statechart example

For instance, the Statemate Magnum tool from i-Logix (i-Logix, 1997) distinguishes between *steps* and *supersteps* during simulation for resolving conflicts arising from the specification (see right side of Figure 9). Given a system state consisting of the set of all active states, variable values, signals, internal (timeout) events and history information a *step* is calcualted in the following way:

- Reactions within a step will be executed in the next step.
- Events are alive for one step only.
- Calculations are based on the state at the beginning of the step.

Variables change their values at the end of a step. A *superstep* is completed when no further steps can be executed without external input. The simulation semantics is not compositional.

Other Statechart simulators realize a different semantics not based on the notion of steps and supersteps and hence do not follow the synchronous paradigm any more. Coupling of Statechart modules following different semantics usually raises the same problems like coupling of entirely different specification languages.

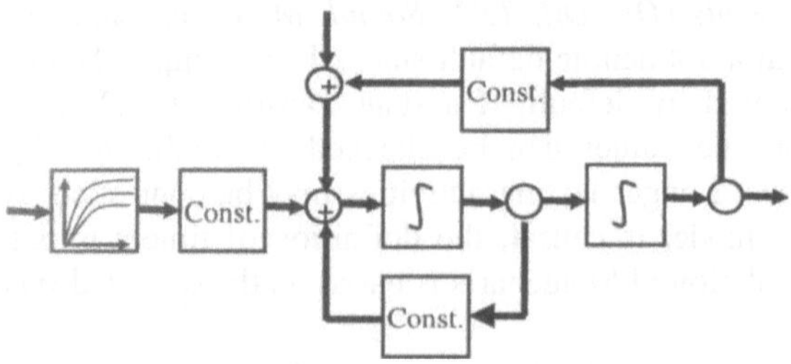

Figure 8 Block diagram example

The second notation used in our example are *differential equations*. Many tools are available that represent differential equations by block diagrams (see Figure 8). Each block may contain mathematical operators, differential or integral operators, and timing delays. The specification of characteristic curves is usually supported, too. Design tools and methods that perform discretization of continuous differential equations are beyond the scope of this tutorial. For further processing the results obtained by these tools can be represented as dataflow graphs, whose outputs have to be provided at defined points of time. Real time applications often require a periodical evaluation depending on a fixed sampling rate.

For the coupling of event based specifications and solutions of discretized, timed differential equations the first step is to determine which events should be exchanged between these models at which times. An event may for instance be triggered by an interval exceeding of a differential equation. The event driven model part may for instance determine input values, activate continuous input functions, or even change entire parameter sets of the model part specified by differential equations. Furthermore, it may switch between semi continuous models.

A second step is to determine the timing points for data exchange (see Figure 9). For Statecharts data exchange is only reasonable at the beginning of a superstep, since the system reacts in zero time (synchrony hypothesis). For system parts specified by differential equations, for instance, a concept based on timers may be developed to guarantee the correct execution of periodic events.

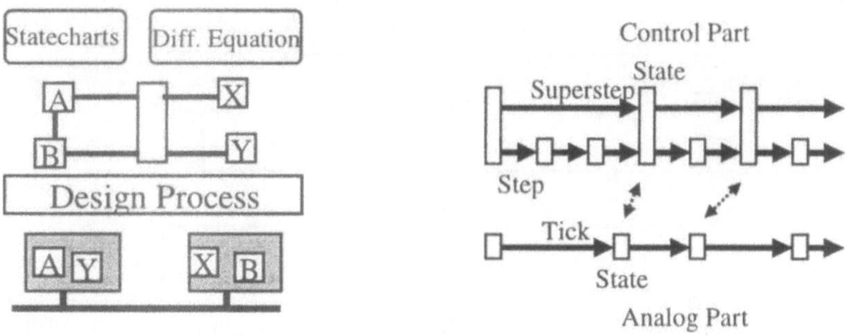

Figure 9: Coupling of Statecharts and differential equations

Using the above explained concept of language coupling, usually, has the following consequences for subsequent steps in the design process (left part of Figure 9). *Optimization* steps can only optimize the distribution of entire model parts in the overall controller topology or perform local optimizations w.r.t. a single model part (A, B, X, Y in Figure 9). A shift of functionality between model parts specified in different notations cannot be done automatically but has to be done manually by altering the specification. Furthermore, the simulation of coupled model parts causes performance loss due to the communication overhead of (at least) two simulator kernels involved for the corresponding model parts. Commercial tools supporting the coupling of Statecharts and block diagrams are already available (ISI, 1998, Tanurhan, 1995). The scientific community often uses the concepts of language coupling to integrate tools with reasonable effort. An example is the approach described in (Rust, 1998) which is based on Software Circuits (Hansson, 1997). Here existing, pre optimized modules are used for system realization. The control part is realized by software running on a real time operating system. The interconnection of existing hardware modules is done by predefined interface modules and protocols.

The goal of a design method should be reuse support at even higher levels of abstraction with largely automatic generation of realizations from a specification.

5. Language Integration

Language integration assumes that all involved specification paradigms are mapped onto a common internal model. Henzinger describes, for example, the integration of finite state machines with differential equations into a common model called hybrid automata (Henzinger, 1996). Hybrid automata combine the specification of event based state transitions (e. g. due to exceeding of intervals) with differential equations. For this purpose states in the state transition graphs can be annotated with systems of differential equation. This work describes also refinement rules for sub graphs fulfilling certain constraints. Hybrid automata do not provide constructs for the specification of complex information processing tasks like e. g. SDL. Therefore, they cannot be used as a common model for embedded systems.

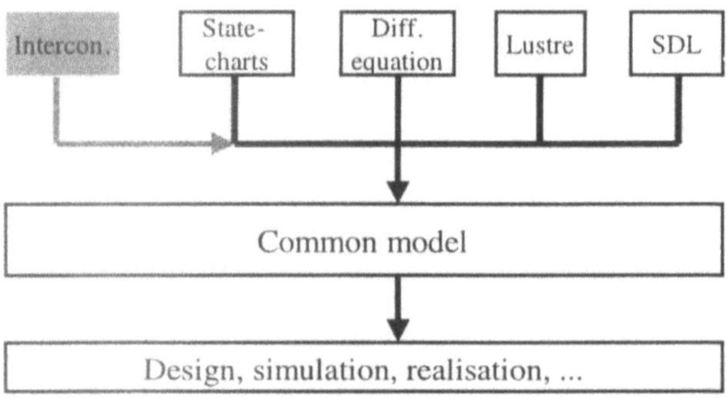

Figure 10: Language integration

A common model has to provide constructs that cover all concepts of the specification languages that should be mapped to it. Hence, a common model tends to become very complex and unwieldy resulting in the fact that established design methods cannot be easily transferred to fit with a common model of the required complexity. To overcome these difficulties and transfer at least parts of a design method some restrictions have to be considered during definition and application of a common model.

At first it should be possible to identify and separate a part of the common integration model generated from a specification (part) in a certain language from the rest of the specification. This results in the requirements for modularity and hierarchy.

Secondly, for such a part in the common model restrictions should be definable in order to allow a transfer of the design methods applicable for the original specification language to this "restricted" common model. Such a transferred design method should then be applicable for all common model parts fulfilling these restrictions. This approach makes design methods also available outside their original application domain.

Furthermore, it allows to shift functions between modules specified in different languages. Hence, the common integration model provides the basis for inter module optimizations.

Last but not least, it should be possible to recognize constructs of the original specification languages also in the common model. This feature on the one hand eases the translation into the common model, on the other hand design steps are more easily traceable.

The remainder of this section will present extended Predicate Transition Nets (Pr/T nets) as an example of such a common integration model. Pr/T nets were derived from Petri nets (Peterson, 1981) by Genrich and Lautenbach (Genrich, 1987). Pr/T nets are a reactive event driven modelling paradigm with a formally defined execution semantics.

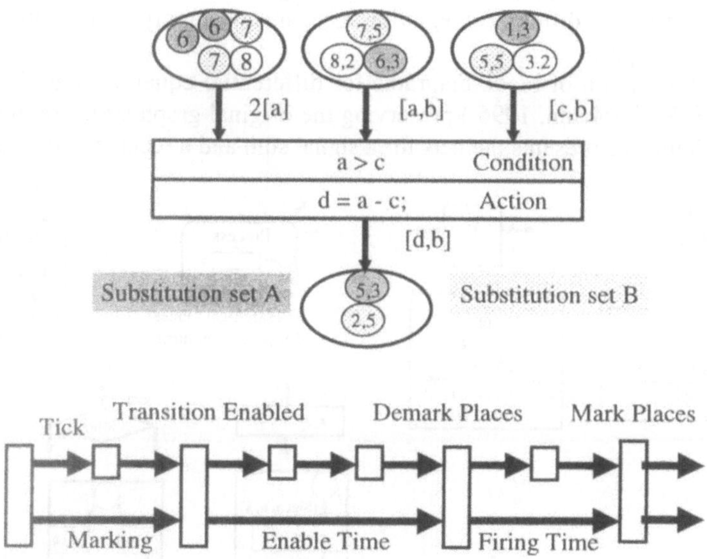

Figure 11: Pr/T net example

A Pr/T net is a bipartite directed graph consisting of *places* (represented as circles, see Figure 11) and *transitions* (represented as boxes, see Figure 11). *Places* serve as data storage and may contain distinguishable *tokens*. *Tokens* may contain structured data items (in our example (tuples of) integers). *Transitions* can be annotated with conditions (a > c) and actions (d = a-c). Edges are annotated with formal variables ([a,b], [c,b], etc.). The execution semantics is defined by the *firing* of transitions. A transition t is *enabled* or may fire in the current *marking* if appropriate tokens are available in its input places, i. e. there exists a valid substitution of the formal variables at t's input edges that fulfills also the conditions in t's annotation. The firing cycle starts by deleting the appropriate tokens from t's input places (demark places, Figure 11). Then the actions annotating t are executed and finally the calculated tokens are generated in t's output places (mark places, Figure 11). Furthermore an *en-*

able delay and a *firing delay* may be specified for a transition t. The *enable delay* specifies an interval how long the appropriate tokens may be in t's input places before t fires. The firing delay specifies a time interval for the length of the firing cycle. Delays may be infinitely long. A delay value (upper/lower bound of delay interval) may be altered by the actions annotating the transition t depending on the data values of the tokens in the actual firing cycle. These changes become valid for the next firing cycle.

Pr/T nets that contain only a bounded number of tokens can be mapped to finite state machines. The above presented timing model fulfills the synchrony hypothesis if enable delays are restricted to the interval [0, 0] and firing delays are restricted to the interval [1,1]. In this case the specification of nondeterminism (forward conflicts) in the net structure is not allowed. In principle these concepts allow to map Statecharts to Pr/T nets. If additionally hierarchical constructs as described in (Cherkasova, 1981, Kleinjohann, 1996) are used, states may be mapped to hierarchical places and state transitions to net transitions. Then the resulting net model resembles also in its graph structure the original Statechart. During design the hierarchy concept allows, for instance, the use of different integration mechanisms simply by instantiating the corresponding net part.

The translation of block diagrams for differential equations into Pr/T nets is also feasible (Kleinjohann, 1996) preserving the original graph structure of the block diagram. Figure 12 presents the nets for a signal sum and a rectangle integrator.

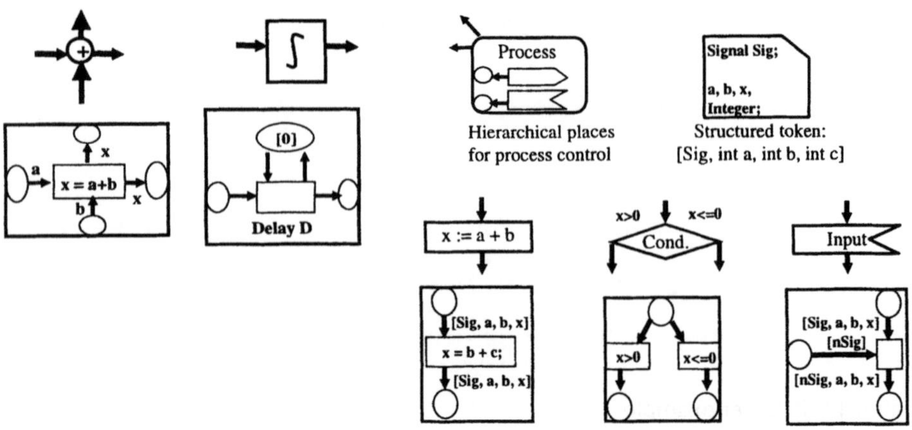

Figure 12: Mapping of block diagrams and SDL to Pr/T nets

The right part of Figure 12 shows the mapping of some SDL constructs to Pr/T nets. SDL is an asynchronous language widely used in telecommunication applications. The control diagrams of SDL provide among others, rectangles for statements, rhombs for conditions, and arrows for communications. Data types are represented in separate diagrams. For a mapping of SDL into Pr/T nets, at first, the data types and defined variables have to be mapped to token types and appropriate annotations. The evaluation of conditions and the execution of statements can be directly mapped to transition annotations. Process diagrams can be transferred similarly to block diagrams for differential equations. The asynchronous communication mechanisms of SDL can be easily mapped to the asynchronous execution of Pr/T nets.

We have developed the SEA Environment for specification and animation of extended Pr/T nets (Kleinjohann, 1996). The handling of foreign language constructs is supported by an abstract graphics that can be linked to the underlying Pr/T net. This graphics can be animated in the desired way when the according net is simulated. By providing appropriate libraries for Statecharts, SDL, block diagrams etc. users can directly use the constructs they are familiar with, without knowledge of the underlying Pr/T net.

Currently some other integration approaches are developed. On the basis of UML (Rational, 1997, Booch, 1996) efforts are undertaken to integrate Statecharts, SDL, Message Sequence Charts, and synchronous data flow notations. Many specification languages relying on the synchronous paradigm like Lustre, Signal, or Esterel (Halbwachs, 1993) can be integrated on the basis of a common synchronous automaton model (Maffeïs, 1996). VHDL and C in the hardware/software codesign domain are often integrated by means of control data flow graphs. However, a commonly suitable solution is not yet known. Here additional research is necessary.

6. Conclusion

In this tutorial we investigated the semantic problems in multilanguage design with regard to the composition of system parts specified in several languages and with regard to their environment behavior. Secondly, we introduced the concepts of language coupling and language integration and explained them by two examples. The third part of the tutorial introduced Pr/T nets as an integration model. Furthermore, we showed exemplary how Statecharts, block diagrams for continuous models, and SDL as an asynchronous language can be integrated by mapping some constructs of these specification languages onto Pr/T nets. If such subnets fulfill some restrictions the design methods provided for the original models can be adopted for Pr/T nets as the integration model.

Solutions for language coupling are already available for specific subsets of languages. But no general solution exists. Common integration models also exist for specific subsets of application domains. However, considerable research is necessary in this field. This research should be directed towards the extension of application domains and more general common models, which cover a broader set of modeling paradigms. By applying appropriate restrictions in the use of such a broad common model the design methods used in the original application domains can be transferred to the common model.

Actually we perform some work on language coupling in the COMITY project (EU 2305) based on previous nationally funded work in the METRO project. We perform further research on language integration and an according design method in a nationally funded project (SFB 376 on massive parallelism).

References

Booch, G., Rumbaugh, J., Jacobson, I. (1996). The Unified Modeling Language for Object Oriented Development, Version 1.0.

Cherkasova L. A., Kotov V. E. (1981). "Structured nets". J. Gruska and M. Chytil, editors, *Mathematical Foundations of Computer Science*. Volume 118 of Lecture Notes in Computer Science. Springer Verlag.

Genrich, H. J. (1987). *Predicate/Transition Nets*. Advances in Petri Nets Part I. Volume 254 of Lecture Notes in Computer Science. Springer Verlag.

Halbwachs, N. (1993). *Synchronous Programming of Reactive Systems*. Kluwer Academic Publishers.

Harel, D. (1977). "StateCharts: A visual formalism for complex systems". *Science of Computer Programming* 8(3), pp. 231-274.

Henzinger, T.A., (1996). " The theory of hybrid automata". *Proceedings of the 11th Annual Symposium on Logic in Computer Science*. IEEE Society Press.

I-Logix (1997). *STATEMATE, User Reference Manual, Magnum 1.0*. I-Logix Inc.

ISI (1998). "Design Automation Solutions". Integrated Systems Inc.. http://www.isi.com/Products/DAS

ITU-T (1992)."ITU-T Specification and Description Language SDL", Recommendation Z.100 (SDL-91), ITU General Secretariat, Geneva. http://www.itu.ch/ITU-T.

Kleinjohann, B., Kleinjohann, E., Tacken, J. (1996). "The SEA Language for System Engineering and Animation". *Applications and Theory of Petri Nets*. Volume 1091 of Lecture Notes in Computer Science. Springer Verlag.

Kleinjohann, B., Tacken, J., Tahedl, C. (1997). "Towards a Complete Design Method for Embedded Systems Using Predicate/Transition-Nets". *Proc. of the XIII IFIP WG 10.5 Conference on Computer Hardware Description Languages and Their Applications*, Toledo, Spain, Chapman & Hall.

Maffeïs, O., Morley M., Poigné, A. (1996), " The Synchronous Approach to Designing Reactive Systems". *Arbeitspapiere der GMD*, No. 973. GMD, St. Augustin, Germany.

OSEK (1997), *OSEK/VDX operating system*. ftp://www-iiit.etec.uni-karlsruhe.de/pub/osek/os20ra.pdf

Peterson, J.L. (1981). *Petri Net Theory and the Modelling of Systems*. Prentice Hall.

Rational (1997). *UML Summary, Version 1.1*. http:/www.rational.com/uml/resources/documentation/ summary

Rust, C., Stroop, J., Tacken, J. (1998). "The Design of Embedded Real-Time Systems using the SEA Environment". *Proc. of the 5th Annual Australasian Conference on Parallel And Real-Time Systems (PART '98)*, Adelaide, Australia.

Tanurhan, Y:, Schmerler, S., Müller-Glaser, K.D. (1995). "A Backplane Approach for Cosimulation in High-Level System Specification Environments". *Proceedings of EURO-DAC*.

van de Snepsheut, J.L.A. (1985). *Trace Theory and VLSI Design*. Springer Verlag.

2 SYNTHESIS FROM SYNCHRONOUS/ASYNCHRONOUS SPECIFICATION

FROM SYNCHRONOUS SPECIFICATIONS TO ASYNCHRONOUS DISTRIBUTED IMPLEMENTATIONS

Technische Universität München

Peter Scholz

In this contribution, we sketch a design process for reactive systems, specified with the visual formalism Statecharts. In particular, we discuss how to come from a synchronous Statechart specification to an asynchronous, distributed implementation. Synchronous in this context means that these specifications are based on the assumption that all ist subcomponents interact synchronously with a global clock and in addition perfect synchronous `a la Berry.

1. Introduction

One particularly interesting application field of reactive systems are aircrafts or automobiles: reactive systems can, in the form of embedded systems, be a part of automobile electronics. In a modern upper class car, more than 50 processors or electronic control units can be integrated. These electronic systems increasingly take over tasks of the driver and assist him or her in safety critical or standard situations.

More and more functions will be implemented by software in the cars of the future. However, these systems do not act standalone, but interact to solve complex problems. Today up to 30 percent of the development costs of an upper class car are caused by electric and electronic units. Hence, every single unit must have a high performance so that the additional costs to implement it in the car are justified. Thus, there is a growing interest in industry to use not only one processor for a single task, but to appoint it to different tasks which may not be related at all. However, the specification of a task still should be implementation independent. Hence, a description technique is needed that still leaves room for various implementation strategies, but nevertheless provides all necessary prerequisites for arbitrary implementations. Further reasons why reactive systems are implemented on distributed architectures are: the distributed implementation is imposed by the target architecture through sensor and actor locations; the distributed implementation improves the overall performance of the reactive system as the inherent concurrency in the model can be (better) exploited; through several redundant implementations a higher fault-tolerance can be achieved. This is in particular important for safety critical systems.

Altogether, the design of reactive systems and their distributed implementation is a challenging task that requires elaborated and adapted design techniques. We sketch a complete design process for the development of reactive systems with the visual formalism Statecharts. „Complete" in this context means that the designer is guided from the behavioral system specification stage to the final, distributed implementation on a processor network.

2. System Design and Implementation

To achieve this challenging task, we follow the subsequent strategy. First, we define the compositional Statechart dialect μ-Charts that is suited for both centralized and distributed implementation. For this language, a precise semantics is formalized (Scholz, 1998a) (Scholz, 1998b) . Second, we present a refinement calculus for this dialect (Scholz, 1998a). Then, we show how μ-Chart specifications can be formally verified by model checking (Philipps, 1997b) (Scholz, 1998b). Finally, we discuss how single μ-Charts specifications can be partitioned and implemented on both single processors (Philipps, 1997c) and processor networks (Scholz, 1998b). The aim of this paper is to sketch this design process in more detail, where we mainly concentrate on the presentation of partitioning.

2.1. Specification and Refinement

First of all, we develop the theory of μ-Charts. μ-Charts are a dialect of Statecharts, a visual specification language for reactive systems. In recent years, much scientific work has been invested to improve the Statecharts language. However, up to now most approaches focus more on defining new semantics for Statecharts than on providing solid specification techniques. Several informal and formal semantics for Statecharts and related dialects have been proposed.

We define the semantics $[S]_{io}$ of a μ-Chart S in terms of sets of I/O behaviors or, in other words, I/O histories (Scholz, 1998a). We illustrate that three syntactic concepts, sequential automata, signal hiding, and a composition operator including multicasting are sufficient to express also more complex Statecharts constructs; hierarchy and pure parallel composition can be defined on top of them as syntactic sugar. This strategy has several advantages. First, we restrict ourselves to the most essential language concepts and so can motivate that Statecharts are not as complex as assumed in the hitherto existing literature. Second, we get a semantics that leads to simple proofs when reasoning about the semantics itself. Third, treating hierarchical decomposition as parallel composition and communication is an elegant way to establish distributed implementation of charts in different hierarchical levels.

Our μ-Charts formalism is considered to be a specification technique rather than a (synchronous) programming language like Argos, ESTEREL, LUSTRE, SIGNAL. Therefore, we show how to use μ-Charts in an incremental development process. We demonstrate what it means to develop a system step-by-step. We present a refinement calculus with rules that are easy to understand, but at the same time describe formal design steps towards the final system. One of our goals is to show that μ-Charts are more than a simple two-dimensional programming language. A design methodology is needed, supported by a set of purely syntactic refinement rules that tell the user how to transform an abstract, under-specified system description into a more concrete one. The essential rules we presented in (Scholz, 1998a) are thought to be applicable not only for μ-Charts, but also for any other version of Statecharts. On the semantic level, under-specification is reflected by non-determinism.

2.2. μ-Charts

Statecharts are a graphical description technique for the state-based, behavioral specification of control-oriented systems. In this section, we introduce a Statecharts-like language, termed μ-Charts, which we have developed as basis for design and distributed implementation of reactive systems.

The main concept of Statecharts are sequential automata or, in other words, Mealy machines A. These automata consist of states and transitions. An automaton's state denotes a section of a complex state of a reactive system. Transitions connect those states that describe consecutive system states. A transition can be labeled with a pair, consisting of the condition that must be fulfilled in order to establish the transition and an action that specifies more detailed system behavior when taking the transition. Most graphical notions follow the convention that this pair is separated by a slash, *condition / action*, and we adopt this notation for μ-Charts, too.

To enable description of practically relevant systems, these automata can be composed to larger specifications using two principal structuring mechanisms: parallel composition and hierarchical decomposition.

For parallel composition, the basic assumption is that sub-charts S_1 and S_2 composed by $S_1 \bullet S_2$ in parallel proceed in lock-step with respect to a common clock. Without any further assumptions, these automata do not interact at all. However, if specified by the user, they also can interchange messages L (L is the set of those signals that can be sent and received by S_1 and S_2) in order to influence the behavior of each other: $S_1 \bullet L \bullet S_2$. Note that $S_1 \bullet S_2$ is just a special case for $S_1 \bullet 0 \bullet S_2$ and therefore defined as syntactic abbreviation.

Reactive systems possibly have complex system states. Hence, single automata states may not be appropriate for a detailed description of these systems, and more elaborated techniques are needed. Statecharts enable to further structure single states of sequential automata by hierarchical decomposition. The Statechart that describes the systems behavior in a specific state in more detail is simply (graphically) inserted into this state. The behavior of an hierarchically decomposed Statechart is comparable with the one of procedure calls in an imperative programming language. An automaton of an higher level of hierarchy „calls" sub-routines, that is, Statecharts of a lower level, whenever a decomposed state is entered.

To express hierarchical decomposition, which plays a key role in the concept of Statecharts, we do not need a principally new syntactic construct, but derive hierarchy from the composition operator. This facilitates the definition of both formal semantics and refinement calculus. Furthermore, to express hierarchy by parallel composition and multicasting is a convenient way to provide a basis to implement charts of different levels of hierarchy on different processors. With Statecharts semantics that treat hierarchy on the semantic level this could not be achieved that elegantly. In (Scholz, 1998a), it is explained in detail how hierarchical decomposition can be defined by composition and communication.

2.3. Verification

In former publications (Philipps, 1997a), we also demonstrated how to use the semantic model we introduced as starting point for an efficient formal verification, based on symbolic model checking techniques. We gave a scheme, demonstrated by an example, that translates μ-Charts specifications into μ-calculus (Biere, 1997) formulae and the SMV (McMillan, 1993) input language.

2.4. Implementation

As a further result of our work on symbolic verification of μ-Charts, we showed how a μ-Chart can be implemented as a finite state machine, using a register and a combinational logic block that represents the transition relation of the system (Philipps, 1997c).

However, we do not only provide a strategy for centralized implementation, but in addition discuss problems that occur and restrictions that have to be fulfilled when a μ-Chart specification will be realized with more than one processor. The architecture template we focus on is a realistic architecture that is widespread in automobile industry: it consists of a number of electronic control units that get inputs from sensors, deliver outputs to actors, and are connected via one or more field busses.

2.5. Partitioning

Before a single μ-Chart specification can be implemented on this target architecture, however, some deliberation is necessary. We discuss which problems occur when a specification is partitioned in order to implement it on a processor network.

Apart from the aforementioned reasons, we had to develop our own dialect of Statecharts to bridge the gap between an abstract, formal system description and a distributed implementation. The μ-Chart language fulfills several technical requirements that are a prerequisite for distributed implementations.

It only consists of three syntactic constructs: sequential automata, signal hiding, and a composition operator that combines parallel composition and multicasting. Hierarchical decomposition is defined as syntactic abbreviation: it is achieved by parallel composition and message passing. Thus, we can solve the question how to implement charts of different levels of hierarchy on different processors. With Statechart semantics that treat hierarchy on the semantic level this could not be achieved that elegantly. A syntactically rich language, in which every single construct has its own semantics would neither be suited as starting point for the definition of refinement techniques nor for partitioning nor for distributed implementation.

A further prerequisite for distributed implementation is compositionality of the underlying description technique. Our μ-Chart semantics is compositional and therefore builds a solid basis for partitioning.

Since their syntax is defined incrementally with sequential automata as basic construct, μ-Charts straightforwardly lend themselves to partitioning specifications on the granularity level of automata. A more fine-grained granularity would yield a far too complex partitioning strategy and a more coarse-grained granularity possibly would yield inefficient partitionings.

When partitioning a specification in μ-Charts, care has to be taken that communication between the different parts is deadlock-free or, in other words, does not contain any causality errors. The fixed point semantics we define for the deterministic μ-Charts version exactly reflects the signal causality relationships within one instant and therefore also the communication of distributed μ-Charts components in detail. As a consequence, this semantics serves as mathematical basis to value the partitioning and to verify that no communication deadlocks arise.

As the overall result, this paper offers a design process for a Statecharts dialect that spans the gap between visual formalization of reactive systems up to their distributed implementation on a processor network in an embedded system. Apart from the very early development phase requirements engineering, all important stages of system development (description, refinement, formal verification, partitioning, and implementation) are covered. In each design step, we use equivalent formal semantics for μ-Charts. As a consequence, we do not loose any information between the different stages. Thus, the designer can be sure that the system he or she gets in the final product is semantically equivalent to the one that has been abstractly specified, refined, and formally verified. Hence, we follow the principle of „what you specify and verify is what you implement" and all concepts presented here harmonize with each other.

2.6. Entire Design Process

Our design process for reactive systems starts with the state-based *system description* by the Statecharts-like specification language μ-Charts. As a user might not have a precise imagination how the system under development shall look like in detail in this phase, the system yet might be *under-specified.* Roughly speaking, this means that design alternatives for certain system parts or, more precisely, certain sequential automata yet have been left open by him or her. In the context of this paper, under-specification is a purely syntactic notion that only refers to sequential automata. An automaton can be under-specified because of the following three reasons.

First, the user may have specified more than one initial state for the automaton. Second, the designer may have specified more than one transition for at least one input event in one or more states. Last but not least, no transition might be defined for at least one input event in one or more states. The last type of under-specification is termed *non-responsiveness.* If for every state and every input event of an automaton at least one transition has been specified, we call the automaton *responsive* because it can fire a transition in every state on every input event. This is not the case for non-responsive automata. In the first two cases of under-specification, we say that the system under development is *(syntactically) non-deterministic.* An automaton where exactly one transition is defined for each possible input event in each state and that only has one single initial state is both *deterministic* and *responsive.* We call such an automaton also *completely specified.* If all automata of a μ-Chart specification are completely specified, we also call the overall μ-Chart itself completely specified and under-specified otherwise. If all automata are responsive, we also term the μ-Chart itself responsive and non-responsive otherwise.

Here, we would like to add a warning: apart from this purely syntactic notion of non-determinism, there also exists a semantic notion of non-determinism. A μ-Chart is *(semantically) non-deterministic* if and only if its semantics contains more than one input/output history (see (Scholz, 1998a)). For sequential automata, under-specification is isomorphic to semantic non-determinism. However, for the composition operator of μ-Charts this is in general not true. Later on, we will see that syntactic non-determinism also is semantic non-determinism, but that the opposite is not true. With μ-Charts, semantic non-determinism cannot only be caused by syntactic non-determinism or, more generally, under-specification, but also by composition. This phenomenon is common to most synchronous languages. While syntactic non-determinism is intended by the user, semantic non-determinism that is caused by composition is not. Detecting semantic non-determinism caused by composition requires subtle analysis techniques which have been discussed in detail for centralized implementations in the literature (cf. ESTEREL). In this paper, we will present an approach for distributed implementation.

We recognize that non-responsive automata do not have a defined semantics since the designer did not define any behavior. In order to ease the mathematical formulation of the behavior, that is, the semantics, and the mathematical reasoning with it, we provide a technique to unify both syntactic notions, non-determinism and non-responsiveness, on the semantic level. The technique we use is *chaos completion* (Scholz, 1998b). It allows to interpret non-responsiveness as non-determinism, too. Whenever a sequential automaton of a μ-Charts specification is non-responsive in a state, we assume that this automaton can perform every possible reaction in this state, that is, outputs an arbitrary event that is included in its output interface and has an arbitrary successor configuration. The latter means that the subsequent control and data states can have an arbitrary value within their admissible ranges.

Instead of no system reaction we so get all possible system reactions. Therefore, we say that this part of the system behaves *chaotically*. The mathematical result of the discussion above is a stream semantics for μ-Charts with chaos completion. This stream semantics is tailored for both the mathematical definition of the behavior of possibly non-deterministic and non-responsive μ-Chart specifications and the formal reasoning about how to get implementable specifications: since reactive systems must behave reliably and completely predictably in all situations, we want our final systems to behave (semantically) deterministic.

As a consequence, in the course of system development, under-specification has to be resolved in order to get an implementable system. Hence, in the next design phase, the *refinement* phase, we provide the system developer with easy-to-apply refinement techniques. These are based on a set of syntactic refinement rules. Each rule supports the designer with context restrictions that must be fulfilled in order to get correct refinement steps. All rules are combined to a *refinement calculus* (Scholz, 1998a) that guarantees the correct step-wise concretization of a system under development towards a final deterministic and responsive description that fits for implementation. We would like to mention that through refinement also those specifications that include (unintended) semantic non-determinism that has been introduced through composition may be transformed into deterministic specifications.

As soon as the system engineer comes up with a responsive specification, which yet may be non-deterministic, she or he can begin to formally verify certain properties of the system by *model checking* (Phillips, 1997b) (Scholz, 1998b). Note that we do not support the model checking of non-responsive μ-Charts. This is because of methodological and technical reasons. If no behavior is specified, any system reaction is possible. Hence, the system does not have any longer a „reasonable" behavior, for which interesting properties could be verified. Moreover, since our semantic view of non-responsiveness is chaos, we would have to explicitly encode chaotic behavior with the input language of a model checker, too. If we skipped these explicit encodings, our model for formal verification, a Kripke structure, possibly could perform deadlocks in those configurations where the μ-Charts is non-responsive. However, the explicit encoding of chaos is impracticable. As a consequence, we decided to support model checking of responsive μ-Charts only, which is not a strong restriction in practice. Notice that in contrast to the explicit encoding for model checking, we can formulate chaos implicitly with the theoretical semantics.

Model checking must not necessarily be performed in a separate phase of development shortly before the implementation. Rather, system properties of different levels of abstraction can be verified at different phases of development. These properties can be divided into liveness and safety properties. Informally, the first guarantees that eventually something good will happen and the latter that nothing bad will happen. Once having verified a certain safety property, the application of correct refinement rules guarantees that this property still holds after the application of this rule. While safety properties are not affected by refinement steps, liveness properties are. This is explained by the fact that non-determinism is restricted through refinement. As a consequence, behavioral alternatives that have been included on an earlier design stage possibly are excluded by subsequent refinement steps.

When we finally arrive at a complete specification for which all required properties have been formally verified, we can implement it either on a centralized or on a distributed target architecture. While the first is relatively unproblematic, this is not the case for the latter. Locations for every single sequential automaton have to be defined. We call this process, which can be optimized by tool support, *allocation*. However, before a complete specification can be implemented on a distributed target architecture, a number of considerations is needed. First, this specification has to be partitioned. However, not every partition is feasible. In (Scholz, 1998b) and Section 2.2, we discuss context restrictions and provide the system engineer with guidelines how to partition a μ-Chart specification.

In order to reason about partitioning and distributed implementation, we consult the formal semantics of μ-Charts again. However, the mathematical discussion of multicast communication in the case of distributed implementation requires a slightly different semantic view: in each instant, distributed components send and receive signals according to a chain reaction until the overall system reaches a stable configuration. This stabilization process can be mathematically understood as fixed point computation. Hence, we provide a tailored semantics for deterministic and responsive μ-Chart specification to do so. For deterministic and responsive specifications this semantics is just a concretization of the original stream semantics.

3. Partitioning

In this section, we discuss the problems that potentially may occur when one tries to partition a design with Statecharts and to implement the different parts on a processor network. Problems of this type are the lack of a global clock for a loosely coupled network, communication deadlocks, and the scanning for signal absences in synchronous languages. Note that these aspects are not problematic in case of centralized implementations, but are common to most synchronous languages.

Problems

Partitioning a specification written in a synchronous language, we are faced with a number of interesting problems that are common to most synchronous languages, such as ESTEREL, LUSTRE, SIGNAL, Argos, and μ-Charts. In (Scholz, 1998b), we discussed these problems in detail by means of μ-Charts and presented strategies to remedy them. These strategies provide partly automated solutions and partly syntactic restrictions to the design process of reactive systems with synchronous languages. We begin with a classifications of the envisaged problems and then sketch appropriate solutions.

First, synchronous languages are based on a perfect synchronous time model (Berry, 1998); in particular, the assumption is that all components of a specification interact in lock-step. While this assumption can be fulfilled when the specification is implemented on centralized and tightly coupled target architectures, respectively, this is not the case for loosely coupled systems. Distributed processors in embedded systems, as they occur in automobile industry, are mostly loosely coupled: they communicate via one or several field busses. For these systems, we cannot longer assume that all distributed components are triggered by one single global system clock. Hence, it is difficult to guarantee that also distributed implementations of synchronous specifications interact in lock-step. In particular, care has to be taken that all distributed components start to react in the same instant. Since external input signals are responsible to start reaction in each step, we have to examine these signals and their mutual dependence in more detail.

Second, while external signals are produced by the system environment, internal signals are sent from other system components. The classification into external and internal signals plays an important role in our analysis. If components written in a synchronous language are partitioned and implemented on a distributed architecture, the logical communication of the specification becomes a physical communication. Now, it is important to guarantee that this communication, which possibly consists of a number of sending and receiving actions and in which a number of components can be involved, does not have deadlocks.

The third problem is common to external and internal signals. As a global clock is not available in loosely coupled systems, it is not possible for a distributed reactive system to react on the absolute absence of a signal. The problem here is to decide when to react on the absence of a signal; it is difficult to argue about the relative presence or absence of external signals. As a consequence, we require for distributed implementation that each component can only scan single external input signals in each instant, but not groups of them.

Solutions

To overcome the problems with *external input signals* of distributed implementations, we have proposed two different strategies. We can either restrict the feasible trigger conditions of sequential automata to conditions that only can react on single input signals or we can make assumptions to the system environment by using an rely/guarantee-like specification style. In the former case, give syntactic restrictions that help the designer to specify sequential automata in a way that they always react on just one single external input signal. However, for composed charts we cannot give easy-to-understand syntactic guidelines. Here, tool support is necessary. In (Scholz, 1998b), we discuss how this in principle has to look like. Since for some reactive systems it may be too restrictive to require that its distributed implementation merely reacts on the presence of single signals, but also on the relative presence or absence of more than one, we sketch how this restriction can be weakened using additional information about the external signals of the environment. Of course, in principle, a centralized implementation has to overcome the same problem because its input interface also has to collect signals to events, that is, sets of signals. However, this can be done much easier by a clock signal in the case of centralized implementation. Hence, the problem with external input signals can be avoided for centralized implementations. Using the same clock for all processors of a loosely coupled distributed target architecture is not possible due to technical reasons.

The same argument with the global clock also applies to the problem of dealing with *signal absences* using only one single clock in a centralized implementation enables the scanning of signal absences.

However, the situation is somewhat different in case of the problems *internal input signals* cause in distributed implementations. While for centralized implementations it is sufficient to know that a specification or, more precisely, its semantics, is continuous, we had to require additionally for distributed implementations that their signal graphs, that is, visualizations of the signal dependencies, do not contain any harmful cycle in any reachable configuration. This is necessary to avoid communication deadlocks. In (Scholz, 1998b), we provided an algorithm to detect deadlocks that is similar to the approach for causality analysis suggested by ESTEREL. For centralized implementations, this kind of causality analysis is not needed. Here, already monotonicity alone is adequate, because monotonic charts always have a least fixed point. In order to generate a centralized implementation this is a sufficient property. Since signal graphs can only be constructed for monotonic charts, the existence of a signal graph without harmful cycles also guarantees the chart's monotonicity.

Last but not least, we give syntactic guidelines that support the specifier in writing specifications that do not cause problems in case of distributed implemented due to scanning of absolute absence of external or internal input signals.

In (Scholz, 1998b), we have discussed these three problems and their solutions in more detail. Here, we merely could give a short overview of our solutions due to space limitations.

4. Conclusion

This work was driven by the idea of supporting a design method for Statecharts that covers the design phases description, refinement, verification, and generation of centralized and distributed code, independently of whether the code is implemented in hardware or software. As a first step towards this goal we developed the visual formalism μ-Charts, a dialect of Harel's Statecharts. In contrast to Statecharts and many related approaches, μ-Charts overcome many semantic problems inherent in the former notation. The core language of μ-Charts consists of only three constructs: sequential automata, signal hiding, and a composition operator.

Starting with a lean core language and then extending it by means of abbreviation mechanisms has several advantages. First, it eases the task of obtaining specifications that can be partitioned and implemented on a distributed processor network. Second, it eases reasoning about the semantics itself. Finally, the task of partitioning a monolithic specification is simplified.

5. Acknowledgement

I thank Martin Rappl for carefully reading a draft version of this paper.

References

Berry, G. (1998). *The Foundations of Esterel*, In G. Plotkin, C. Stirling, and M. Tofte, editors, Proof, Language and Interaction: Essays in Honour of Robin Milner, MIT Press.

Biere, A. (1997). *μ-cke - Efficient μ-Calculus Model Checking*. Number 1254 in Lecture Notes in Computer Science, pages 468-471, Springer Verlag.

McMillan, K.L. (1993). *Symbolic Model Checking*. PhD thesis, Carnegie Mellon University.

Philipps, J., Scholz, P. (1997a). *Compositional Specification of Embedded Systems with Statecharts*. In TAPSOFT'97: Theory and Practice of Software Development, volume 1214 of Lecture Notes in Computer Science, Springer Verlag.

Philipps, J., Scholz, P. (1997b). *Formal Verification of Statecharts with Instantaneous Chain Reactions*. In TACAS'97: Tools and Algorithms for the Construction and Analysis of Systems, volume 1217 of Lecture Notes in Computer Science, Springer Verlag.

Philipps, J., Scholz P. (1997c). *System-Level Hardware Design with μ-Charts*. In CHDL'97: Hardware Description Languages and their Applications, Toledo.

Scholz, P. (1998a). *A Refinement Calculus for Statecharts*. In Proceedings of the „ETAPS/FASE'98, Lisbon (Portugal), March 30 - April 03, 1998", volume 1382 of Lecture Notes in Computer Science, Springer Verlag.

Scholz, P. (1998b). *Design of Reactive Systems and their Distributed Implementation with Statecharts*. PhD thesis, Technische Universität München, TUM-I9821.

USING EXTENDED PREDICATE/TRANSITION-NETS FOR THE SPECIFICATION, ANALYSIS AND SYNTHESIS OF EMBEDDED REAL-TIME SYSTEMS

Jürgen Tacken[1]

1. Introduction

In recent years embedded systems have gained increasing importance. Due to the increasing functionality they have to be designed in teams with several specialists, each of them working on one single part of the whole system. But the focus in design is not only more functionality and higher performance but also safety and reliability criteria that have to be fulfilled by the designed components. This includes functional requirements as well as real-time constraints.

By now every single area of application has developed its own well understood techniques for modeling, combined with corresponding methods and tools for analysis and simulation. Already at the state of many individual models many predictions about the temporal and functional behavior of each subsystem can be made. But to validate the behavior of the whole system, the individual models have to be coupled. Especially for the systems' reliability it is important to consider not only each single component on its own but its behavior within the whole context. Many functional errors only expose themselves when all individual components work together in the whole context, observed over time.

Often the models are given in different domain-specific modeling languages, so coupling can only be realized either on the level of simulation or within a hybrid language, that usually does not offer any facilities for further analysis. Coupling of simulators allows a hybrid simulation in the sense of a combined simulation of all subsystems, while each subsystem may be formulated in a different language for a specific simulator. On the level of simulation temporal and functional behavior and

[1] C-LAB, Fürstenalle 11, 33094 Paderborn, Germany, Email: theo@c-lab.de

performance can be studied and validated. But not all errors can be found by simulation because of the exhaustive number of possible simulation runs. Hence it is desirable to run a formal analysis of the static and dynamic properties for formal verification purposes.

A further problem in a separated design process of different subsystems is that each individual domain has proprietary methods of optimization, but for a global optimization of the joint system no facility exists. Especially when coupling different subsystems it may be useful and more cost-effective to export some functionality from one into another subsystem. An overall analysis of the joint system may reveal states that can never be reached and therefore can be eliminated from the design. The prerequisite for this kind of analysis is that all models are given in an uniform language.

In this paper we will describe a new method for the design of embedded real-time systems based on a design flow. During the specification and modeling phase of the design flow it allows the use of several domain-specific modeling languages. All these different languages are transformed into one common model using only one modeling language. So this modeling language has to be very powerful since it must have at least the functionality of every single domain-specific modeling language. After combining all the different designs a global analysis and formal verification of the system may be performed on the common model. To apply efficient and useful analysis and verification methods together with a corresponding software and hardware synthesis the common modeling language is transformed into a less powerful modeling language.

In Chapter 2 we describe our common formal model with all its extensions useful for the integration of different modeling languages. In Chapter 3 we outline our design flow. Chapter 4 deals with the transformation of the powerful model into less powerful versions. Together with these transformations their effect on the analysis results is discussed. In Chapter 5 a timing analysis method for the common model is introduced. The timing analysis results in a partitioning of the system guaranteeing that the real time restrictions are met. This partitioning is the basis for the synthesis into distributed real time software and special hardware. Chapter 6 summarizes the results presented in this paper.

2. Extended Predicate/Transition-Nets

When modeling embedded systems it is important to handle concurrency. As shown in (Dittrich, 94) petri nets are very well suited for the specification of concurrent systems. To handle the complexity they use hierarchical petri nets as specification language in order to support hardware/software-codesign. In our work we also decided to use an extended form of petri nets, namely extended Predicate/Transition-Nets (extended Pr/T-Nets). They have a well defined semantics that allows modular specifications of parallel behavior. Additionally the integration of other specification languages is supported and the representation of the internal model in different specific views is possible. Pr/T-Nets (Genrich, 1987) are bipartite graphs consisting of *places* and *transitions*. In order to define dynamic behavior the places may contain *tokens*. The actual set of all tokens on all places is called a marking of the net. The *edges* between places and transitions (partly) define the possible flow of tokens in a net by the so called *firing* of transitions. To further specify the flow in Pr/T-Nets edges may be annotated by sums of variable tuples. Transitions carry first order formulae over a set of constants and variables together with expressions used to calculate values for variables occurring at output edges of a transition. Transitions are *enabled* (can fire) if appropriate tokens are available on all their input places. When a transition fires it removes tokens from its input places and produces some new tokens on its output places according to the flow specified by the edges and the annotations. In this way the behavior of the Pr/T-Nets is formally defined.

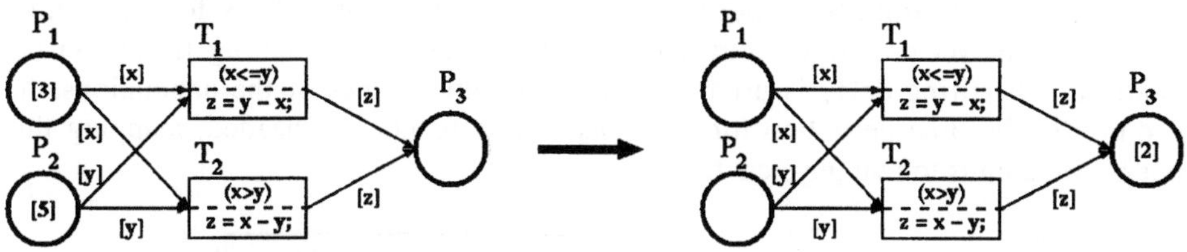

Figure 1: Pr/T-Net example

Figure 1 shows a simple Pr/T-Net calculating the distance of two integers. The places P_1 and P_2 have to be marked with tokens containing the arguments for the calculation. Within the marking shown on the left a substitution of the variables x by *3* and y by *5* determines a valid set of tokens for which the transition T_1 may fire, since *3 <= 5*. The right part of Figure 1 shows the net after firing of T_1.

We extended the basic definition of Pr/T-Nets with hierarchy and timing concepts. Hierarchical specifications are useful to handle complexity in large designs, support a modular specification, and allow the reuse of predefined nets in several models. Our hierarchical Pr/T-Net-model allows the refinement of places and transitions by subnets. Nodes refined by subnets are called structured nodes. The subnet of a structured node is itself an extended Pr/T-Net which may again contain structured nodes. A subnet of a structured node may have connections to nodes in the surrounding net. The connections have to be made via special nodes of the subnet, that are called ports. The net depicted in Figure 1 defines three ports for the inputs and the output of the calculation. Ports are marked by a bold outline. We allow several modes for the semantics of a structured node. In general the semantics is defined via the activity of the subnet. A subnet of a structured transition is active as long as the structured transition itself is active. This is similar to the philosophy of structured nets described in (Cherkasova, 1981). The subnet of a structured place is active as long as the structured place contains at least one token. The concept for structured places is similar to the hierarchical concept in statecharts. The most simple case is a structured place that is initially marked and has no connections to other nodes. Its semantics complies to replacing the node by its refining subnet.

The definition of hierarchical Pr/T-Nets is closely coupled with a mechanism for graphical abstraction of Pr/T-subnets. Based on this graphical abstraction a domain specific representation of the internal model is possible. It provides the ability to define an intuitively understandable abstract graphical representation that is also able to continuously represent the system's behavior and state changes during simulation. The description of the abstract representation may use arbitrary graphical elements. Hence, existing graphical specification languages can be (re)produced by using their predefined symbols as the abstract representation of the petri net elements (Kleinjohann, 1996/1997). Furthermore, an engineer can define his own graphical representation of the system in a way he is familiar with.

Our timing concept supports the integration of real-time aspects like execution and idle times for actions into a Pr/T-Net-model. For each transition an interval or a single integer value may be defined as enabling delay and firing delay. The enabling delay determines the time units before a transition may become active after it has been enabled and the firing delay specifies how long a transition is active. If a transition is active, the tokens from the input places are removed but the tokens for the output places are not yet produced. With the enabling delay idle or waiting times can be modeled. The firing delay is used to specify execution times of the annotations. In addition to the time definition for the transitions a function is needed, mapping the integer time units to real physical times.

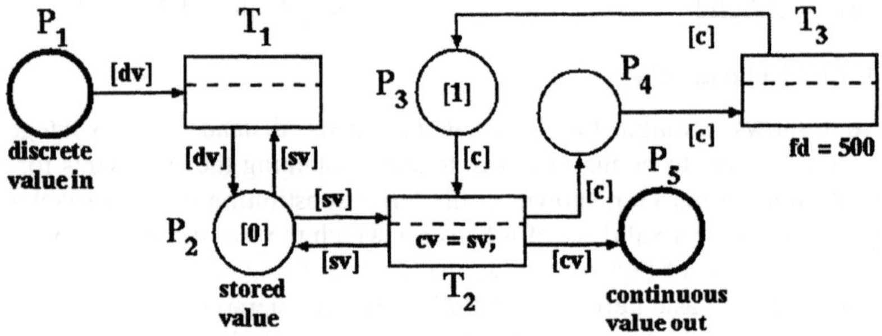

Figure 2: Timed Pr/T-Net example

In Figure 2 an example for a Pr/T-Net with timing specifications is depicted. The net is a typical example for an element used for interfacing models of different system parts, e.g. of a discrete event driven part and a periodic one, that was originally specified by a continuous model. Each value arriving aperiodically at the in-port of the net is stored in place P_2 by transition T_1. The stored value is sent to the out-port by transition T_2. Due to the firing delay defined for transition T_3 the value is sent with a period of 500 time units. If for example the integer time unit is mapped to the physical unit µs, the value would be produced with a frequency of 2 kHz.

For a comfortable specification, simulation, and animation of extended Pr/T-Nets we use the System Engineering and Animation-environment SEA (Kleinjohann, 1996).

3. Design flow

To advance towards a complete design method one has to take the flow of design into account. The process we suggest in this work is divided into the three stages modeling, analysis and synthesis (cf. Figure 3).

3.1 Modeling

The process of modeling usually starts from a concept of a given system the designer has in mind. During a manual prepartitioning phase he roughly defines which components will constitute the system. For the application described here this should be a partitioning into software, controllers having continuous behavior, and digital hardware. This prepartitioning is based upon the experience of the engineer developing the system.

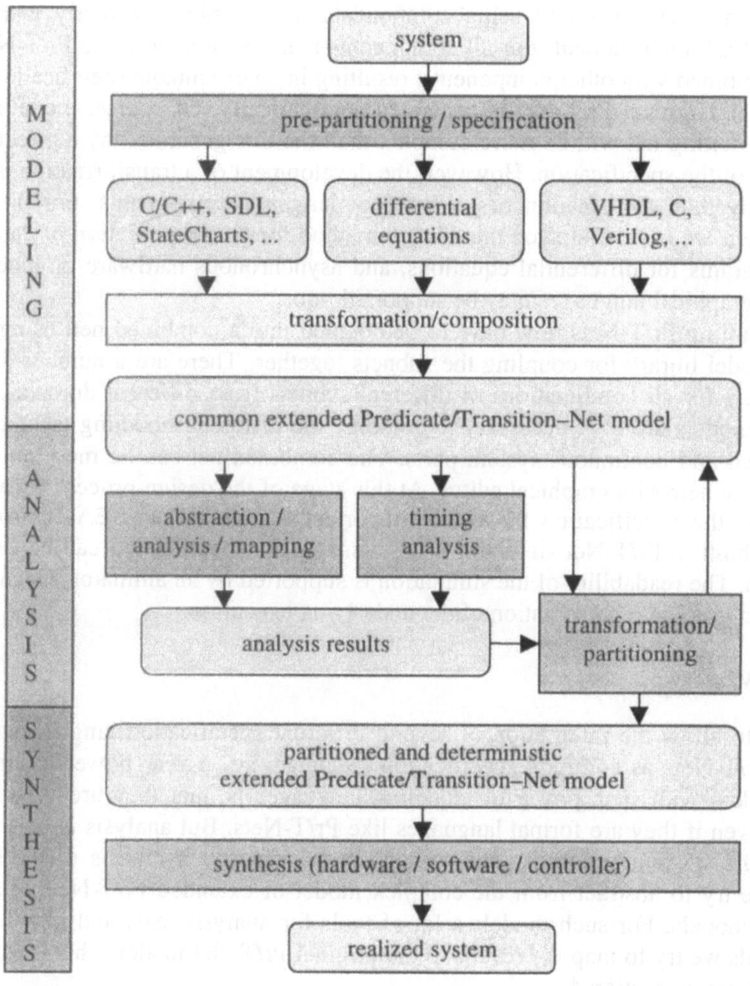

Figure 3: Design flow with the three stages modeling, analysis and synthesis

Typically designers of the individual components choose a specification language they are familiar with and that is appropriate for the area of application. Generally these languages have their own domain-specific tools for analysis and optimization which are not subject of this work. There are two possible ways to transform models given in different specification languages into an extended Pr/T-Net model.Using transformation each individual specification can be transformed, either manually or automatically, into an extended Pr/T-Net. Depending on how skillful this transformation was performed a more or less complex Pr/T-Net is created that realizes the specification. A transformation for differential equations is presented in (Brielmann, 1995). An example for the transformation of SDL (Specification and Description Language) is shown in (Kleinjohann, 1997).

Another method for the SEA-environment is a library construction. The process of modeling may be performed using components from a library directly within the graphical SEA-environment. For all components there is an underlying Pr/T-Net that can be combined with other components, resulting in an executable specification. So a complete hierarchical Pr/T-Net is generated automatically. Of course, modeling this way the resulting net will be more complex than the one generated by a direct transformation of the specification. However, the development of a transformation is much more costly than the creation of a library of language components. For the SEA-environment we have evaluated this library method for the specification of data flow, block diagrams for differential equations, and asynchronous hardware on gate level, but other graphical languages may be supported, too.

All resulting Pr/T-Nets now have to be coupled into a combined net, using an interface model library for coupling the subnets together. There are a number of interface models for all combinations of different subnets from different domains. These interface models are e. g. necessary to combine the different modeling techniques of event-based and continuous system parts. The combined net can be modified manually with the help of a graphical editor. At this stage of the design process we are able to validate the specification by a very important feature of the SEA-environment. With the built in Pr/T-Net simulator and -animator the specification can be executed and tested. The readability of the simulation is supported by an animator which shows an abstract graphic representation of the underlying execution.

3.2 Analysis

In order to allow the integration of several different specification languages the extended Pr/T-Nets as common specification language are a very powerful language. The problem with such powerful modeling languages is, that they are very hard to analyze even if they are formal languages like Pr/T-Nets. But analysis is very important for the systems reliability and to support an effective synthesis of the system. Hence we try to abstract from the complex model of extended Pr/T-Nets to simpler petri net models. For such models a lot of tools for analysis exist and may be used. Afterwards we try to map the results to the original Pr/T-Net model. This is explained in more detail in section 4.

Another aspect of analysis is to do timing analysis, for example to determine the different execution times for alternative realizations of functions for different target architectures. Such alternative realizations can be specified using non determinism. Each alternative may have its advantages or disadvantages for different target architectures or target code languages. The design method should then support an automatical selection of the best alternative for synthesis. This is explained in more detail in section 5. The results of this analysis can either be used for the partitioning or for the synthesis phase. The timing results are for example used to transform non deterministic subnets into deterministic ones.

3.3 Synthesis

After a stable state is reached in the alternating phases of modeling and analysis, the partitioned net graph can be compiled into hardware and real-time software during the phase of synthesis. The compilation process can be supported by results of the analysis. In the case of digital hardware the net is transformed into RT-level VHDL code using the Paderborn MOdular System for High-Level Synthesis and HW/SW-codeSign (PMOSS) (Hardt, 1995). In the case of distributed real-time software one compiles the corresponding Pr/T-subnet using the C-LAB Hard Real-Time System (CHaRy) (Altenbernd, 1997). These tools are both parts of the PARADISE Design Environment (Hardt, 1998).

4. Analysis for the verification of system properties

As described above, we made various extensions to the formal model of Pr/T-Nets in order to meet all requirements for a common modeling language. Unfortunately, these extensions have the drawback that all the well-known analysis methods for petri-net are not applicable to our models. We decided to use existing petri net methods for the analysis phase of our design method. The main properties for the analysis of petri nets are boundness, reachability, deadlock-freeness and liveness (Starke 1990). In the following we describe these properties and their meaning for the modeled embedded systems.

A place is bound if a positive number exist which is an upper limit for the number of tokens on this place for every possible firing sequence within the net. If this upper limit is equal to 1 the place is called safe. If all places are bound/safe than the whole net is bound/safe. If places are unbounded in the model there may exist potentially overflowing buffers or infinite process calls in the realization of the embedded system.

A marking in a net is called reachable if a firing sequence of transitions exists leading from the initial marking to this marking. A marking in the net represents a state of the modeled system. Hence knowing if a marking is reachable means to know if the corresponding state of the embedded system is reachable. With this property one can for example check if in case of emergency conditions a safe state is reached.

A marking is called a deadlock if no transition of the net is enabled for this marking. So there is no further action possible within the modeled system which is often not intended. In case of a deadlock every transition of the net is dead. A transition is called live for a marking M if it is not dead for M and also for all markings that are reachable from M. If all transitions are live for a marking then the marking is called live and if all reachable markings of a net are live the net is called life. If a net is live then it can not have any deadlocks.

Some properties can already be checked with a structural analysis of the net graph. This can be done directly for the Pr/T-Net graph. For example if there exists a transition without input places it is live and all output places are unbounded or if a place has no input transitions it is bounded and all output transitions are live. If t is a transition without output places then t is not live or all input places of t are unbounded and if p is a place without output transitions then p is unbounded or all input transitions of p are not live. More important than these structural results are results of dynamic analysis like for example occurrence graph based analysis. In the occurrence graph of a net a node represents a state in the net. A state is characterized by the actual marking of places with token. This is represented by a tuple containing the set of token for every place.

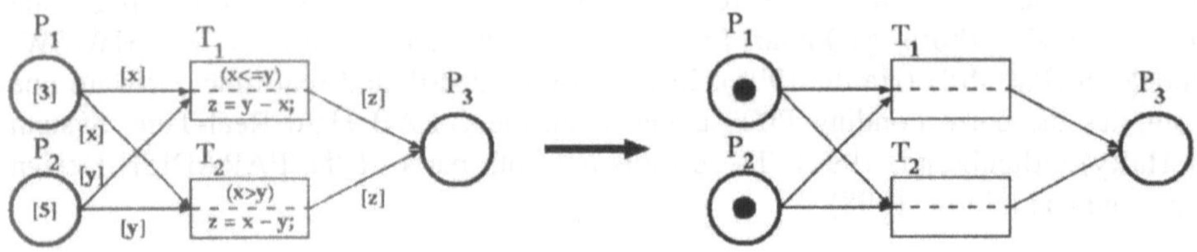

Figure 4: Simple abstraction of an extended Pr/T-Net

To use the occurrence graph based analysis methods for extended Pr/T-Nets we need an abstraction from extended Pr/T-Net models to petri net models. Figure 4 shows an example for a very simple abstraction. If we ignore all the annotations of transitions, edges and token the result is a simple petri net. This has of course effects on the resulting occurrence graph.

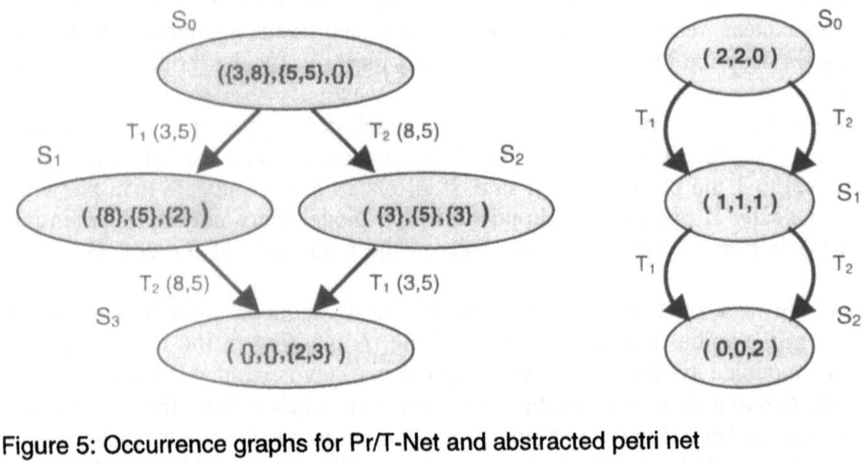

Figure 5: Occurrence graphs for Pr/T-Net and abstracted petri net

In the left side of Figure 5 the occurrence graph for the Pr/T-Net from Figure 4 is depicted. The first state in this graph indicates that P_1 is marked with 3 and 8, P_2 with 5 and 5, and P_3 contains no token. The edges are annotated with the transition, that causes the change of the state and the chosen variable substitution. For example if T_1 fires with the substitution 3 and 5 the state S_1 is reached. The occurrence graph for the abstracted net depicted on the right side of Figure 5 contains less nodes, because the states are not distinct by individual token. Only the number of token on a place is relevant. But if you examine the possible firing sequences of transitions, you get more than in the Pr/T-Net. For example in the petri net the transition T_1 may fire twice but not in the Pr/T-Net. This means the annotations in the Pr/T-Net define a restriction on the token flow.

Based on this fact some results from the analysis of the abstracted nets can directly be mapped to the Pr/T-Nets. If for example a marking is not reachable in the petri net it is also not reachable in the corresponding Pr/T-Net. But if it is reachable in the petri net it is not necessarily reachable in the Pr/T-Net. But of course we can use the petri net analysis to determine all possible firing sequences leading to a marking and than just check if one of these firing sequences also exists in the Pr/T-Net. If a deadlock occurs in the abstracted net it is also present in the Pr/T-Net if the corresponding marking is reachable. But not having any deadlocks in the abstracted net does not mean the Pr/T-Net is deadlock free. For safeness or boundness it holds that the Pr/T-Net is bound/safe if the abstracted petri net is bound/safe. But if the abstracted net is unbounded/unsafe the Pr/T-Net may be bound/safe.

5. Timing analysis

To support a software/software partitioning of the net and the elimination of non determinism we perform a timing analysis (Rust, 1998). As a first step we calculate execution times for every transition annotation in the examined net part using the C–LAB Hard Real-Time System CHaRy (Altenbernd, 1997). CHaRy determines a worst case execution time for each annotation on a specified target architecture. This worst case execution time is used to annotate the transitions in the Pr/T-Net with delay values. Afterwards a reachability analysis is done to determine all possible firing sequences leading from an input to the desired output and a rough worst case execution time for all firing sequences can be calculated. Now the best fitting alternative can be chosen from all alternatives.

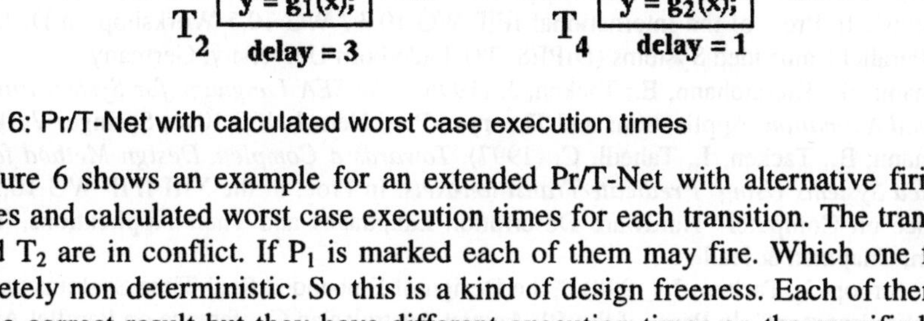

Figure 6: Pr/T-Net with calculated worst case execution times

Figure 6 shows an example for an extended Pr/T-Net with alternative firing sequences and calculated worst case execution times for each transition. The transitions T_1 and T_2 are in conflict. If P_1 is marked each of them may fire. Which one fires is completely non deterministic. So this is a kind of design freeness. Each of them produces a correct result but they have different execution times on the specified target architecture. The same holds for the transitions T_3 and T_4. In this case the best result is achieved for the sequence T_1,T_4 and the worst for T_2,T_3. So the transitions T_2 and T_3

can be eliminated from the model. For the remaining transitions the delay values are used to perform a partitioning on the extended Pr/T-Net model.

6. Conclusion

In this paper we described a new method for the design of embedded real-time systems. Our suggested design flow is an approach towards an integrated, complete design. We have shown how to use an extended form of Pr/T-Nets as a common model for specification. We explained how to use standard petri net analysis methods to achieve results for extended Pr/T-Nets. These results are used for the verification of system properties. Additionally we introduced timing analysis to determine the different execution times for alternative realizations of functions for different target architectures and to support the partitioning of the modeled system. This partitioning is the basis for the synthesis of the system.

References

Altenbernd, P. (1997). CHaRy: The C-LAB Hard Real-Time System to Support Mechatronical Design in International Conference and Workshop on Engineering of Computer Based Systems (ECBS), Monterey, CA.

Brielmann, M. (1995). *Modelling differential equations by basic information technology means.* Proceedings of the 5th International Conference on Computer Aided Systems, Theory and Technology (EUROCAST'95), Innsbruck, Austria.

Cherkasova L. A., Kotov V. E. (1981). *Structured nets.* In J. Gruska and M. Chytil, editors, Mathematical Foundations of Computer Science, volume 118 of Lecture Notes in Computer Science. Springer Verlag.

Dittrich, Gisbert. (1994). *Modeling of Complex Systems Using Hierarchical Petri Nets.* In Codesign: Computer-aided software/hardware engineering, New York, NY: IEEE Press, chapter 6.

Genrich, H. J. (1987). *Predicate/Transition Nets.* Advances in Petri Nets Part I, Vol. 254, Springer Verlag.

Hardt, W. (1995). An Automated Approach to HW/SW-Codesign. In IEEE Colloquium: Paritioning in Hardware-Software Codesings. London, Great Britain, February 1995.

Hardt, W., Altenbernd, P., Böke, C., Del Castillo, G., Ditze, C., Erpenbach, E., Glässer, U., Kleinjohann, B., Lehrenfeld, G., Rammig, F. J., Rust, C., Stappert, F., Stroop, J., Tacken, J. (1998). "Paradise: Design Environment for Parallel & Distributed, Embedded Real-Time Systems", In Proc. of the International IFIP WG 10.3 / WG 10.5 Workshop on Distributed and Parallel Embedded Systems (DIPES '98), Paderborn University, Germany.

Kleinjohann, B., Kleinjohann, E., Tacken, J. (1996). *The SEA Language for System Engineering and Animation.* Applications and Theory of Petri Nets, LNCS 1091, Springer Verlag.

Kleinjohann, B., Tacken, J., Tahedl, C. (1997). *Towards a Complete Design Method for Embedded Systems Using Predicate/Transition-Nets.* In Proc. of the XIII IFIP WG 10.5 Conference on Computer Hardware Description Languages and Their Applications, Toledo, Spain, Chapman & Hall.

Rust, C., Stroop, J., Tacken, J. (1998). "The Design of Embedded Real-Time Systems using the SEA Environment", In Proc. of the 5th Annual Australasian Conference on Parallel And Real-Time Systems (PART '98), Adelaide, Australia.

Starke, P. H. (1990). Analyse von Petri-Netz-Modellen, Leitfäden und Monographien der Informatik, Teubner, Stuttgart.

FROM MSCS TO STATECHARTS

Ingolf Krüger, Radu Grosu,
Peter Scholz, Manfred Broy[1]

We present a first step towards a seamless integration of MSCs into the system development process. In particular, we show how scenario-based system requirements, captured in the early system analysis phase using MSCs, are translated into state-based description techniques like Statecharts. To this end, we sketch a schematic integration of MSCs and Statecharts.

1. Introduction

Message Sequence Charts (MSCs) have gained wide acceptance for scenario-based specifications of component behavior (see, for instance, [IT96, BMR+96, Rat97, BHKS97]). In particular, they have proven useful in the requirements capture phase of the software development process. However, up to now, most development methods do not assign a precise meaning to this graphical description technique. Moreover, MSCs are often used only for documentation purposes, and are not seamlessly integrated into the development process. Therefore, a lot of their potentials are usually left unexploited. Besides the interaction oriented system view provided by MSCs, state-based specification languages, such as Statecharts, are of particular importance in later development stages. For Statecharts, concepts for refinement, verification, and code generation have recently been developed. Aiming at a seamless development process, an integration of both description techniques seems necessary and promising. As a step towards this goal we show how to derive Statecharts from MSCs schematically. To that end, we discuss various interpretations of MSCs with respect to their applicability within the development process we target at, and show how to translate a subset of MSC specifications into Statecharts models.

1.1. MSCs and Development Processes

Typical software development processes of today [V97, Boe86, Boe88, Roy70] suggest to develop the intended product not in one single step, but in successive devel-

[1] Institut für Informatik, Technische Universität München, Arcisstr. 21, D-80290 München, Germany; email: {kruegeri,grosu,scholzp,broy}@in.tum.de

opment phases. Four common phases across different development processes are requirements capture, design, validation, and implementation.

MSCs have gained wide acceptance particularly during requirements capture for all classes of systems, including both business and embedded systems. Due to their intuitive notation MSCs have proven useful as a communication tool between customers and developers, thus helping to reduce misunderstandings in early development stages. In later phases, the most common use of MSCs today is for documentation or explanatory purposes. A lot of information that is illustrated using MSCs is not systematically exploited when transiting from requirements capture to design, let alone the transitions between the development activities occurring even later. This means that, in general, there exists no seamless integration of MSCs into an overall software development process. As a first step towards achieving such an integration, we consider the combination of MSCs and state-based specification techniques, such as Statecharts. The latter are mainly employed during design, and, increasingly often, during validation and implementation of distributed embedded systems. In particular, we aim at deriving Statecharts from a set of given MSCs such that the former exhibit the same interaction behavior as the latter. The resulting Statecharts can then be refined towards an implementation.

1.2. A closer look at MSCs

One of the major obstacles at increasing the integration of MSCs into the overall software development process is that their semantics with respect to other system views, such as the component distribution or state transition views, is either left unspecified, or restricted to a purely scenario-based specification style. The potential for confusion arising in both cases manifests itself in the slightly adapted saying "Everybody understands MSCs, but everybody understands them differently".

Traditionally, the graphical syntax of most MSC dialects provides the following basic symbols: labeled axes, representing part of a component's existence, and labeled arrows, representing message exchange, directed from the sender to the recipient of a message. For simple scenarios these symbols already suffice. Frequently, additional constructs that increase the expressiveness of the notation are added. Examples of such constructs are sequential and parallel composition, choice, repetition, and even hierarchic decomposition (see, for instance, the graphical syntaxes discussed in [IT96, Rat97, BMR+96]). Most of these turn out to be essential when transiting from scenarios to more elaborate system descriptions. To perform this transition, we have to state precisely what we mean when we draw an MSC. To show that there is indeed a lot of room for discussion and, therefore, (mis)interpretation, we raise the following questions. First, what does an MSC mean with respect to the set of components within the system under development? Answering this question results in three different interpretations: the system consists exactly, at most, or at least of the components referenced in the MSC. Second, how "complete" is the information we obtain from a given MSC with respect to the components involved and the messages they exchange? The interaction between the components referenced in the MSC is determined either completely, i.e. there do not occur other message sequences between the components, or partially, i.e. other message sequences are explicitly allowed. Third, at what time instants do successive message exchanges occur? This addresses a problem that is of particular importance when designing reactive systems: may, for instance, two successive message exchanges occur during the same system step? Considering the interpretations obtained by answering these questions yields a classification of possible MSC semantics. Each element of this classification can be investigated for its usefulness in enabling a methodical transition from MSCs to state-based description techniques. To base this discussion on more solid grounds we formalize our notion of systems and interaction.

1.3. Statecharts

Statecharts are a graphical description technique for the state-based, behavioral specification of control-oriented systems [Har87]. The language was developed for the description of reactive systems. Statecharts combine the operational notions of Mealy machines (sequential automata) with graphical structuring mechanisms to concisely describe large state spaces.

The main concept of Statecharts is that of sequential automata. These automata consist of states and transitions. An automaton's state denotes a section of a complex state of a reactive system. Transitions connect consecutive system states. A transition is labeled with a pair, consisting of the condition that must be fulfilled in order to trigger the transition and an action that specifies more detailed system behavior to be executed when the transition is performed.

To enable description of practically relevant systems, these automata can be composed to larger specifications using two principal structuring mechanisms: parallel composition and hierarchic decomposition. Here, the basic assumption is that automata composed in parallel proceed in lock-step with respect to a common clock. Without any further assumptions, these automata do not interact at all. However, if specified by the user, they also can exchange messages in order to mutually influence each other's behavior. Reactive systems may have complex system states. Hence, single automaton states may not be appropriate for a detailed description of these systems, and more elaborate techniques are needed. Statecharts allow the designer to structure single states of sequential automata by hierarchic decomposition. The Statechart that describes the system's behavior in a specific state in more detail is simply (graphically) inserted into this state. The behavior of a hierarchically decomposed Statechart is comparable with the one of procedure calls in an imperative programming language.

However, a specification formalism is of limited value without its integration into an appropriate system development process. What we need is to give guidelines how to develop a concrete implementation or realization from an abstract system specification. This transition from an abstract specification to a concrete implementation covers a number of different development steps such as specification, verification, efficient compilation, and refinement. For the Statecharts dialect μ-Charts, such a development process has been presented in [Sch98a].

1.4. Integrating MSCs and Statecharts

In the development process using Statecharts as sketched above, we factored out the requirements engineering phase. Hence, there is still a gap between this phase and the state-based description of a reactive system with Statecharts. This gap can be filled by applying techniques that are based on MSCs. In contrast to Statecharts, these provide a possibility for event- or scenario-based development of a system in its early design phase. In order to get a seamless development process that also covers requirements engineering, it is interesting to develop an appropriate MSC-like description technique that is based on the same semantic model as Statecharts and therefore can be automatically translated to an equivalent Statechart specification. Furthermore, these MSC-like techniques can serve to represent counter-examples and witnesses from model checking results, or simply as a front end for the input language of an appropriate model checker. Finally, MSCs can be used to restrict communication between Mealy machines combined in parallel to only those signal interactions that are free of causality errors [Sch98b], which is one of the major problems when specifying larger systems with Statecharts.

Integrating MSCs and Statecharts to form a seamless development process, a number of interesting questions have to be solved. First of all, both languages have to be unified on the semantic level. To this end, we define their semantics by means of a relational stream semantics. The stream semantics of one component, specified either as an MSC or as a Statechart reflects its, potentially non-deterministic, input/output behavior. Dealing with a non-deterministic semantics has the advantage that we can treat abstract specifications and concrete, implementation-level descriptions with the same mathematical machinery. Furthermore, this approach makes it possible to allow mixed MSC and Statechart specifications. This is a prerequisite to capture the behavior also of those systems under development, where different system parts reside in different development phases. Of course, a common, homogenous semantic model further eases specification of complex systems: not only can components in different development phases be described with different techniques, but also those in identical phases. Thus, it is possible that some system parts are merely specified in MSCs and others just in Statecharts.

2. Translating MSCs into Statecharts

In this section we discuss a general procedure for deriving state-based component descriptions from a set of MSCs. To that end, we first sketch the underlying semantic framework that we use to achieve a smooth integration of Statecharts and MSCs (Section 2.1). We give an overview of our translation scheme in Section 2.2, and present an example of its application in Section 2.3.

2.1. Semantic Model

As we have mentioned already in Section 1, there is a lot of freedom in interpreting MSCs. Here, we introduce a simple, yet expressive formal framework, on top of which we can both discuss possible MSC semantics, and establish an integration of MSCs and Statecharts.

The systems we are interested in consist of a set of components, and a set of directed channels. Components that have to communicate must be connected by channels. Each component operates by reading input on its input channels, calculating its output, and writing the output to its output channels. Furthermore, we assume that the system is driven by some global, discrete clock. This is a quite natural assumption considering the current hardware technology and it allows us to determine exactly at what time unit a message occurs on a given channel. We call the sequence of messages passed along a channel over time a channel history. Our basic assumption here is that communication happens message-asynchronously: the sender of a message is never blocked by the receiver of the message. A simple strategy to assure this kind of communication is buffering messages.

Given a system specification *Sys* and an MSC *msc*, we can now define how the two relate. Each such relationship defines one possible interpretation of *msc*. There are two interesting questions concerning the semantics of any given MSC: what sequences of messages does it represent, and when – with respect to a complete execution of the system under design – do they occur. We assume that we know the set of sequences defined by an MSC so we can focus on answering the second question. Suppose the system *Sys* is characterized by a set of channel histories V and that *msc*, msc_0 and msc_1 are MSCs. We distinguish the following interpretations of the MSCs with respect to *Sys*:

- **exact**: the interaction sequences specified by *msc* occur exactly once in all $v \in V$, and no other interactions are possible;
- **existential**: there are elements $v \in V$ that exhibit the interaction sequences specified by *msc*;
- **universal**: all elements $v \in V$ exhibit the interaction sequences specified by *msc*;
- **trigger condition**: we say that msc_0 triggers msc_1, if, after an interaction sequence as specified by msc_0 has occurred in a valuation $v \in V$, an interaction sequence as specified by msc_1 will also occur in v within a finite amount of time;
- **negation**: using logical negation, we obtain the dual interpretations of the ones given above.

Each of these interpretations has its place within the software development process. During requirements capture each of them is of value and in use. The exact interpretation is the one we use for the transition from MSCs to Statecharts. For testing, and documentation the most prominent use of MSCs today is under the existential, and universal interpretation, together with their negations. The bottom line of this discussion is that in whatever phase of the development process we employ MSCs, we should state clearly what interpretation we have in mind.

2.2. Roadmap for the translation procedure

In the previous section we have explained the semantic model for the systems we are interested in, together with a number of possible interpretations for MSCs in that model. Here, we select the exact interpretation in a slightly modified form as the basis for our translation procedure from MSCs to Statecharts.

The basis for the translation is the procedure explained in detail in [BGK98]. We assume given a set of MSCs that describe all the interaction sequences among a set of components, i.e., we make a closed world assumption with respect to the interaction sequences occurring in the system under development. The procedure we suggest makes use of information on the component's control/data-state provided by the designer, for instance, via the condition symbols found in the MSC standard [IT96, IT98]. Each condition will be translated into a corresponding automaton state. We assume further that we try to obtain an automaton for exactly one of the components, say c, occurring in the MSCs. The second input we expect, besides the set of MSCs, is the name of the starting state for c's automaton. The procedure for obtaining that automaton consists of five successive phases: projection, normalization, transformation into an MSC-Automaton, transformation into an automaton, and optimization.

2.2.1. Projection

During the first phase we project each of the given MSCs onto the component c, i.e. we remove all other instance axes, as well as message arrows that neither start, nor end at c.

2.2.2. Normalization

Then, in the second phase, we normalize the projected MSCs. An MSC in our normal form consists of exactly two condition symbols and a (possibly empty) sequence of message arrows in between. To normalize an MSC that does not start or end with a condition symbol, we add the one representing the given initial state. We split MSCs that contain more than two conditions at any of the intermediate ones. Thus, we replace each such MSC by two new ones; the first of these is the original MSC up to (and including) the condition at which we split, the second one is the original MSC from that condition on.

2.2.3. Transformation into an MSC-Automaton

To obtain what we call an MSC-Automaton, we now identify the condition labels occurring in the resulting MSCs with states of the automaton for component c. Furthermore, we create a transition from state s_0 to state s_1 labeled by MSC M if and only if there is a normalized MSC M whose start and end conditions are labeled with s_0 and s_1, respectively. As the initial condition for this automaton we use the one provided as an input to the procedure. The result of this phase is an automaton that provides a high-level view on the states of the component we are interested in.

2.2.4. Transformation into an Automaton

In the fourth phase of our procedure we expand the transitions that are labeled with MSCs by intermediate states and transitions. We replace all transitions that are labeled with an MSC containing only conditions by an ε-transition. Let M be any other MSC label. It defines $k > 0$ communication actions that we denote by (d_1, n_1, c_1), ..., (d_k, n_k, c_k), recorded in the order of the corresponding arrows of M. Here d_i, n_i, and c_i represent the direction of the message exchange ("!" for an outgoing, and "?" for an incoming arrow), the message label, and the name of the corresponding sender or receiver, respectively (for $1 \leq i \leq k$). For $k = 1$ we replace the transition labeled with M by one labeled with (d_1, n_1, c_1). For $k > 1$ we add k-1 new states, labeled by s_1 through s_{k-1}, as well as k new transitions to the automaton. The first transition starts in the state corresponding to the start condition of M, ends in s_1, and its label is (d_1, n_1, c_1). The k-th transition, labeled with (d_k, n_k, c_k), starts in the new state s_{k-1}, and ends in the state corresponding to the final condition of M . All other transitions start in state s_{i-1}, end in state s_i, and their label is (d_i, n_i, c_i), for $1 < i < k$. After applying these steps to all transitions labeled with MSCs we obtain a nondeterministic automaton with input/output actions.

2.2.5. Optimization

To optimize the resulting automaton we may now use standard algorithms from automata theory; examples of such algorithms are the elimination of ε-transitions, the subset-construction, and the Myhill-Nerode construction for minimization (cf. [HU93]). Other optimizations are motivated by the semantics of the underlying communication system. For Statecharts we might, for instance, condense transition sequences of the form "?, !, !, ..., !"[2] into a single transition labeled with "?/!!...!". The symbol "/" separates input and output actions that occur during the same time instant [Sch98a]. This corresponds to identifying the occurrence of a sequence of outputs with their triggering input.

The next section provides an example application of the procedure we have outlined here.

2.3. Example

As the running example we use a simplified specification of a central locking system (CLS) for cars. This example is inspired by a case study from automotive industry. The principal structure of the CLS is sketched in Figure 1; it gives an overview of the locking system of a two-door car.

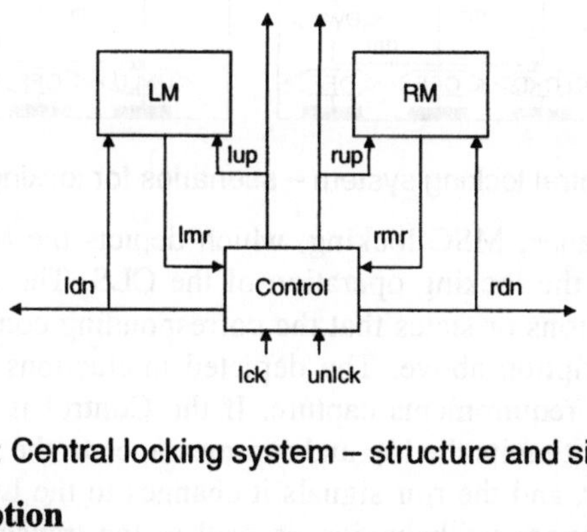

Figure 1: Central locking system – structure and signals

2.3.1. Informal Description

The CLS consists essentially of three main parts: the Control and the two door motors LM (short for "left motor") and RM (short for "right motor"). These parts are composed in parallel. In this system structure, we also describe the signal flow between different components by arrows, which connect output and input interfaces of possibly communicating components.

---

[2]Here we consider the direction of the communication only.

The default configuration of the system is that all doors are unlocked (UNLD) and both motors are OFF. The Control is the central component of the central locking system.

The driver can unlock or lock the doors either from outside by turning the key or from inside by pressing a button. Locking and unlocking the doors leads to complex signal interactions. Both actions generate the external signals lck (for "locking") or unlck (for "unlocking"). The Control generates the internal signals ldn and rdn and changes to its locking configuration LCKD.

Instantaneously, influenced by ldn and rdn, respectively, both motors begin to lock the doors by entering their DWN configurations. As the speeds of the motors depend on external influences like their temperature, each motor either needs one or two time units to finish the lowering process. Only when both motors have sent their ready messages lmr (for "left motor ready") and rmr ("right motor ready"), the Control enters its LCKD configuration.

2.3.2. Scenario-based View

The MSCs of Figure 2 illustrate most of the requirements stated informally in the previous paragraphs; for reasons of brevity we have omitted the handling of simultaneity and of the possibly different speeds of components.

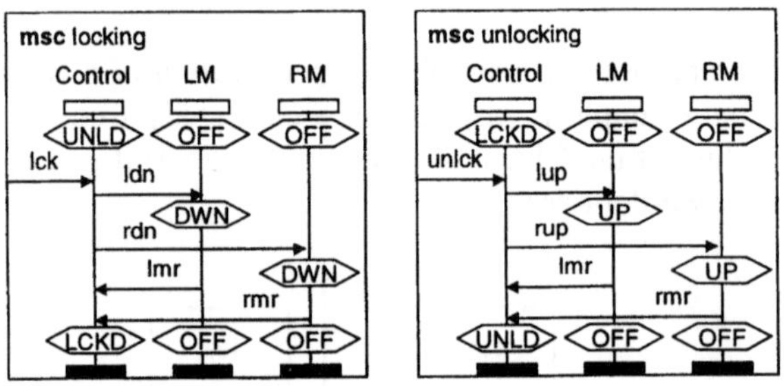

Figure 2: Central locking system – scenarios for locking and unlocking

Consider, for instance, MSC locking, which depicts the behavior of the Control, LM, and RM during the locking operation of the CLS. The angular boxes in MSCs denote the configurations or states that the corresponding component is in, according to the informal description above. The depicted interactions also proceed along the lines of the informal requirements capture. If the Control is in state UNLD and receives the lck signal, it emits the lup and rup messages to the two motors. After it has received both the lmr, and the rmr signals it changes to the LCKD state. The translation of the other components' behavior, as well as the translation of the second scenario (see MSC unlocking) are equally direct.

2.3.3. Translation into Statecharts

In this section we apply the translation procedure as described in Section 2.2 to the MSCs depicted in Figure 2. We illustrate the results of the individual phases of the procedure using the Control component.

In the first step we project the two MSCs onto the axes that represent Control. The resulting MSCs (see Figure 3, left) are already in normal form. Note that we would have to split the projections of LM and RM at the intermediate UP and DWN conditions to obtain normal forms for these components. We derive the MSC-automaton for Control as it appears in Figure 3, right, because MSCs LC and UC take that component from state UNLD to LCKD, and from LCKD to UNLD, respectively.

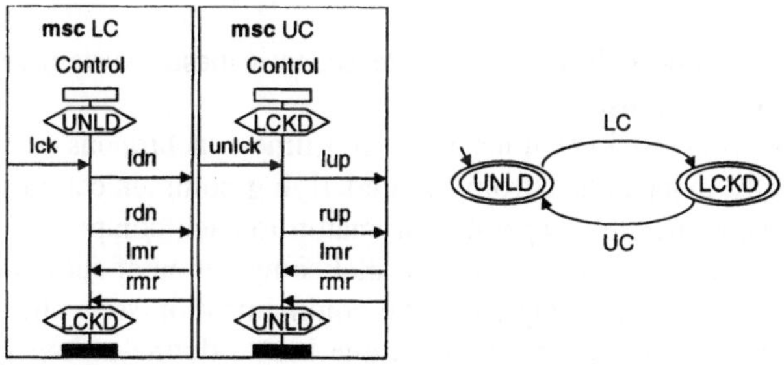

Figure 3: Projected MSCs for component Control and corresponding MSC-Automaton

By expanding the MSC-labeled transitions in the fourth phase of the procedure, we obtain the automaton depicted in Figure 4. Note that we have omitted the receiver in the transition labels because in the broadcasting communication model of Statecharts this information is redundant.

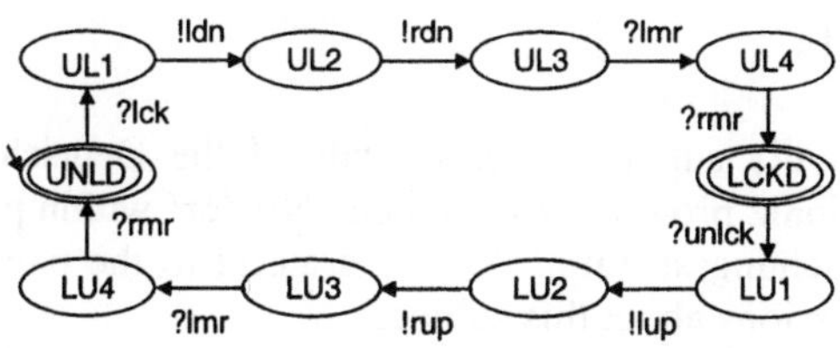

Figure 4: Automaton for component Control

Using the optimization suggested in Section 2.2, and combining the result with the result of deriving also the automata for LM and RM, we obtain the Statechart depicted in Figure 5.

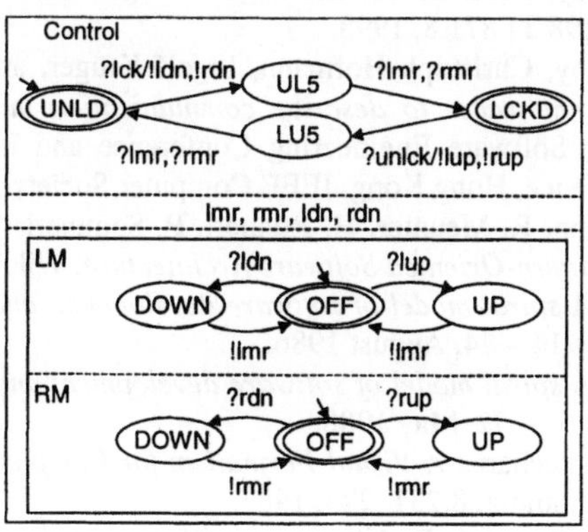

Figure 5: Overall Statechart for component Control and both motors

Having translated the set of MSCs into a Statechart, we may further refine the system under development towards the final implementation as shown in [Sch98b].

3. Conclusion

In this paper we showed how to translate scenario-based system requirements into state-based system designs.

Although we presented the translation in a time-synchronous communication setting, it is actually independent from the underlying communication mechanism. The reason is that we associate a separate automaton to each component occurring in the MSCs. Communication is captured by parallel composition of automata.

The composition can be adapted to the communication style chosen for MSCs. If this communication is time-synchronous, one has to define a time-synchronous parallel composition of automata (as done in this paper). If the communication is time-asynchronous, one has to define a time-asynchronous parallel composition. Similarly, one can consider a communication mechanism using one, two or several communication buffers. In all these cases, our translation remains the same. One only needs to change the automata composition.

Acknowledgments

Our work was partially supported with funds of the Deutsche Forschungsgemeinschaft under the Leibniz program, by Siemens-Nixdorf within project SysLab, and by the Bayerische Forschungsstiftung. We are grateful to the participants of DIPES'98 for interesting discussions about this subject.

References

[BGK98] Manfred Broy, Radu Grosu, and Ingolf Krüger. Deutsche Patentanmeldung, Aktenzeichen 198 37 871.8, 1998.

[BHKS97] Manfred Broy, Christoph Hofmann, Ingolf Krüger, and Monika Schmidt. *Using extended event traces to describe communication in software architectures.* In Asia-Pacific Software Engineering Conference and International Computer Science Conference, Hong Kong. IEEE Computer Society, 1997.

[BMR+96] F. Buschmann, R. Meunier, H. Rohnert, P. Sommerlad, and M. Stal. *A System of Patterns. Pattern-Oriented Software Architecture.* Wiley, 1996.

[Boe86] B. Boehm. *A spiral model of software development and enhancement.* ACM SIGSOFT, pages 14 – 24, August 1986.

[Boe88] B. Boehm. *A spiral model of software development and enhancement.* IEEE Computer, pages 61 – 72, May 1988.

[Har87] D. Harel. Statecharts: *A Visual Formalism for Complex Systems.* Science of Computer Programming, 8:231–274, 1987.

[HU93] J. E. Hopcroft and J. D. Ullman. *Einführung in die Automatentheorie, Formale Sprachen und Komplexitätstheorie.* Addison Wesley, 2. korrigierter Nachdruck, 1993.

[IT96] ITU-TS. Recommendation Z.120 : *Message Sequence Chart (MSC)*. Geneva, 1996.

[IT98] ITU-TS. Recommendation Z.120 : *Annex B*. Geneva, 1998.

[Rat97] Unified modeling language, version 1.1. Rational Software Corporation, 1997.

[Roy70] W.W. Royce. *Managing the development of large software systems*. IEEE WESCON, pages 1 – 9, August 1970.

[Sch98a] P. Scholz. *A Refinement Calculus for Statecharts*. In Proceedings of the ETAPS/FASE'98, Lisbon (Portugal), March 30 - April 03, 1998, volume 1382 of Lecture Notes in Computer Science. Springer, 1998.

[Sch98b] P. Scholz. *Design of Reactive Systems and their Distributed Implementation with Statecharts*. Ph.D. thesis, Technische Universität München, 1998.

[V97] Entwicklungsstandard für IT-Systeme des Bundes, Vorgehensmodell. Allgemeiner Umdruck Nr. 250/1. Juni 1997, BWB IT I5.

SOFTWARE SYNTHESIS FROM STATECHART MODELS FOR REAL TIME SYSTEMS

Claude Ackad[1]

Formal description techniques like Harel's statecharts offer a great potential to facilitate the design of complex real time systems. The systems are modeled and simulated at a high level. Automatic translation from the abstract models into implementations significantly reduces overall development time. This paper contributes to the optimized code generation from statechart models. The worst-case execution time of the generated code is reduced.

1. Introduction

Real Time (RT) systems gain increasing importance through the widespread use of embedded systems like automative systems. Computations must fulfill RT requirements such as worst case execution times (WCET), i. e., the maximal required computation time with arbitrary input to the system.

Formal description techniques like SDL [Itut93] and statecharts [Hare87] allow the formal and unambiguous description of systems at a high level enabling the simulation of the (informal) system specification.

Statecharts employ parallel, hierarchical state diagrams. Concurrent processing as well as high-level interrupts can be specified appropriately. The semantics are formally defined supporting simulation and analysis of dynamic properties.

To avoid an error-prone manual translation into an implementation and to save design time, automatic code generation is seeked bridging the gap between abstract model and implementation. Although some code generators for statechart models do exist, yet no generator takes into account optimizing the code for small execution times. This paper contributes to the optimized translation of statechart models into implementations w. r. t. a small WCET.

---

1. Technische Universität Braunschweig, Abteilung Entwurf integrierter Schaltungen, Gaussstrasse 11, 38106 Braunschweig, Germany, email: ackad@eis.cs.tu-bs.de

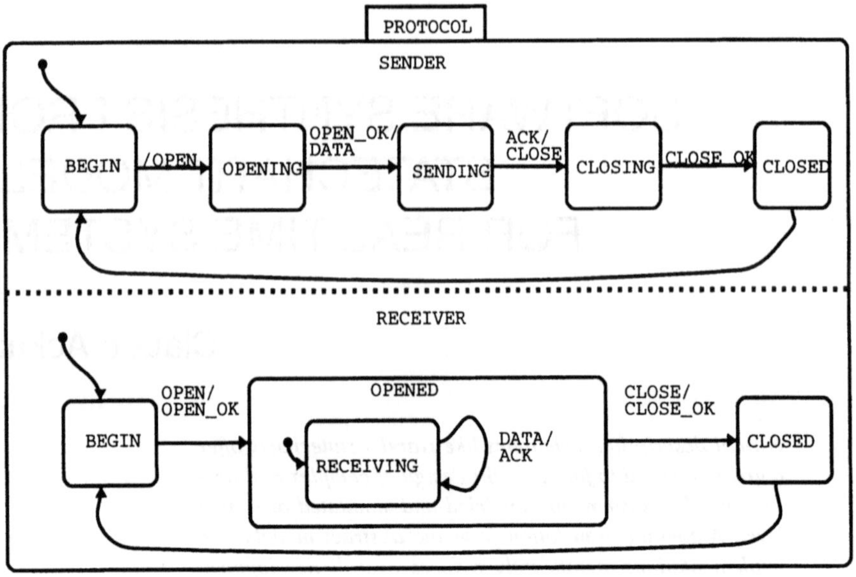

Figure 1: A simplified Transfer Protocol

2. Statecharts as a Modeling Language for RT Systems

Figure 1 shows a statechart example of a simplified transfer protocol consisting of the two parallel finite state machines (FSM) SENDER and RECEIVER. In a typical statechart, concurrent FSMs exchange data through normal variables such as integers or using abstract *events* which remain valid for one step only. In the remainder, we use "variable" for normal variables as well as events.

All variables are global to the whole model. Each FSM may read or write any variable. Multiple write accesses to the same variable in one step are forbidden and considered to be a model error.

In the example, the sender opens a connection by generating the event OPEN, the receiver acknowledges with OPEN_OK, enters the hierarchical state OPENED and its sub-state RECEIVING. Data are transmitted generating DATA. The transmission is terminated by sending CLOSE in which case a transition occurs from OPENED to CLOSED (high-level interrupt).

Parallel activities, inherent in most real world systems, can be modeled appropriately at different levels in the statechart model. Parallel FSMs may be started dynamically. Similar behavior of states can be expressed using high-level transitions leading to more comprehensible models.

3. Design Flow of RT System Design using Statecharts

Figure 2 shows the design flow using statecharts. The abstract (textual) specification for the system often contains contradictions and ambiguities. It cannot be simulated because the specification is not formal, thus leaving errors unrevealed.

The specification is modeled using statecharts. This model is on the one hand "near" the specification by means of the abstract nature of the statecharts and on the other hand simulateable because the statechart semantic is formal and unambiguous. Specification errors are discovered quickly and different design architectures are explored in short time at this abstract level.

After validation of the model, an implementation must be developed. A manual translation is error-prone as well as time consuming violating a short time-to-market. Therefore, an automatic transformation into an implementation is required.

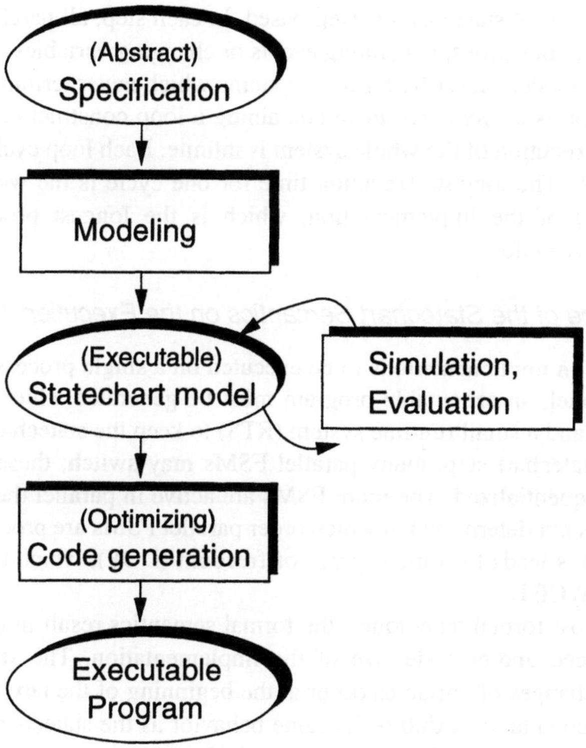

Figure 2: Design Flow using Statecharts

4. Software Synthesis of Statechart Models

After designing the statechart model, an *implementation* is derived automatically which essentially exhibits the same functionality as the statechart.

The real time systems we consider must fulfill constraints on the WCET, e. g. for scheduling calculations. Each piece of implementation code takes some amount of *execution time* depending on the actual state and the input. The implementation must be structured in a way to provide for an automatic execution time analysis to determine the WCET of the program. Therefore, recursive function calls and unbounded loops are prohibited.

The WCET of the implementation should be as small as possible, that is, the implementation should be optimized w. r. t. a small WCET.

Of course, there are many valid implementations with different WCETs for a given statechart. Our contribution lies in the optimized code generation from statechart models into implementations for single processor target platforms. We consider only a special class of implementations derived from *parallel execution graphs* as explained below.

The execution of statecharts is step-based. In each step, all parallel FSMs synchronously execute transitions, generating events or changing variables.

Statechart models describe reactive systems which never terminate. Therefore, the implementation is a *cyclic executive* containing a loop construct at the top level. The time for the execution of the whole system is infinite. Each loop cycle corresponds to a statechart step. The longest execution time for one cycle is the worst-case execution time (WCET) of the implementation, which is the longest processing time of a response to a stimulus.

4.1. Influence of the Statechart Semantics on the Execution Time

We focus on implementations to be executed on a single processor. Starting with a statechart model, an executable program must be generated which has the statechart functionality and a small runtime system (RTS) to keep the statechart semantics.

In each statechart step, many parallel FSMs may switch; these parallel activities have to be sequentialized. The more FSMs are active in parallel the longer the execution time. It is not determined in which order parallel FSMs are processed in the implementation. This leads to some degrees of freedom (DOF), which can be exploited to improve the WCET.

Like in most formal techniques, the formal semantics result in overhead regarding execution speed and/or code size of the implementation. The statechart semantics require that changes of variables occur at the beginning of the next step. It is essential that the implementation exhibits the same behavior as the statechart model, thus variable changes must be buffered until the end of the current step (*variable buffering*). This buffering consumes execution time delaying writes after all reads to the same variable are done. Often, no buffering is needed; the execution time may be improved in these cases.

Events are valid for only one step; after generating the event, it is cleared in the following step. Because non-trivial statecharts contain quite a few events, an efficient RTS event handling is crucial.

4.2. Existing Code Generators

Statemate [Ilog97] is a toolkit containing a statechart editor, a simulator as well as a code generator. Unfortunately, the generated code is not optimized for a small WCET; furthermore, the implementation contains unbounded loops and calls to library functions like *malloc*, such that execution time is unpredictable.

Procors [Spre96] is a code generator developed at BMW AG, Germany. Although the code is optimized w. r. t. a small WCET, the generator imposes severe restrictions on the allowed statechart models. For example, only one event is consumed by the model at each step. Furthermore, the statechart semantics are altered in that variable changes occur immediately, even "inside" a step, resulting in behavioral differences between the statechart model and its implementation.

5. SCOT[2] Project Description

Because of the lack of an optimizing code generator for statecharts, we launched the project SCOT. The main project objective is the efficient translation of statechart models into implementations. The generated machine code should exhibit a small and computable WCET, which is to be optimized for a single 68000 processor system.

Statemate is our statechart modeling tool. It was successfully applied to the rapid prototyping of airplanes [RJJC95], automobiles as well as specification of home automation systems [ScSc96].

5.1. Transformation Flow Using SCOT

Figure 3 shows the transformation flow using SCOT. After designing the statechart model with Statemate, we transform it into an intermediate format, a *parallel execution graph* (PEG). The PEG is an acyclic directed graph, which is an abstract scheme for the final implementation. The rather complex statechart semantics (evaluation of transition trigger expressions, calculation of priorities) are significantly reduced to simple branches depending on variable values, and assignments. The time required for one step can be estimated more accurately because of the simpler constructs.

The PEG execution contains some degrees of freedom (DOF), for example, the FSM execution order, which are represented using *parallel blocks*; segments contained in parallel blocks can be executed in an *arbitrary* order. In an iterative optimization cycle, this freedom is eliminated.

The WCET estimator analyzes each node in the graph for its type, data-dependency to other nodes, number and type of operands etc., and estimates the execution time depending on timing information of the target platform. To all nodes containing variable read or write references, an overhead for the double buffer handling is added. This overhead may be reduced later upon fixing the execution order.

The longest path through the PEG is determined and optimized yielding a new PEG with a smaller WCET and less DOF. This step is repeated until no more optimizations are possible.

2. Statechart Compilation for Optimized worst-case execution Time

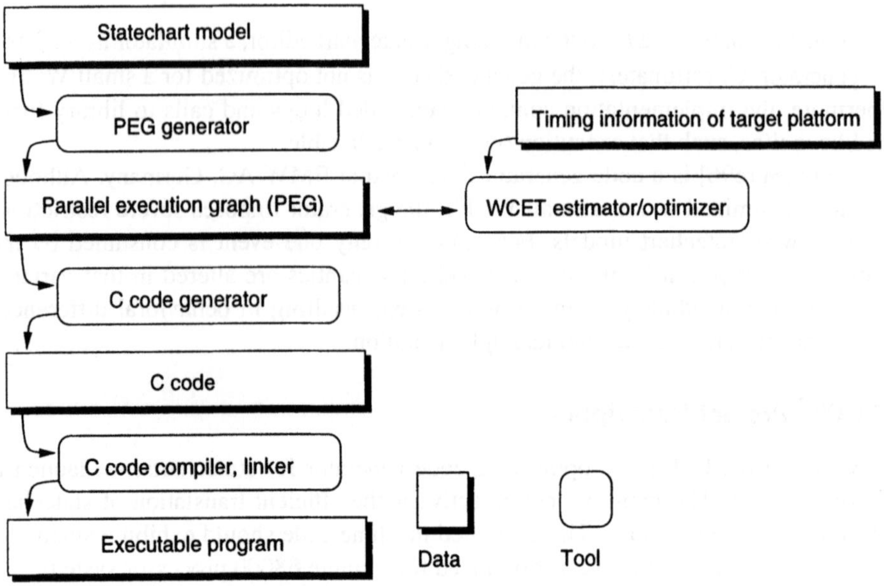

Figure 3: SCOT Transformation Flow

The C code generator produces C code for the PEG together with a tailored RTS which can be compiled, linked, and executed.

5.2. PEG Optimization

The PEG consists of conditional branches, variable assignments, parallel blocks, and join nodes to collect several path segments. Each path through the PEG corresponds to one possible statechart step. Thus optimizing the longest PEG path means optimizing the WCET of the implementation.

To calculate the WCET, the execution time of each node must be estimated. The estimation is based on the analysis of the node execution time on a 68000 platform.

Optimizations are possible for variables, when a variable is buffered and the buffering can be eliminated. Remember that in this case, the execution time of all nodes referencing this variable, is shortened.

Figure 4 shows a PEG example. Each path leads from START to END. Both path

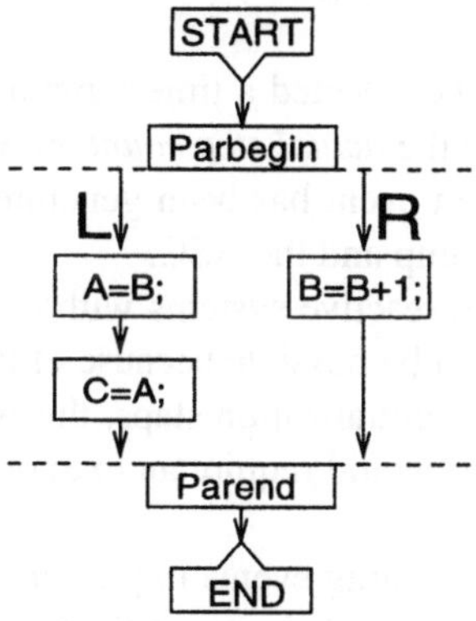

Figure 4: PEG Example

segments between Parbegin and Parend must be contained in all paths through the PEG, but the order is arbitrary. Because of the statechart semantics, changes to variables must not be observable by other statements before the next step. In all paths, no write to a variable may be followed by a read, otherwise, the variable must be buffered (changes are applied upon reaching END). In the figure, variable B needs no buffering if segment L is executed before R. Thus, selecting the order "L before R" reduces variable buffering, hence execution time of the nodes referencing B.

On the other hand, A needs buffering, since it is read after being written in segment L.

For each optimization step, the path through the PEG with the longest WCET is determined. All referenced variables with buffering along the path are collected. For each variable all references are checked w. r. t. data dependencies to path segments before and after the reference as well as parallel segments.

The variable contributing most to the execution time of the path is selected for optimization. If an execution order of segments is possible so that the buffering is unnecessary, this segment order is fixed, the buffering is deleted, and the execution time is fixed. In some situations, no order can be found because of cyclic data dependencies. In this case, one variable is marked as unoptimizable breaking the cycle. If there is still some DOF left, the next iteration is started.

5.3. WCET-Optimized Runtime System

Generated events must be cleared. Both generating and clearing is associated with an RTS overhead, in that the event must be generated during step *n* and cleared at the end of step *n+1*. Generating an event contributes to the execution time of the PEG nodes; the RTS is responsible for clearing events. Good *average* execution times can be achieved using an event clear list like in the Statemate-generated code, where all generated events are inserted for clearance after the next step. Unfortunately, the length of the list contributing to the *WCET* depends on the number of generated events in the execution of the implementation, which cannot be determined at compile time. Counting all existing events as maximal length would result in an unrealistic WCET estimation.

To alleviate this problem, we selected a timestamp approach. Generating an event means setting the timestamp to the *actual step counter* (ASC), which is incremented in each step. Checking whether an event has been generated in the last step results in a comparison between its timestamp and the ASC.

Since statechart models are reactive systems with continuous use, a simple incrementation of the ASC would not be possible because of the overflow due to the limited range of integers. At special re-initialization steps, the ASC and the timestamps must be set to zero. This special step would require an extraordinary amount of time resulting in a loose WCET prediction.

Therefore, we partition all existing events in p *event groups*. Each group is associated with a *individual* ASC. In each step, one of the p groups is re-initialized together with its ASC. Using this approach, the overhead for the re-initialization is distributed equally to p steps.

6. Application Example

As an example for the optimization process, a system for an elevator control is used. Figure 5 shows the statechart model; it contains parallel and hierarchical con-

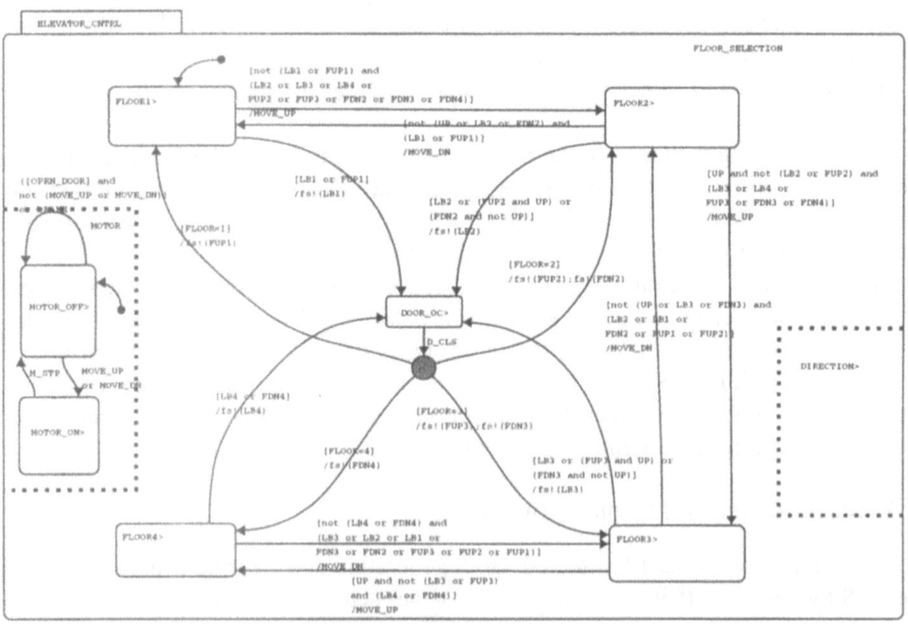

Figure 5: Application Example: Elevator Control System

structs as well as complex transition triggers. 19 variables and 8 events are used; a standard code generator would use double buffering for all of them.

After model analysis and selecting an appropriate execution order, the SCOT code generator needs buffering for only three variables and three events reducing the execution time from 1142 to 842 clock cycles (26 % less).

References

[Hare87] D. Harel; Statecharts: *a Visual Formalism for Complex Systems*; Science of Computer Programming, Vol. 8, August 1987.

[Ilog97] *Statemate Magnum Reference Manual*; i-Logix Inc., Andover, USA, 1997.

[Itut93] *CCITT Specification and Description Language*; Recommendation Z.100, ITU-T, Geneva, Switzerland, 1993.

[RJJC95] M. Romdhani, A. A. Jerraya, A. Jeffroy, P. de Chazelles, A.-El-K. Sahraoui; *Modeling and Rapid Prototyping of Avionics Using STATEMATE*; 6th IEEE International Workshop on Rapid Systems Prototyping, Chapel Hill, North Carolina, USA, 1995.

[ScSc96] S. Schulz, M. Schütze; *Modeling and Simulating an Home Automation System Using STATEMATE* (in German); 4th German User Meeting for STATEMATE, Munich, Germany, 1996.

[Spre96] M. Spreng; *Rapid Prototyping of electronic Control Systems in the Car Development* (in German); Thesis, University of Karlsruhe, Germany, 1996.

3 PARTITIONING AND LOAD-BALANCING

COMBINING STATIC PARTITIONING WITH DYNAMIC DISTRIBUTION OF THREADS

Ronald Moore, Melanie Klang, Bernd Klauer and Klaus Waldschmidt

This paper presents a hybrid approach to automatic parallelization of computer programs which combines static extraction of threads (tasks) with dynamic scheduling for parallel and distributed execution. Fine-grain scheduling decisions are made at compile time, and coarse-grain scheduling decisions are made at run time. The approach consists of two components: compiler technology which performs the static analysis (thread extraction), and an architecture which takes over the responsibility for scheduling and distributing the threads. Each processor is augmented with a ***broker****, whose responsibility it is to* ***shop*** *for tasks for the processor to perform. This approach aims to provide an adaptive run-time distribution of computation for irregular problems such as the simulation of embedded systems. Finally, this approach is general enough to allow the seamless incorporation of heterogeneous hardware, in particular including dynamically reconfigurable hardware, e.g. FPGAs.*

1. Introduction

1.1 Motivation and Overview

Programming parallel computers is hard. In fact, the difficulty of designing parallel software is increasingly seen as the main barrier to wider acceptance and usage of parallel computers (e.g. Patterson 1997). Programming parallel computers is inherently harder than programming sequential computers, since computation as well as data must be *distributed* amongst the available resources.

This paper presents a hybrid approach to automatic parallelization of computer programs which combines static extraction of threads with dynamic scheduling. Fine-grain scheduling decisions are made at compile time, and coarse-grain scheduling decisions are made at run time. The approach consists of two components: compiler technology which performs the static thread extraction, and an architecture which takes over the responsibility for scheduling and distributing the threads amongst the available processors.

This architectural component is itself distributed: Each processor is augmented with a *broker*, whose responsibility it is to *shop* for tasks for the processor to perform. See figure 1. Taken together, these brokers implement not only a Distributed Shared Memory (DSM), but also a Distributed Shared Scheduler. Each combination of a processor, a broker and a local memory is called an "attraction memory site", and functions like a giant, slow cache in a *Cache Only Memory Architecture* (COMA), compare (Hagersten et. al., 1992).

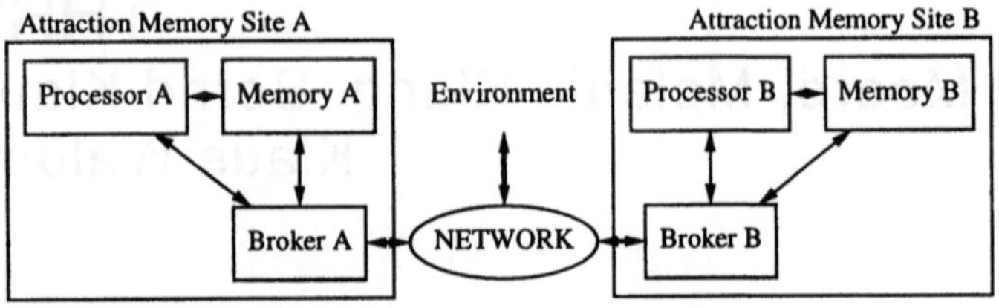

Figure 1: Abstract Schematic for a system with a Distributed Shared Memory (DSM) and a Distributed Shared Scheduler.

The architecture described in this paper has two goals. One goal is to provide an adaptive run time distribution of computation for irregular problems and for applications which will be used in dynamic, unpredictable environments.

However, the main goal is to attack the problem of *programmability*. The system presented in this paper takes over the complete task of distributing both data and computation, and as such has the potential to make programming parallel systems approximately as easy as programming sequential systems.

1.2. Background

The approach outlined in this paper draws together concepts from two previously independent fields of: Multithreaded Architectures on the one hand, and Cache Only Memory Architectures (COMAs) on the other: The concepts from the Multithreaded Architectures are used to define the basic scheduling terms (see Culler, 1993 or Nikhil, 1993); The concepts from COMAs are used to provide a DSM where data is free to migrate from one local memory to another (Hagersten et. al., 1992, Saulsbury et. al., 1996).

Previously, the questions of data distribution and computation distribution were strictly separated. Multithreaded architectures had little to say about data distribution, and COMAs were content to provide a DSM and leave the problems of program partitioning and scheduling to the programmers. This division of labor simplified the development of each camp. However, a point has been reached where significant further development can be obtained by lifting the division and optimizing each component (scheduling and DSM), based on knowledge of the other.

We call this combination of COMA and multithreading SDAARC, for *Self Distributing Associative ARChitecture* (Moore et. al., 1998a and 1998b).

The rest of this paper is organized as follows: Section 2 provides an Overview, describing first the overall SDAARC Strategy, and then the hardware and software (compiler) prerequisites of SDAARC. Section 3 discusses the compiler technology in more detail, and section 4 discusses the run-time distribution protocol. Section 5 discusses possible extensions for embedded systems. Section 6 presents conclusions.

2 Overview

2.1. Strategy

In SDAARC, we treat both data and computation as a *population of migratory objects*. The central idea is to first select objects of an appropriate granularity, and then distribute those objects adaptively, responding to conditions that arise at run-time. The distribution must balance the conflicting goals of *locality* (to reduce communication costs) and *parallelism* (to reduce total run-time).

This strategy divides the distribution problem into two subproblems: First, appropriately sized objects must be extracted at compile-time from a program's source code. Second, these objects must be mapped at run-time onto the available attraction memory sites. As such, SDAARC consists of two major technologies: compiler technology for the extraction of objects, and run-time technology for their distribution.

2.2. Hardware Requirements

SDAARC makes a small number of very basic demands on the hardware utilized to implement the system. As described above, the hardware is to be organized into a collection of *attraction memory sites*, where each site consists of one or more processors, a broker, a memory, and a network connection. Additionally, multiple sites can be clustered together, and represented by a *cluster broker*, to build hierarchical systems.

The brokers can be implemented in hardware, software, or both. Many different network topologies are possible. Examples include standard tree topologies and a novel crossbar topology described in (Moore et. al. 1998a).

The brokers together with the network are responsible for supporting the SDAARC strategy. Since the program together with its data are treated as a population of migratory objects, almost all messages sent on the network will be addressed to objects, and not to locations. Each message needs to be sent to all brokers whose sites *could* currently contain the recipient.

2.3. Compiler Requirements

SDAARC assumes that each program has been represented as a set of *microthreads*. Compiler technology for translating programs into threads is illustrated in figure 2.

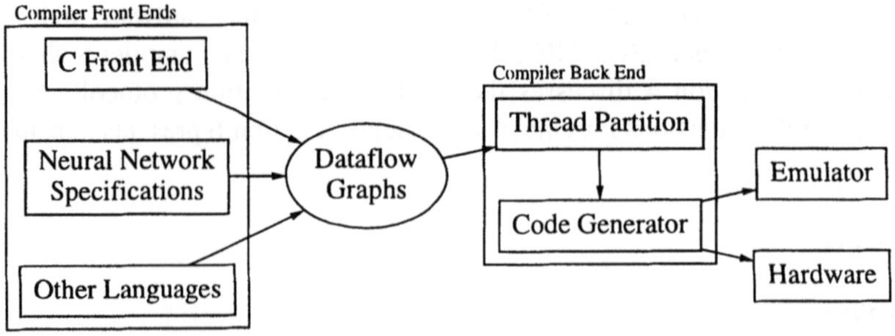

Figure 2: Compiler Technology for Representing Programs as Threads.

The compiler technology can be split into two groups: the front ends and the back ends. The fronts ends are responsible for translating a program into a dataflow graph. The choice of source language is left open to the programmer, and can be chosen according to which language best facilitates problem solving for a given application. Front ends for a subset of ANSI C and for a declarative neural network specification language are described in (Moore et. al. 1996 and 1997).

Dataflow graphs are chosen as an intermediate format for two reasons: first, to facilitate source language independence, and second, to represent all the parallelism implicit in the program.

The back end consists of two steps: First, the dataflow graph is partitioned into microthreads. Second, code is generated for each thread separately. While the code generation is done largely with conventional techniques, the graph partitioning receives closer examination below in section 3. Before closing this section however, we define the meaning given the term *thread* in this paper (since the term "thread" is unfortunately used with various, often contradictory meanings in the literature). We use the terminology from (Nikhil, 1993), where a *microthread* is an atomic subset of a dataflow graph, which never waits for data or an event. Should a *process* have to wait for some form of input, then that process is divided into (at least) two microthreads: one which performs the calculations up to the point where the input is necessary, and a second microthread which is triggered by the arrival of the input.

3. The Compiler Technology

3.1. Graph Partitioning Algorithm

The authors have implemented a prototype graph partitioning tool in order to evaluate the SDAARC approach empirically. The tool accepts dataflow graphs from the front ends described in (Moore et. al. 1996 and 1997), and assigns annotations to the vertices, assigning each vertex into a hierarchically organized tree of subgraphs. The algorithm proceeds in two passes:

In the first pass, nested control structures are identified and assigned to macrothreads. The result of this pass is a hierarchical graph partitioning tree, the leaves of which contain directed acyclic dataflow.

In the second pass, each directed acyclic subgraph is further partitioned into microthreads. This is done, at the moment, with a greedy, bottom-up clustering algorithm which attempts (heuristically) to minimize a cost function. In the beginning of the second pass, each vertex is assigned to an individual microthread (each starting microthread thus has exactly one vertex). Pairs of microthreads are then selected and merged if and only if the merge reduces the cost, and introduces no cycles in the macrothread.

In the cost function, each vertex is assigned a static cost representing the time required for the computation, and each edge between two microthreads is assigned a cost representing an average of communication time and context-switch time. The cost of the subgraph is then the costs along the *critical path* within the subgraph.

The calculation of the critical path serves three purposes here: first, we select pairs of vertices to merge from the critical path. Second, having identified a pair for merging, we calculate a new critical path to obtain the new cost estimate. Finally, the critical path calculation determines whether the merge introduces cycles.

The partitioning tool is described in more detail in (Klang, 1997).

3.2 Initial Results

We show two examples of the results of the second pass: one regular and one irregular. For each example, we show two possible partitionings, one where we assume extremely optimistic (low) edge costs, and one where the edge costs are more realistic (higher).

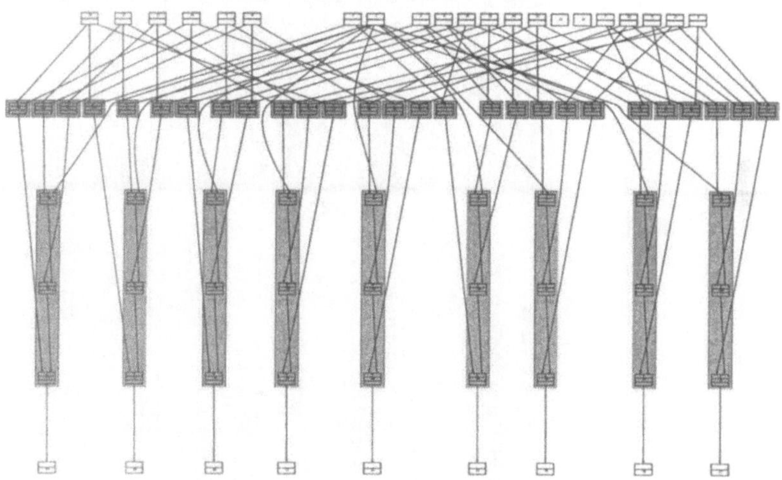

Figure 3: Partitioning a 3x3 matrix multiplication, assuming optimistic communication costs, results in 36 microthreads.

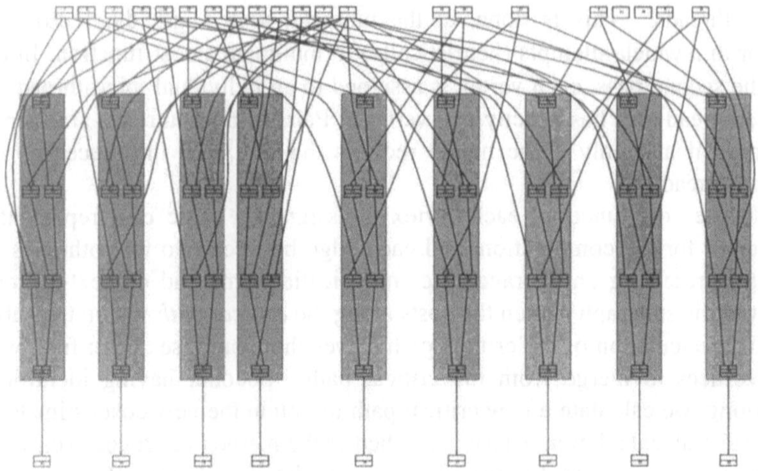

Figure 4: Partitioning a 3x3 matrix multiplication, assuming more realistic communication costs, results in 9 microthreads.

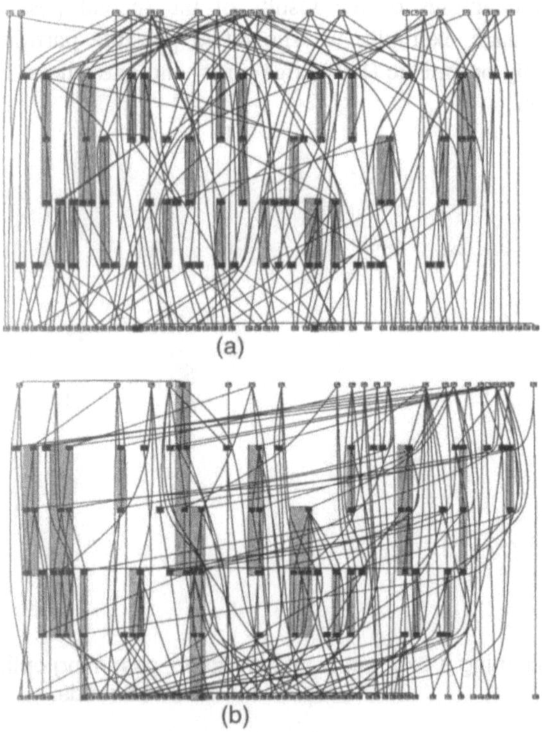

Figure 5: Partitioning a randomly generated dataflow graph with 160 vertices produces
(a) 52 microthreads when assuming optimistic costs, and
(b) 39 microthreads when assuming realistic communication costs.

The regular graph represents the calculations in a 3x3 matrix multiplication. This example has been chosen, not because it is necessarily typical, but rather because the structure is familiar, and illustrates the trade-off between parallelism and locality. When we assume optimistic edge costs, the graph is partitioned as shown in figure 3. Here, the partitioning algorithm has decided to obtain the maximum practical parallelism by performing all the multiplications in parallel, while the additions are merged into 9 microthreads.

In figure 4, the same graph has been partitioned under the more realistic communication assumptions. This time the algorithm has sacrificed some parallelism, and increased the locality. Here, each of the 9 results is calculated in a separate microthread.

Figures 3 and 4 demonstrate that the algorithm is capable of discovering and exploiting implicit structure in a regular dataflow graph. In order to see how the algorithm would deal with *irregular* graphs, we tested the partitioning algorithm with randomly generated dataflow graphs. In figure 5 we see the partitioning of a randomly generated 160 vertex dataflow graph. In figure 5(a) we again assumed optimistic communication costs, and the algorithm produced 52 microthreads. In figure 5(b) we assumed realistic communication costs, and the algorithms produced 39 microthreads.

4. Dynamic Distribution of Threads and Data

4.1 Adapting COMA for SDAARC

As discussed in Sections 1 and 2, SDAARC builds upon COMA technology. COMAs (e.g. Hagersten, 1992 or Saulsbury, 1996) implement a transparently distributed shared address space for parallel processors. Data blocks move from local memory to local memory in response to read and write operations. As in all cache technology, this strategy represents a gamble on locality: as long as the assumption of locality holds, the odds are good that the data needed at a site will be needed there again in the near future. When the assumption is not correct, data can be unnecessarily shuffled back and forth between sites (the so-called *ping pong* effect).

The first insight in SDAARC is that, if we could associate each thread with a data object, we could let the COMA distribute those objects amongst the attraction memory sites. We could then schedule tasks for each local processor corresponding to the thread-objects currently residing in its local memory. We do not have to search very far to find such objects: in the multithreaded architecture literature, for every thread there exists a *frame* which holds the arguments and return addresses for the thread. These frames closely resemble the *stack frames* in conventional (sequential) architectures, except that they are not organized in a stack. Instead, the frames are effectively contained in a distributed, common heap. Usually, several threads can share one frame (Nikhil 1993, Culler, 1993), but more recent literature suggests that performance enhancements can be obtained when each thread has a frame of its own, called a *framelet* (Annavaram and Najjar, 1996).

Having found a data object which represents each thread, and thus allowing the

COMA technology to be used to distribute *computation* as well as data, it soon becomes apparent that further optimizations are possible. We now have a system where not only data migrates to adapt to the program distribution, but where the program distribution simultaneously adapts to the data distribution. This provides a solution to the *ping pong* effect. In a conventional COMA, there is no effective way for data to adapt to a poorly distributed program: if a data block is utilized simultaneously in two sites, then the block needs to migrate back and forth between those sites. In SDAARC, it is possible for the competing portions of the computation to be redistributed to reside on the same site.

4.2. The Brokers and the ECOLI Cache Coherency Protocol

The brokers in SDAARC are an extension of the cache coherency controllers in the COMA literature. They are responsible for handling network traffic, for providing the processor with frames (threads) to execute, and with ensuring that the transparently distributed, shared address space remains consistent and coherent.

As in a standard COMA, the brokers enforce a *cache coherency protocol.* By combining computation and data, we have been able to significantly simplify the protocol compared to other COMAs. In our protocol (Moore et. al., 1988b), objects can be in one of five states: Exclusive, Cloned, Original, Leaving or Invalid (ECOLI). This can be compared to the standard SMP (non-COMA) MESI (Modified, Shared, Exclusive and Invalid) protocols, or the the 7 state COMA protocol in (Haridi and Hagersten, 1989).

The shared address space in SDAARC is separated into three partitions. As in a standard Harvard Architecture, there exists data and instruction partitions. However, we add a third partition for frames, to allow special optimized handling of these essential data objects. Further, as discussed in section 5, the instruction partition can also be extended to incorporate heterogeneous architectures.

4.3. Distribution Events

As explained above, the brokers must balance the conflicting demands of parallelism and locality (in order to reduce communication costs). To do this, they need to assemble collections of more or less connected threads and data objects. The goal is always to provide the shortest run-time, and not necessarily to provide an even load balance. Tasks should be distributed over only as many processors as they can efficiently exploit (especially in multi-tasking environments).

To accomplish this balancing act, we define a number of *forces* which drive the migration of objects and threads. The forces fall into two categories: *dissipative* forces drive objects apart, maximizing parallelism, potentially at the cost of locality; while *attractive* forces bring related objects together, maximizing locality, potentially at the cost of parallelism. These forces operate at precisely defined *distribution events.* When these events occur, the brokers make decisions about which objects migrate, and where they migrate to.

There are two dissipative distribution events:

1 We assume that the attraction memories are set-associative: Each object is statically mapped onto a *set* which holds a small, constant number (e.g. 4 or 8) of objects. When an object is inserted into a set, and that set is full, then some other object must migrate to make room

2 When the broker is idle, it can identify sets which are *almost* full, and spontaneously evict objects from these sets.

Similarly, there are two groups of attractive distribution events:

1 When one thread calculates an argument for another frame, and the receiving frame is resident on another site, then the receiving frame's broker can decide whether to simply accept the argument, or instead to send the receiving frame to the site sending the argument.

2 In SDAARC, data loads and stores always produce an acknowledgment, to enable barrier synchronization and mutex locking of data objects. When data is loaded or stored from the data partition, the broker can decide whether to send the entire data block to the site waiting for the acknowledgment.

5. Extensions for Embedded Systems

5.1. Extending Dynamically Reconfigurable Hardware

As mentioned above, the SDAARC address space contains a data partition, a frame partition and an instruction partition. We have until now tacitly assumed that the instructions can be used on all the processors. This need not be the case. If the architecture contains heterogeneous processors, the instruction partition can contain instructions for each processor type present. Of course, the compiler technology will have to be enriched with new code generators each time a new processor type is added to the system. Those programs which wish to exploit the new processor type will need to be recompiled. Recompilation will only be necessary when new processor types are added (changing the *number* of processors does *not* force recompilation), and only for those programs which need to exploit the new technology.

Perhaps the most interesting possibility is to incorporate not only instruction-driven processors, but also dynamically reconfigurable processors. Modern FPGAs store configurations in RAM, and FPGAs are now coming to market which can store multiple configurations on chip, and have configuration times on the order of (or less than) 1 millisecond. The best way to integrate this interesting new performance potential into conventional computing systems is the object of intensive research. Dynamically configurable logic has the same programmability problem as parallel processors, but in a much more extreme form. The performance potential is clear; what is unclear is the best way to bring applications to the hardware. Configuration times under 1 ms are too fast to be used only for rapid prototyping (with reconfiguration performed every few days or weeks), but still too slow to be performed, for example, at every function call in a conventional program (see

Villasenor and Mangione-Smith, 1997, Page, 1998, or Brebner, 1998).

A SDAARC system could be extended with sites consisting of a (specialized) broker, optional RAM and one or more FPGA's. We then view these FPGAs as both processors and, simultaneously, as *instruction caches*. The broker's decision to accept storage of a frame is thus equivalent to the decision to store a block of instructions in instruction cache. As with all cache logic, storing data (i.e. reconfiguring the FPGA) is a gamble on sufficient locality. We effectively bet that this configuration will also be useful for other frames in the immediate future. This provides an automatic, dynamic and adaptive way of deciding when to reconfigure and which reconfiguration to perform.

5.2. Extending SDAARC for Real Time Systems

Another fascinating potential for extending SDAARC lies with embedded systems. SDAARC could be useful either as a simulation platform or even as a target platform for embedded systems.

SDAARC as a simulation platform is attractive if we extend the concept to allow some objects (frames or data objects) to be *fixed,* that is, labeled as non-migratory. (This will be necessary in any case to allow the programming of device drivers). The designer of a distributed embedded system could then initially leave the distribution of the objects unspecified, use SDAARC to see which distributions arise naturally at run-time, and then tie objects to sites, arriving iteratively at a static distribution. Alternately, if SDAARC is also to be used as a target platform, the designer could leave some or all of the system migratory, depending on the criticality and performance of the simulation.

If SDAARC is to be used as a target platform for real time systems however, the scheduling decisions made in the brokers will need to respect *timing constraints.* To support these decisions, the compiler technology will need to be extended to produce *annotated* dataflow graphs, allowing the user to specify, and later the broker to respect, this timing information. Much research has been done in the field of real time operating systems (e.g. Ditze, 1995) and development environments (e.g. Kleinjohann et. al. 1997) which can be leveraged to extend SDAARC in this direction.

Of course, no target architecture can always guarantee that timing constraints will be met. Further since a certain degree of non-determinism is inherent to SDAARC's adaptivity, SDAARC will occasionally fail to meet timing constraints which other systems might have met. Nonetheless, many embedded systems include both critical and less critical subsystems, and the critical systems often leave significant resources unused, which can be assigned to the less critical systems in a dynamic and adaptive fashion. A similar approach was taken in, for example (Grewe et. al., 1998).

6. Conclusion

In this paper we have introduced a hybrid system for partitioning and distributing data and computational load in a parallel and distributed system. Fine-grain decisions are made at compile-time: A program is translated into a dataflow graph, from which microthreads are extracted using a heuristic clustering algorithm. Coarse-grain decisions are made at run-time: Each processor is augmented with a *broker* whose job it is to: first, enforce a cache coherency protocol which implements a transparently distributed shared address space; second, select from the local portion of a shared collection of *frames* those frames which represents threads suitable for the local processor, based on dynamic load information.

This system, called SDAARC (Self-Distributing Associative ARChitecture), is an extension of COMA (Cache Only Memory Architecture) techniques. Whereas COMAs are content to offer a Distributed Shared Memory, SDAARC goes further and incorporates automatic distribution of computation.

SDAARC becomes interesting for embedded systems when extended in (one or both of) two directions: First, since the SDAARC concept is hardware-independent, it can be used to integrate heterogeneous processor technologies. In particular, dynamically reconfigurable logic can be incorporated, providing an adaptive automatic method for selecting the configurations for FPGAs. Second, if SDAARC's dataflow graphs are annotated with timing constraints, techniques from real time operating systems can be utilized to obtain a simulation architecture which evolves seamlessly into a target platform for distributed embedded systems.

Acknowledgments

This work was supported in part with funds of the Deutsche Forschungsgemeinschaft under reference number WA 357/11-2 within the priority program "System and Circuit Technology for Massively Parallel Computation"

References

Annavaram, Murali and Najjar, Walid (1996), *Comparison of Two Storage Models in Data-Driven Multithreaded Architectures,* Eighth IEEE Symposium on Parallel and Distributed Processing (SPDP), New Orleans, LA., Oct. 1996, IEEE Computer Society Press, 122-129.

Brebner, Gordon (1998), *Field-Programmable Logic: Catalyst for New Computing Paradigms,* Proc. 8th International Workshop on Field-Programmable Logic and Applications (FPLA '98), Springer Verlag.

Culler, David E., Goldstein, Seth Copen, Schauser, Klaus Erik and von Eicken, Thorsten (1993) *TAM - A Compiler Controlled Threaded Abstract Machine*, Journal of Parallel and Distributed Computing, Special Issue on Dataflow, June, 1993.

Ditze, Carsten (1995), *DReaMS - Concepts of a distributed real-time management system,* Proc. 1995 IFIP/IFAC Workshop on Real-Time Programming.

Grewe, Claus, Obelöer, Wolfgang and Pals, Holger (1998), *Kombination von anwendungs- und systemintegrierter Lastverwaltung mit Mobilen Agenten*, Proc. 17. PARS Workshop, Karlsruhe, 16.-17. September, PARS Mitteilungen Nr. 17, 98-107.

Hagersten, E., Landin, A. and Haridi, S. (1992), *DDM - A Cache-Only Memory Architecture,* IEEE Computer, 25(9), 44-54.

Haridi, Seif and Hagersten, Erik (1989), *The Cache Coherence Protocol of the Data Diffusion Machine*, Proceedings of the PARLE 89, Vol. 1, Springer-Verlag, 1-18.

Klang, Melanie (1997), *Hierarchische Zerlegung von Datenflußgraphen für mehrfädige Architekturen,* Diplomarbeit, Fachbereich Informatik, J. W. Goethe-Universität, Oct. 1997.

Kleinjohann, Bernd, Tacken, Jürgen, and Tahedl, Christoph (1997), *A Design Environment Using High-Level Petri-Nets as Common Model for Specification, Analysis, and Validation of Hybrid Real-Time Systems,* 3. ITG/GI/GMM Workshop Hardwarebeschreibungssprachen und Modellierungsparadigmen, Holzau (Germany), Febuary 1997.

Moore, Ronald, Zickenheiner, Stefan, Klauer, Bernd, Henritzi, Frank, Bleck, Andreas, and Waldschmidt, Klaus (1996), *Neural Compiler Technology for a Parallel Architecture,* International Conference on Parallel and Distributed Processing Techniques and Applications (PDPTA '96), Sunnyvale, CA, Aug. 1996.

Moore, Ronald, Klauer, Bernd and Waldschmidt, Klaus (1997), *Compiler Technology for Two Novel Computer Architectures,* 14th ITG/GI-Fachtagung Architektur von Rechensystemen (ARCHS '97), Rostock, Germany, Sept. 1997.

Moore, Ronald, Klauer, Bernd and Waldschmidt, Klaus (1998a), *A Combined Virtual Shared Memory and Network which Schedules*, International Journal of Parallel and Distributed Systems and Networks, 1(2), 51-56, 1998. Originally appeared at the International Conference on Parallel and Distributed Systems (Euro-PDS '97), Barcelona, June, 1997.

Moore, Ronald, Klauer, Bernd and Waldschmidt, Klaus (1998b), *Automatic Scheduling for Cache Only Memory Architectures*, Third International Conference on Massively Parallel Computing Systems (MPCS '98), Boulder, Colorado, April, 1998.

Nikhil, Rishiyur S. (1993), *A Multithreaded Implementation of Id using P-RISC Graphs*, Proceedings of the Sixth Annual Workshop on Languages and Compilers for Parallel Computing, Portland, Oregon, Aug. 1993, Springer Verlag LNCS 768, 390-405.

Page, Ian (1998), *Design of Future Systems,* Proc. Design Automation and Test Europe (DATE '98), IEEE Press, 343-347.

Patterson, David A. (1997), *Microprocessors in 2020*, Scientific American Special Issue: The Solid-State Century, 8(1), 86-88.

Saulsbury, Ashley, Wilkinson, Tim, Carter, John and Landin, Anders (1996), *An Argument For Simple COMA*, First IEEE Symposium on High Performance Computer Architecture, Rayleigh, North Carolina 276-285.

Villasenor, John and Mangione-Smith, William H. (1997), *Configurable Computing,* Scientific American, June, 1997.

DISTRIBUTED HIL SIMULATION FOR THE DESIGN OF DECENTRALIZED CONTROL STRUCTURES

Ralf Stolpe, Oliver Oberschelp

Abstract: In technical systems of the future the combination of local components from different technical disciplines with local information processing will increase. One example is a series hybrid vehicle. It consists of an auxiliary power unit, e.g,. an internal combustion engine, and a generator coupled to the crank shaft of the combustion engine, a battery and a drive unit with two electric motors. Each of these vehicle units has its own electronic control unit. Design and interplay of distributed intelligent aggregates in future technical systems will gain ever more importance. Parallelisation will be used not only for the purpose of reaching real time, but also for structuring purposes. The aim of mechatronics is the overall design of those systems. A toolset which supports the distributed HIL simulation as part of the mechatronic design cycle will be presented.

1. Mechatronic Systems

The mechatronic design cycle is characterized by taking into account and integrating mechanics, electronics, and information processing in the design process. For complex mechatronic systems a promising procedure is the decomposition of the entire system according to physically reasonable criteria. To describe the function of such combined subsystems we use the expression "mechatronic function" (Lückel 1997). Each discipline contributes its own specific function to the mechatronic function. Many technical systems boast an inherent physical parallelism, their setup showing parallel structures. Maintenance of the inherent physical parallelism in the design process means the design of parallelized mechatronic functions.

Therefore, such subsystems can be called Mechatronic Function Modules (in short: MFMs) (Honekamp 1997). An MFM consists of actuators, sensors, continuous and discrete information processing, and interfaces for mechanical coupling and information exchange.

For the hybrid vehicle two subsystems are obvious: one subsystem for the generation of electric energy, the MFM "generate energy", and another for driving the vehicle wheels, the MFM "drive wheels". The mechatronic functions "generate energy" and "drive wheels" and their assigned subsystems of the hybrid vehicle are only coupled via the battery. This characteristic allows the decoupling of the mechatronic functions. A mechanical coupling would complicate parallel decentralized control arrangements. An increasing control effort must be invested to develop a suitable decentralized control concept for these systems.

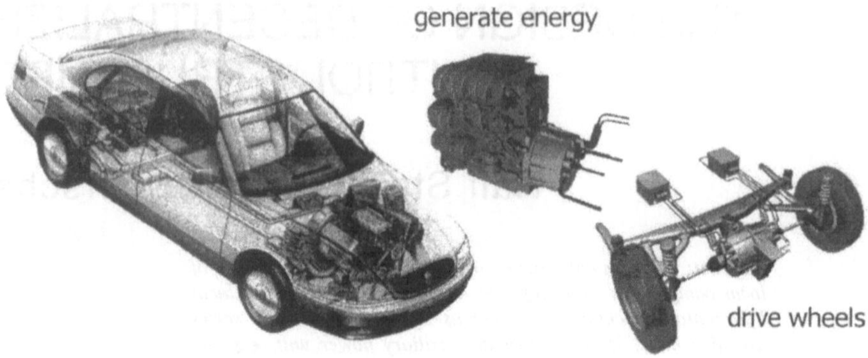

Figure 1. Functional decomposition of the series hybrid vehicle

2. IPANEMA Toolset

If you want to apply the MFM structuring approach on the realization, two features are required:
- comfortable, well-designed modelling tools which allow to arrange the components from different disciplines in a flexible way. One of the approaches to a structuring of the modelling process is represented by the MOOMo concept (Mechatronic Object-oriented Modelling) (Wolf 1998). MOOMo allows to model systems on the basis of their respective discipline-specific physical model. For realization, the concept combines elements from object-orientation and from graph theory, thus providing the condition to integrate formalisms for the derivation of the mathematical model (Hahn 1998);
- a strategy to organize parallel processes within a system and a software library supported by tools that can be used to make up distributed real-time processing. The IPANEMA toolset described in the following is designed to support this procedure.

In the mechatronic design cycle the step-by-step testing and realization of subsystems (Hardware-in-the-Loop) take an important position. The term "Distributed Hardware-in-the-Loop Simulation" means that one or more parts of a system actually exist on a testbed and that the other parts of the system are simulated on a multiprocessor hardware in real time. This requires a suitable hardware support with scalable and manageable hardware components for the tasks of computing and coupling real technical systems.

The software must also correspond to the demands on scalability and manageability. This could be achieved through a functional decomposition of the software. One part is the coupling of real technical components, mandatory for digital control and HIL. Another part is the computation, e.g., the solution of the system ODEs via numerical integration. Because of the application to different technical systems, a reusable infrastructure is important. An easy exchange of subsystems and coupling of different technical components must be possible and the supervision of real-time conditions guaranteed. Handling tasks that are not under hard real-time conditions will fall to administrative parts. There are special demands on the administrative tasks since they should be designed for parallel simulation. Important features are the simultaneous start and stop of the subsystem simulation and the simultaneous alteration of distributed parameters online. Data-logging of distributed variables is necessary for visualization and documentation purposes.

All these points were taken into account in the design of the distributed simulation platform IPANEMA (Integration Platform for Networked Mechatronic Applications) (Honekamp 1998, Stolpe 1998). IPANEMA is a library and consists of simple elements for assembling complex mechatronic applications. Parallelized computing applications become more manageable by if only a few basic element types are assembled. Furthermore, the concept will be more transparent to application engineers who like to become familar with the concept.

In order to make available defined interfaces and satisfactory portability, IPANEMA disposes of a software layer between the real-time operating system and the information processing of the mechatronic application. This software layer was introduced to encapsulate operating-system services against their application and vice versa.

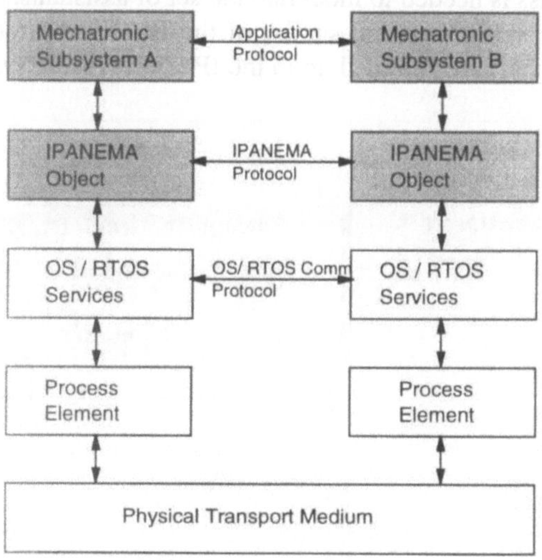

Figure 2. Software layers for the distributed mechatronic application

Additionally the application does not need to "know" specific details of the underlying basic services. This leads to a platform-independent application code and portability. The hardware supported up to now is a cluster of workstations with the operating systems Unix or NT, transputer networks with a hardware-encoded mini operating system and USAP (Power PC 604/transputer) networks (ETAS 1996). There are two different implementations on the USAP: one version uses the transputer as the owner of the control flow and the PPC with a small operating system kernel on it as a coprocessor for the computational task. The other version was designed and implemented in the METRO project (Kleinjohann 99). Therefore the operating system PEACE (Process Execution And Communication Environment) on the PPC and the real-time communication system DREAMS (Distributed Real-Time Management System) on the transputer were used (METRO 1998).

Because of the above-mentioned functional decomposition of the software, IPANEMA consists of the following objects: the first object is responsible for the processing of the application-relevant data. If implemented on a real-time hardware, such calculator processes are able to perform real-time data processing. These processes have interfaces among a set of such processes in order to exchange data needed for computation. The number of interfaces is determined by the particular application and therefore not standardized by the concept.

The second object with the name adaptor is employed for the coupling of technical components. This means the coupling of real technical components to a calculator process or to a set of calculator processes. As discussed above, real-time ability is mandatory for adaptor processes. Both adaptors and calculators are quite busy in normal applications. Therefore it seems reasonable to install additional processes in order to support the real-time tasks wherever possible. For that purpose the assistant process class was created. This process is employed for the administration of the calculators and adaptors, e.g., to start and stop the simulation and to alter parameter values online. As each calculator/adaptor has its exclusively accessible assistant, another process class is needed to moderate the set of assistants.

Figure 3 shows an architectural survey of the IPANEMA toolset with the objects mentioned. The objects are summed up in the IPANEMA library.

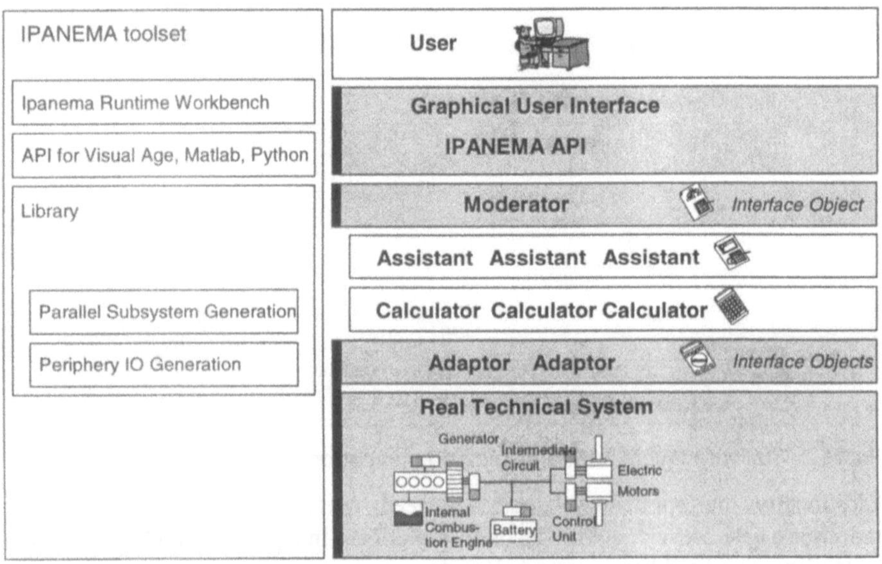

Figure 3. The Ipanema toolset

The moderator of the distributed simulation is the interface object to the user input level. On the user input level, we have an API to VisualAge, Matlab, and Python. A graphical user interface with comfortable plotting features is also part of the toolset. One important property of the moderator is net-transparency. If the user is willing to alter a system parameter or to trace variables during simulation, the moderator is able to determine the physical processor where the particular variable is stored. It is not the user's responsibility to know the physical residence of the particular variable.

Also the adaptor could be seen as an interface object to the technical system. The entire information-processing unit is distributed to a set of calculatos and adaptors. This means that each calculator processes a part of the entire system. The adaptors are generated from I/O description objects by the tool ElBaCo (see chapter 4). The calculators and adaptors are located on the level of hard real-time conditions. The calculators are generated from O-DSS (Hahn 96) by a tool concatenation for distributed simulation-code generation. This tool is still under development and will be integrated into Visual-MOOMo. These are the basic components to manage a distributed simulation.

3. Series Hybrid Vehicle

Hybrid vehicles allow to combine the advantages of the conventional drive (high performance and operating range) with those of the electric one, e.g., the opportunity of emission-free operation and regenerative braking. Figure 4 shows the basic components of a series hybrid vehicle. The hybrid vehicle consists of two electric traction motors that directly drive the two rear wheels. These motors receive their energy either from a Nickel-Cadmium battery or from a generator driven by an internal combustion engine. This aggregate is called the Auxiliary Power Unit, or just APU.

Figure 4. Arrangement of the components on the testbed

On the left-hand side of Figure 4, you see a photo of the APU with the combustion engine on our testbed. It is a Mercedes-Benz 1.8 liter spark-ignition engine from the current C-Class. It has a maximum power of 90 kW at 6000 rpm. The maximum torque is 170 Nm. The generator is a permanent-magnet synchronous machine by Mannesmann-Sachs with 53 kW. For a compact construction the rotor of the generator is directly coupled to the crank shaft of the combustion engine. The right-hand side shows the drive system of our configuration with the tandem motor in the middle and the electric brakes. The tandem motor has a maximum power of 2x30 kW and a maximum torque of 2x650 Nm. The electric brakes are inserted to act like the real vehicle with inertia (Wältermann 1998).

The testbed control is implemented on the distributed real-time PPC hardware mentioned before (Stolpe 1998). Figure 5 shows the testbed configuration with the parallelized mechatronic functions "generate energy" and "drive wheels". Several more parallel functions can still be indicated, but for more clarity, only these two will be considered in the following. The parallel control flows of the mentioned mechatronic functions are shown in Figure 5, right hand.

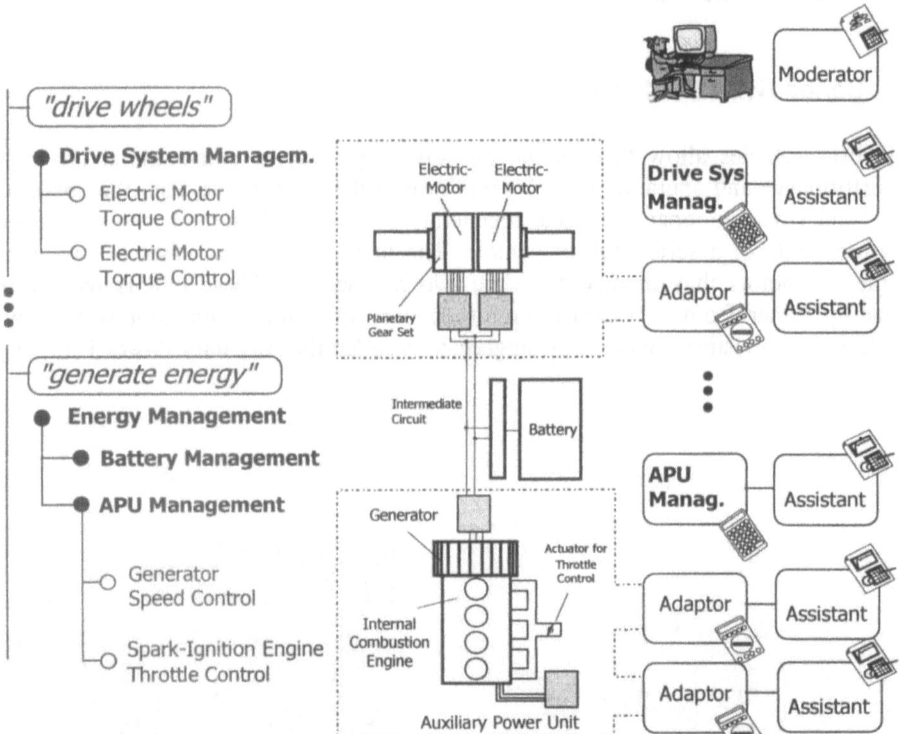

Figure 5. Testbed configuration with parallel control flows and distributed HIL simulation with the IPANEMA objects

The energy management can be divided into the auxiliary power unit management and the battery management. The former can be divided into the spark-ignition Engine control and the permanent-magnet generator control. The drive system consists of the two electric motor controllers.

In the vehicle the entire functionality will be realized by distributed controller units. The controllers working in parallel can be simulated on a parallelized hardware already at the design stage. For this and the realization of parallel mechatronic functions, the IPANEMA toolset can be used.

The energy management with the auxiliary power unit management and the battery management is assigned to one calculator and two adaptors. The adaptors are coupled to the throttle unit and to the ECU of the internal combustion engine. The drive system management is also assigned to one calculator and one adaptor. This adaptor is responsible for the access to the electric motor control units.

Already on the lowest control level, i.e., on the ECU level, you can find the speed control for the generator and the torque control of the electric motors. The task of this HIL simulation was the development of the APU management and the drive system management. Yet, this concept can also be applied to the development of the low-level control functions, e.g., the electric motor torque control. After testing and optimizing the drive system management the calculator with the developed control algorithm and the assigned adaptor could be ported to an ECU of their own.

4. Coupling of Periphery Hardware

The transition of a simple simulation to a Hardware-In-The-Loop simulation requires the embedding of real technical systems into the simulation environment. As a first step the drive system management and the electric motors with their corresponding controllers can be simulated completely. To link the technical process, one or several simulated subsystems can be extracted from the entire system and replaced by a real system. In this case, this means for the simulation platform IPANEMA that a calculator process has to be replaced by an adaptor process. However, this is only a simplified representation. In reality, the corresponding peripheral boards must of course be equipped for the measurement and excitation of the real process.

With this additional hardware higher demands on the coupling process arise than on the calculator. Calculators could be generated automatically from the model description. For the generation of the adaptor code, additional information about the peripheral boards and the mounted technical process is required. These information are usually not included in the physical model description. Answers are required for the following questions:

- Which peripheral board is employed?
- Which connection of the board is employed?
- To which physical quantity does the measured value correspond?

In the IPANEMA toolset these informations are summed up in one or more hardware-coupling descriptions (HCD).

However, even further information is required for embedding into the IPANEMA topology. The main topics are the following:

- Which channels to which calculators are necessary?
- Which measured and controlled value is transmitted via which channel?

These are the coupling informations, which are summarized in the process-coupling description (PCD).

5. Element-based Compiler for Argument-depending Problems of Code Generation

Since the adaptor code depends strongly on the inserted peripheral boards and, what is more, since these may change often, a flexible, fast, adaptable code generation is required. This demand is met by an instrument developed within the context of the METRO project. It is called ElBaCo.

The name ElBaCo stands for **el**ement-**ba**sed **co**mpiler for argument-depending problems of code generation (Oberschelp 1998).

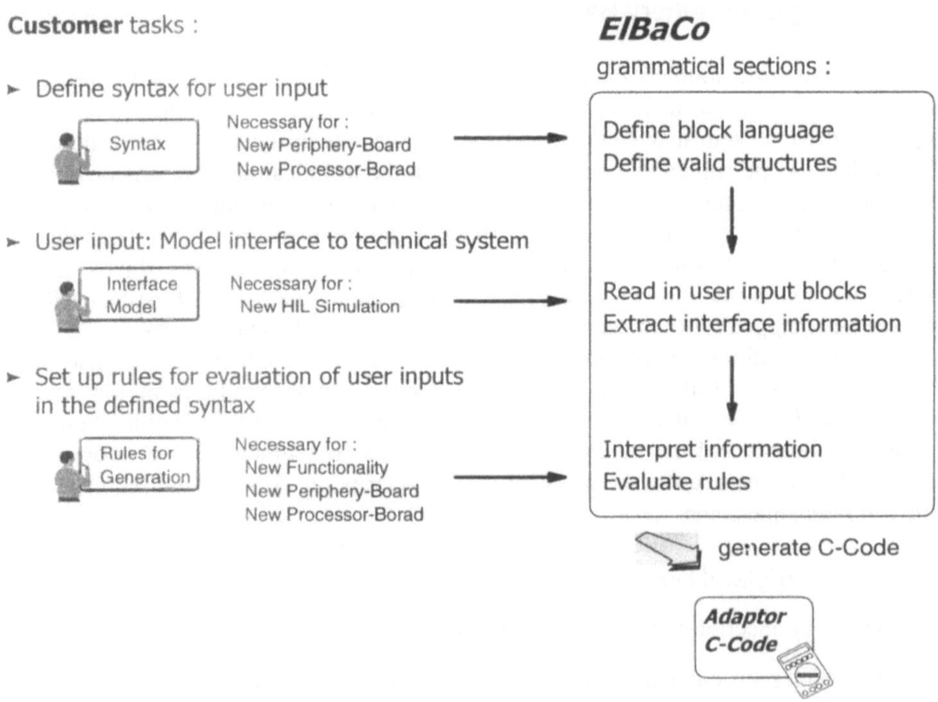

Figure 6. The working method of ElBaCo

ElBaCo is a simple tool for the generation of ASCII source code. It uses a configurable block language which is assembled from predefined grammatical elements as input language. The relevant information is extracted by an interpreter from the input language and code created according to it.

ElBaCo puts moderate demands on the computer hardware and the operating system and is easily portable onto different platforms since it was implemented completely in ANSI-C. It is a flexible compiler since its input language is adaptable.

The syntax is defined by selection from fixed grammatical constructs and the definition of parameters, variables, and constants. These information are stored in a text file which represents the language specification. The interface information contained in the user input file is structured by the syntax and transformed to a data structure. The information in the data structure could be evaluated by an integrated interpreter and used for the generation of code. The syntax definition and the interpretative evaluation rules are written only once for the compilation tasks. The task is finished by an expert for the code to be generated. The user will only use the syntax definition and evaluation. See Figure 6 for the user tasks and the grammatical sections of ElBaCo.

ElBaCo is implemented by means of a special instrument for the generation of compilers. This programming environment of the name ELI (Environment for Language Implementation) is a joint effort of the University of Paderborn, the University of Colorado (USA), and the James Cook university (Australia) (ELI 90).

It offers complete solutions for commonly encounted language-implementation subtasks. ELI contains libraries of reusable specifications, allowing to elaborate high-quality implementations from simple problem descriptions. The environment is problem-oriented instead of tool-oriented, which is the common working method in other tools. The user describes the problem to be solved and then ELI automatically employs the tools and components needed for that particular problem. The compiler construction set is an integrated system, and as a result it generates a complete set of C modules that leads to an easy portability to different platforms.

6. Conclusion

The recognition and installation of parallel control flows are an essential starting point for the design of decentralized control concepts of mechatronic systems. Installation of those subsystems is often physically motivated. This was illustrated by the testbed of the series hybrid drive train. For the realization of the distributed HIL simulation, the IPANEMA toolset was used. The user is supported by the flexible code-generating tool ElBaCo for the coupling of real components on the testbed, by an interpretative user interface and also by a comfortable graphical user interface.

References

dSPACE GmbH. 1991. *DSP-CITpro Hardware.* Paderborn, Germany.

ETAS GmbH & Co. KG. 1996. *USAP Transputer Module.* ETAS PC604-2000 V2 Documentation. Stuttgart, Germany.

Hahn M., Lückel J., Naumann R., Rasche R. "Ein Objektmodell für den Mechatronikentwurf." *ASIM'98. 12. Symposium Simulationstechnik* (Zürich, Switzerland., Sept. 15-18, 1998).

Hahn M., Meier-Noe U. 1996. "Classification in the Object-Oriented Modelling Language Objective-DSS, Exemplified by Vehicle Suspensions." *International Symposium on Computer-Aided Control.* IEEE. (Dearborn, MI, USA, Sept. 15-17, 1996).

Honekamp U. 1998. *IPANEMA - Verteilte Echtzeit-Informationsverarbeitung in mechatronischen Systemen.* Diss., Mechatronics Laboratory Paderborn, Germany.

Jäker K.-P., Klingebiel P., Lefarth U., Lückel J., Richert J., Rutz R. 1991. "Tool Integration by Way of a Computer-Aided Mechatronics Laboratory (CAMeL)." 5th *IFAC/IMACS Symposium on CADCS 91* (Swansea, UK, 1991).

Kleinjohann B., Rammig F., Schmitfranz B.-H., Schröder-Preikschat W., Stolpe R., Wältermann P. 1999: "Parallel Computing for the Design and the Implementation of Mechatronic Systems: Lessons Learned from the METRO Project." *3rd International HEINZ NIXDORF SYMPOSIUM on Mechatronics and Advanced Motion Control* (Paderborn, Germany, May 27 – 28, 1999).

Lückel J., Wallaschek J. 1997. "Functional Modelling and Simulation in Mechanical Design and Mechatronics." 2nd *MATHMOD* (Vienna, Austria, Feb. 5-7, 1997).

Honekamp U., Stolpe R., Naumann R., Lückel J. 1997. "Structuring Approach for Complex Mechatronic Systems." *30th ISATA Conference* (Florence, Italy, June 16-19, 1997).

METRO 1998. "Einsatz massiv paralleler Rechner beim Entwurf und der Realisierung komplexer mechatronischer Systeme." Abschlußbericht BMBF Verbundprojekt METRO. Daimler-Benz AG, ETAS GmbH, GMD-FIRST, Mannesmann-Sachs AG, TU Chemnitz (IfM), Uni-GH Paderborn (C-LAB, MLaP, HNI).

Oberschelp O. 1998. "Design and Implementation of a Flexible Code Generator to Couple Technical Processes in Hardware-in-the-Loop Simulations" (in German). Internal Paper, University of Paderborn, Mechatronics Laboratory Paderborn, Germany.

Stolpe R., Zanella M.C. 1998. "A Distributed Hardware-in-the-Loop Simulation Environment in Use on a Testbed of a Series Hybrid Drive." *ESM 98, 12th European Simulation Multiconference* (Manchester, UK, June 16-19, 1998).

Stolpe R. 1997. "Verteilte Simulation und Realisierung mechatronischer Systeme am Beispiel einer hybriden Roboterregelung". *PEARL 97, Workshop über Realzeitsysteme* (Boppard, Germany, Nov. 27-28, 1997).

ELI 1990. Übersetzerbau, Band 3.3. Handbuch der Informatik, R. Oldenburg Verlag, München/ Wien, 1990.

Wältermann P., Neuendorf N. 1998. "A Testbed for the Design and the Optimisation of a Series Hybrid Drive Train". *International Conference on Combustion Engines and Hybrid Vehicles* (London, UK, April 28-30, 1998).

Wolf M. 1998. "Visual MOOMo – A Graphical Object-Oriented Modelling Environment for the Design of Mechatronic Systems". MECHATRONICS 98, 6th UK Mechatronics Forum International Conference (Mount Billingden, Sweden, Sept. 9-11, 1998).

DISTRIBUTED HIL SIMULATION OF MECHATRONIC SYSTEMS APPLIED TO AN AGRICULTURAL MACHINE

Mauro Cesar Zanella, Ralf Stolpe

This paper presents an approach to a new software platform for distributed hardware-in-the-loop simulation applied to mechatronic systems.
An agricultural machine is presented as an example of a complex hierarchical mechatronic system. The decomposition of this machine into a hierarchical function-oriented form is shown in detail. To evaluate the communication and signal propagation as well as the I/O behaviour of a part of the complete system, a hardware-in-the-loop simulation of an active wheel suspension was implemented. The software approach to HILS is designed to support a hierarchical distributed control algorithm with the possibility of handling errors and dynamic coupling at run-time.

1. Introduction

Mechatronic systems consist of components from different disciplines, such as mechanical engineering, electrical engineering, and information science; each of them contributing their own specific functions to the generation of the utility. The concept of function in mechatronics can in most cases be seen as a synonym for the desired controlled motion behaviour of a system. A basic feature of mechatronic design is its decomposition into smaller subsystems based on the different functions of the system components. In addition to the mechanical supporting structure, actuators, sensors, and components are employed to put the mechatronic functions into effect (Honekamp 1997).
A proposal for the structuring of mechatronic systems as a basis for a generalized design method is presented in (Honekamp 1997). The approach discussed is a combination of hierarchical and modular organization with a distinction between the mechatronic system components. On the lowest hierarchical level, physically related sensors, actuators, mechanical structures, and information-processing units are combined to make up Mechatronic Function Modules (MFM). Two or more MFMs form an Autonomous Mechatronic System (AMS) which, in contrast to an MFM, excludes sensors or actuators. The highest hierarchical level is occupied by a combination of two or more AMSs to make up a Cross-linked Mechatronic System (CMS).

Inside a CMS, the AMSs provide only passive mechanical coupling with one another; and are interconnected by means of informational devices.

The information-processing unit of the entire system can be implemented by means of a parallel software system. In this case each of the MFMs is equipped with a local information-processing unit made up of hard- and software. The MFMs (including information processing) can be tested separately by means of the hardware-in-the-loop simulation technique. For this purpose the subsystem is embedded in a realistic environment which interacts with the subsystem as if the real operational environment were present. This paper will introduce a new approach to support real-time information processing in mechatronic systems.

The decomposition already mentioned and the new approach will then be exemplified by an agricultural machine, and we will give an overview of the complete machine with the HILS hardware.

Due to the large number of sensors and actuators in the machine, ECUs will been distributed along it with the propose to interface I/Os with the control hardware. Communication with the ECUs will be effected via a CANbus.

To evaluate the ECUs, I/O and software as well as the time delay (sampling/setting signals and communication) of the system, a partial simulation of the agricultural machine has been implemented in the laboratory.

We will then present a novel concept of a software platform allowing a flexible distributed HIL simulation of the complete agricultural machine with error-handling at run-time. The main features of this software platform will be explained, as will be its elements. The concept will be implemented in three consecutive stages. The first and the second are an off-line simulation, one with one processor and the other, with two processors. The third stage is an HILS with two processors.

2. Mechatronic Function Module (MFM) and Autonomous Mechatronic System (AMS), Exemplified by an Agricultural Machine

The MFM is the lowest level of the hierarchical structure of a mechatronic system. It has sensors and actuators as its main features and comprises also passive mechanical couplings. The information-processing of the control has to be quasi-continuous and under hard real-time conditions. Security and emergency mechanims also have to be provided for.

As an example of MFMs, we use a wheel control of one vehicle (see Figure 1). Each wheel has three activated degrees of freedom (DOFs): driving, steering, and elevation (suspension of the vehicle). To control each DOF of the wheel, sensors and actuators as well as a control algorithm (in this case SWD, SWS, and ECS) are of vital importance. Thus every degree of freedom (mechanical part, sensors, actuators, control algorithms, and information processing) makes up one MFM.

The coupling of two or more MFMs produces an AMS. The AMSs include neither sensors nor actuators, and the mechanical couplings between two MFMs are purely passive ones. The AMS includes an energy supply for the actuators and sensors on the MFM level, e.g., a battery bank in a hybrid vehicle (Stolpe 1998). An example of the AMS level is also displayed in Figure 1.

This 8-wheel vehicle can be a part of another mechatronic system. In this case, it is an agricultural machine. A machine of this kind is usually also equipped with a loader. Such a loader is made up of joints, each of them regarded as an MFM because it contains sensors, actuators, and local control. If any of these elements are coupled, the result will be another AMS.

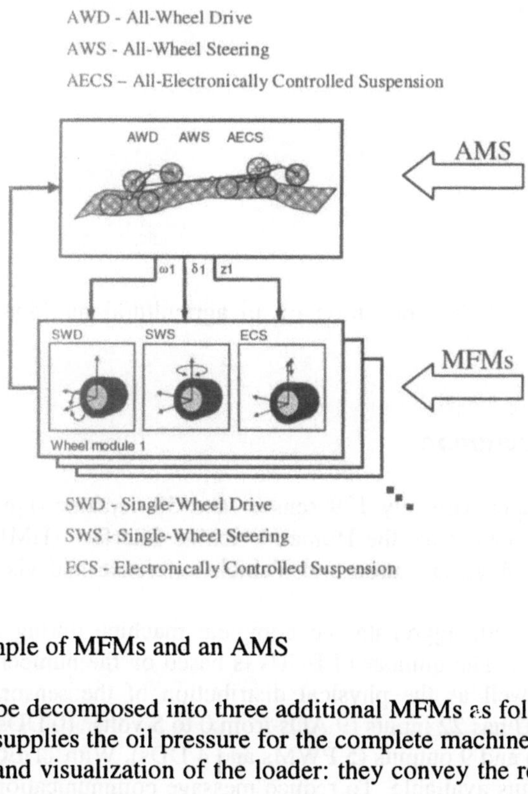

Figure 1. An example of MFMs and an AMS

The machine can be decomposed into three additional MFMs as follows:

1. engine: it supplies the oil pressure for the complete machine;
2. reference and visualization of the loader: they convey the reference values for the loader;
3. reference and visualization of the vehicle: they convey the reference values for the loader.

The main control (see Figure 2) is the result of the coupling of MFMs and AMSs. This is the AMS on the highest hierarchical level on the system.
The complete hierarchical decomposition of the system is shown in Figure 2.

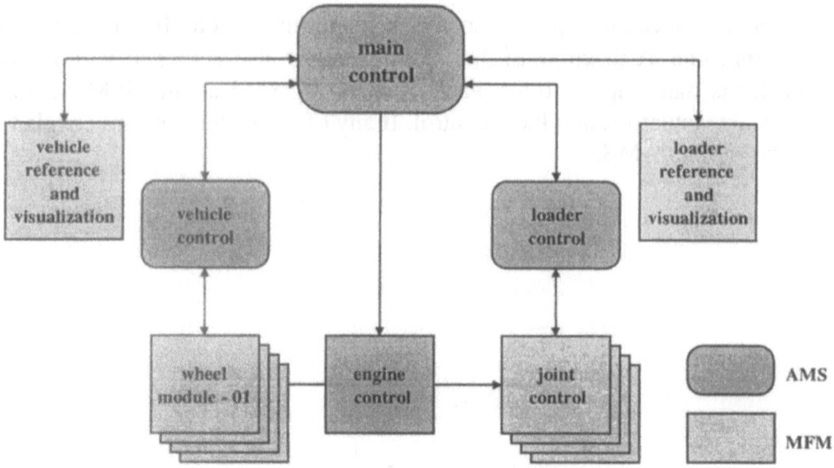

Figure 2. Hierarchical decomposition of an agricultural machine into MFMs and AMSs

3. Hardware Description

For this example approximately 139 sensor- and 50 actuator signals are estimated. The sensors and actuators for the Human-Machine Interface (HMI), generated from Loader reference and visualization and Vehicle reference and visualisation, are not included in the sum.

The hardware that will aggregate the complete machine during the design stages consists of 11 ECUs. The number of ECUs is based on the number of inputs/outputs of the system as well as the physical distribution of the sensors/actuators in the machine. Each ECU has 22 inputs (9 ADs from 0 to 5 volts, 10 DDs and 3 frequency-measuring devices) and 9 outputs (5 PWMs and 4 DDs). With 11 ECUs, there are 242 inputs and 99 outputs available. To reduce message communication and respectively the bus load, 4 CANbuses are designed for the entire machine. On the basis of the control algorithm, the ECUs are distributed into four main subsets: loader, vehicle front, vehicle rear, and reference and visualization. For every pair of CANbuses, a T-CAN (composed of 2 CAN controllers and one transputer) by ETAS (ETAS, 1997) will be used. The control algorithms will be implemented on USAPs (made up of one PowerPC and one transputer in communication via shared memory) also by ETAS (ETAS, 1996). In this configuration, the transputers links are responsible for the communication between the processors as well as that with the user. Figure 3 displays the projected hardware.

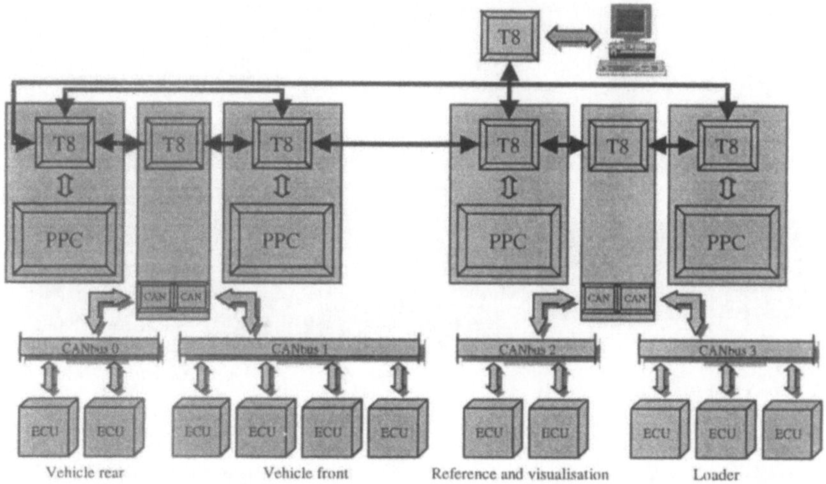

Figure 3. Hardware description for HILS of an agricultural machine

With the aim to perform a realistic simulation of CAN communication and signal propagation as well as to test the controller and the I/O behaviour, a part of the entire hardware was tested in the laboratory. The test consisted of a suspension control of one wheel of the agricultural machine. The model and the control law were tested.
The hardware configuration employed for this simulation is shown in Figure 4. It consists on the right-hand side of a dSPACE C40 hardware with Matlab/Simulink and on the other side of a USAP and a T-CAN on an INMOS B008 with the IPANEMA (Stolpe 1998, Honekamp 1998) software platform. In-between are the ECUs.
A dSPACE C40 hardware was used for the simulation of the testbench dynamics, for the I/O of missing sensors/actuators, and the generation of test stimuli. At first we did an off-line simulation to evaluate the model and the control law of the wheel suspension. For this simulation we used only the dSPACE hardware. The model and the control law were described by Matlab/Simulink. The control law was programmed in one Simulink block.
The next step was to replace the control algorithm by a Simulink I/O block. The physical variables were converted in electric signals and sent to an ECU. This ECU sampled the signal and sent it to the USAP via CAN where the IPANEMA software platform was running at the moment. The control algorithm that was implemented by a calculator object from IPANEMA is the same as in the offline simulation. The output of the control was returned to the ECU via CAN and converted into a PWM signal. The dSPACE I/O read the signal and transferred it to the model. The minimal cycle time of the control was 10 ms, due to the delay time of the ECU.
A connection panel was linked to the ECU and to the dSPACE hardware, thus allowing easy access to input and output signals.

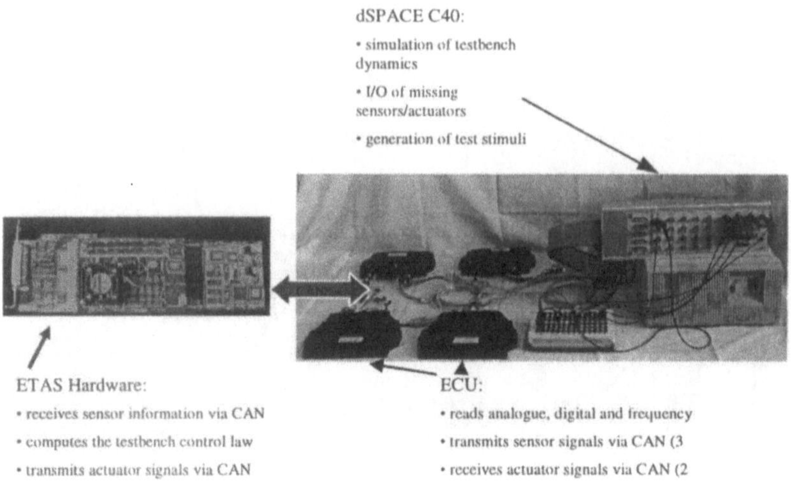

Figure 4. Hardware for the CAN and ECU tests in the laboratory

4. HIL Simulation Platform

IPANEMA (**In**tegration **Pla**tform for **Ne**tworked **M**echatronic **A**pplications) (Stolpe 1998, Honekamp 1998) can be used for a distributed HILS of a mechatronic system with the possibility of changing parameters and starting/stopping the complete system during simulation. The concept of MFMs and AMSs allows simple coupling and exchange of real elements for simulated elements. For highly complicated mechatronic systems, however, other functions gain ever more importance. One aspect is the possibility to handle errors during simulation. The following classes of errors may occur in a system:

1. Error from the simulation platform

   Example: In the agricultural machine an error in the CAN communication could happen. This means that one process will wait for one message and not receive it. As a result, the other processes will wait in vain for a message from this particular process, and the entire system will become unstable. This is an effect of the hard connections between the control laws resp. the processes/processors.

2. Errors from a security system

   Example: Due to security requirements, it is necessary for the operator to turn his chair to the front side to drive the machine. If the operator alters the position of the chair, an error will be generated and the error message sent to all processes responsible for the drive-motor control.

The error messages generated in both examples need not be sent to all processes/processors, just to a pre-defined group of them. A different communication level is necessary to support this feature.

Another important aspect is the possibility to implement the simulation with different step-times between the processes and their respective processors. For example, the

step-time of the suspension control has to be shorter than that of the vehicle reference and visualization.
For other systems, e.g., an intelligent intersection management (Naumann 1997), a dynamic coupling of control processes (Sanden 1998) is required.

4.1 Software Platform Description

For a flexible HILS of the entire system, a software platform is currently being under way at MLaP. The main features of this platform are the following:

- possibility to connect the MFMs and AMSs like in the real system
- high performance of the system because of direct access to variables
- different levels of communication where it is possible to send a message to one processor node or to all processor nodes
- error messages on different levels
- different simulation rates, because each processor node has one real-time clock
- support of dynamic coupling

The Dispatcher/Worker model described in (Tanenbaum 1996) is used as a basis to control the processes on a processor and the communication with processes located on other processors.
The concept is made up of the following elements:

- ♦ Dispatcher: this element is the process manager on one processor. It is responsible for emitting the sequential order of processes that have to run. The dispatcher is also responsible for supervising the real-time on the processor (for more details, see next chapter). Starting and stopping of the simulation, parameter changes, communication and co-ordination of the dynamic coupling fall also into the dispatcher's responsibility.
- ♦ Worker: the description of the system and the data exchange with the real system fall into the worker's responsibility. There are two classes of workers:
  - worker Model/Controller: here you find the equations that describe the dynamical behaviour or the control algorithm of the system. The C code is automatically generated from CAMeL tools (Homburg 1995).
  - worker Adapter: gateway to the inputs and outputs of the system. The C code is automatically generated from ELBACO (Oberschelp 1998).
- Mailbox: The final element of the simulation platform is the mailbox. The mailbox is responsible for the communication with other MFMs, for the consistency of the variables, the composition/decomposition of messages, message-flow control and the coupling between the workers.

In this approach the system is non-preemptive, i.e., the workers cannot be interrupted during its run. Another novel feature of this system is a clock timer added to the model described in (Tanenbaum 1996) to indicate/set the step-time of the MFM (see Figure 6). Thus it is possible to have different time steps for each MFM.
The sequence of activated workers has to be pre-programmed in the dispatcher and cannot be altered during simulation. The dispatcher can also be programmed to run a worker more than once in a single time step.

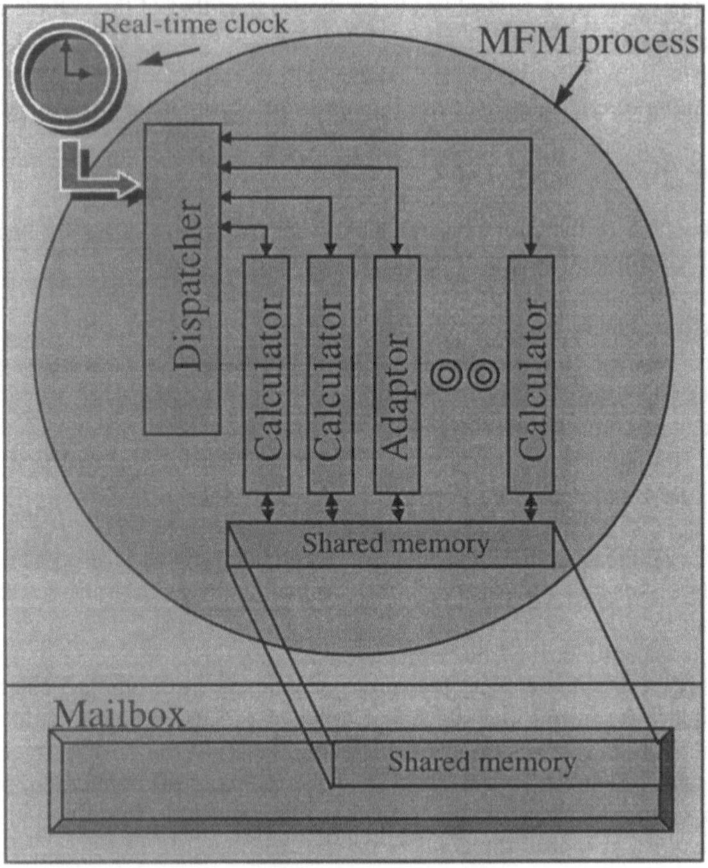

Figure 6. General approach to the HILS software platform

The number and types of workers in one MFM are not limited. A set of one dispatcher and multiple workers makes up an MFM that is encapsulated on one processor. The workers are based on the calculator and adaptor classes of IPANEMA.

4.2 Steps for the HIL Simulation Software Platform

This platform will be implemented at first on a USAP hardware. The objects (dispatcher, workers, and mailbox) can also run in parallel on this platform. In this hardware configuration, the mailbox and the dispatcher will run in parallel. They will be synchronized by means of messages transmitted via shared memory.
Implementation will be executed in three progressive stages:

1. Off-line simulation with one USAP - test of the dispatcher, worker and mailbox on a basic configuration of the platform without communication with other processors.
2. HILS with one USAP and one T-CAN - test of communication with another processor under real-time conditions.

3. Distributed HILS with 2 USAPs and one T-CAN - test of distributed control algorithms and error-handling through error simulation (for example CAN communication).

The configuration of the last phase is illustrated in Figure 7.

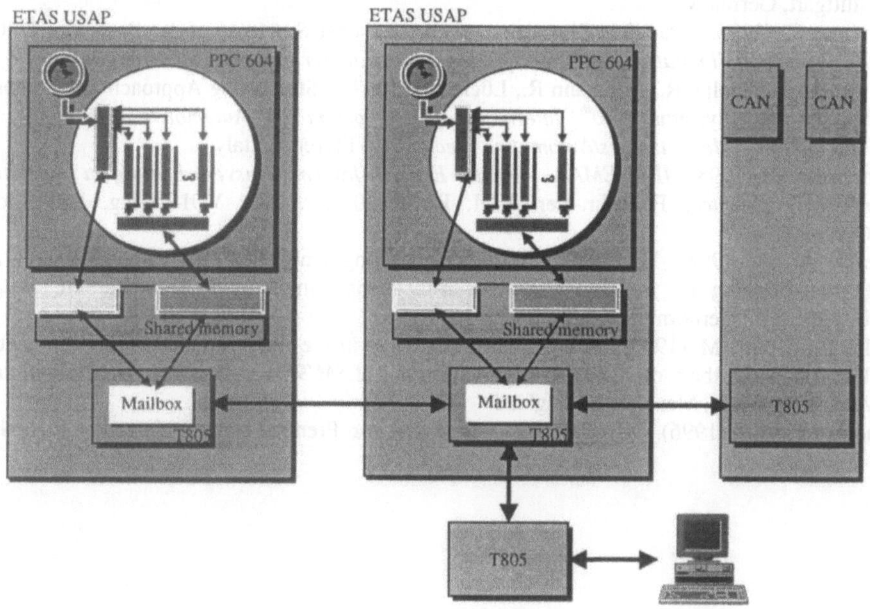

Figure 7. Hardware configuration of the HILS software tests

End Notes

A new approach to an HILS of a mechatronic system by distributed real-time information processing and a case study of an agricultural machine were presented. The division of the system elements is based on their respective functions (MFMs, AMS, and CMS).

The platform is based on a dispatcher/worker model. With this approach it is possible to connect subsystems the same way as in the real-system and to maintain the system hierarchy. It is also possible to alter the connections and the code of the workers. Another feature is the possibility of setting different time-steps for each MFM.

As an application, the example of an agricultural machine was presented. As far as hardware architecture is concerned, a PowerPC/Transputer combination was employed. Communication with the sensors is done via CANbus. The HIL simulation was used to test ECUs and CAN communication The concept presented is going to be implemented in a project to design a novel agricultural machine.

References

ETAS GmbH & Co. KG. (1996). *Usap Transputer Module. ETA PC604-2000 V2 Documentation*, Stuttgart, Germany.

ETAS GmbH & Co. KG. (1997). *TCAN V4.0 Transputer-CAN-Modul.* Documentation, Stuttgart, Germany.

Homburg C. (1995). "Parallele Simulation mechatronischer Systeme auf der Basis von DSC." *10. Workshop Simulation verteilter Systeme und paralleler Prozesse.* Dresden, Germany.

Honekamp U., Stolpe R., Naumann R., Lückel J. (1997). "Structuring Approach for Complex Mechatronic Systems." *30th International Symposium on Automotive Technology & Automation – Mechatronics/Automative Electronics*, Florence, Italy.

Honekamp U. (1998). *IPANEMA - Verteilte Echtzeit-Informationsverarbeitung in mechatronischen Systemen,* Fortschr.-Ber. VDI, Reihe 20, Nr. 267. VDI-Verlag, Düsseldorf, Germany.

Oberschelp O. (1998). "Entwurf und Implementierung eines flexiblen Codegenerators zur Prozeßkopplung für verteilte Hardware-in-the-Loop Simulation.", Diplomarbeit, MLaP, Universität Paderborn, Germany.

Stolpe R., Zanella M. (1998). "A Distributed Hardware-in-the-Loop Simulation Environment in Use on a Testbed of a Series Hybrid Drive." *ESM'98 – 12th European Simulation Multiconference*, Manchester, England.

Tanenbaum, A.S. (1996). *Distributed Operation Systems.* Prentice-Hall, Englewood Cliffs, NJ.

AGENT-BASED LOAD BALANCING FOR MOBILE ROBOT APPLICATIONS

Ralf Kluthe, Wolfgang Obelöer, Claus Grewe
Medical University of Lübeck, D-23538 Lübeck

1. Introduction

There is an increasing demand for mobile autonomous robots, e.g. in the field of service applications. For the use of mobile service robots in real environments, complex and reactive sensing-perception-action systems are necessary. Many of these models were already developed and/or are subject of current research (Mertsching, et al., 1997), (Wasson, et al., 1998). On the other hand, questions on how these models can be integrated into the software architectures for mobile robots as well as the management of system resources necessary in mobile systems are not well studied. Especially the latter requires mechanisms to handle the different timeliness and priorities of the normally parallel tasks even in dynamic environments.

Especially for algorithms based on high resolution sensors, high computational power is needed which enforces the usage of parallelisms. In addition, typical applications in this area show a dynamic behavior due to changes in the environment. Therefore, load balancing has to be a basic part of such a system.

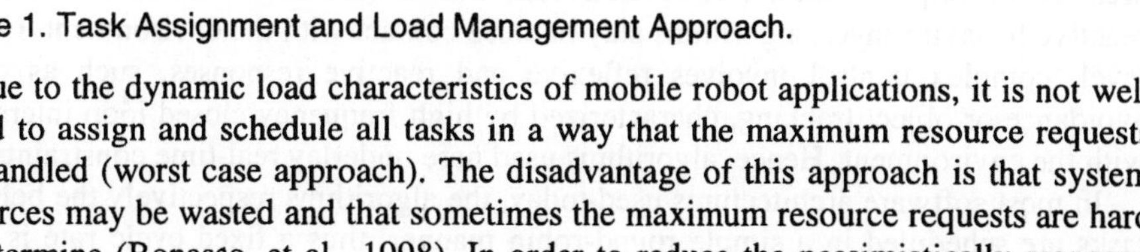

Figure 1. Task Assignment and Load Management Approach.

Due to the dynamic load characteristics of mobile robot applications, it is not well suited to assign and schedule all tasks in a way that the maximum resource requests are handled (worst case approach). The disadvantage of this approach is that system resources may be wasted and that sometimes the maximum resource requests are hard to determine (Bonasso, et al., 1998). In order to reduce the pessimistically managed algorithms, a suitable load management is required. The aim of this management is to reduce the portion of pessimistically managed algorithms (that are algorithms with hard deadlines) to a minimum and handle the rest dynamically (see figure 1).

Therefore, a suitable software architecture is proposed, where the load balancing of mobile robot applications (section 2) is done by mobile agents (section 3). This paper shows a mechanism for migrating processing entities with real-time constraints, which is used by the load balancing approach. For the realization, an existing multiagent environment for load balancing of parallel applications is extended so that it can be used for mobile robot applications (section 4). Finally, first measurements are presented (section 5).

2. Mobile Autonomous Robots

Software systems for autonomous robots are normally decomposed into several layers. Here, the Three-Layer Architecture is a widely applied model (Hasemann, 1996). The three abstraction layers are deliberation, sequencing, and reactive behavior (figure 2).

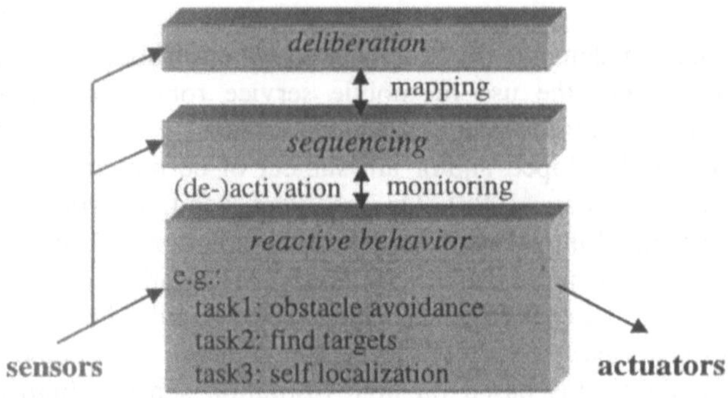

Figure 2. Three-Layer Architecture for Robot Control.

The major tasks of the deliberative layer are planning, scheduling, and resource handling. Activities of this layer correspond to long term planning as well as plan adaptations. The sequencing layer represents tactics, called task nets, i.e. pre-defined, partially ordered sets of actions. The sequencing layer selects appropriate tactics and starts the associated reactive behaviors according to the relationships within the task nets. The reactive behavior layer executes the behavior tasks, activated by the sequencing layer. Several robots have been programmed using some variations of this architecture, e.g. Saphira, 3T, ATLANTIS, LAAS (Bonasso, et al., 1998). In the reactive behavior layer, algorithms stay in close contact with the environment. On this level, complex control involves reflexive and reactive responses, such as object avoidance or object tracking, characterized by high frequency closed loop interaction with the environment. Hence, algorithms used here underlay real-time constraints.

In most software architectures used today, the algorithms respectively the behavior tasks are scheduled in a simple round-robin manner, thus a fixed cycle rate is used. But normally, the behavior tasks have different temporal orders depending on the robot state. So, it is reasonable that at high robot velocity the cycle rate of an obstacle recognition algorithm is higher than that for an object recognition algorithm for person tracking. Hence, modern robot software architectures have to support multi-rate computation (Wasson, et al., 1998). Furthermore, for a reasonable use of system resources, like CPU utilization, cycle rates may be dynamically increased or decreased, e.g. the cycle rate of an obstacle recognition algorithm is proportional to the velocity of the robot.

Due to the increasing demand on high-resolution sensors like laser ranger or cameras, algorithms become more complex. In addition, they are computationally expensive and characterized by a number of computation paths. In this area data flow graphs are normally used for modeling. Often the algorithms are biologically motivated as e.g. attention or fovea control in human perception systems. So, the processing of the data flow chains depends on the dynamics of the environment (Mertsching, et al., 1997) and the robot state. Due to these facts, data flow chains are activated or terminated dynamically. For example, if a special obstacle recognition is needed or some extracted features in the sensor data refer to obstacles, a data flow for further processing is activated additionally. After the obstacle is passed the data flow can be terminated.

Summarized, from system point of view, the reactive part is characterized by the following points:

- Dynamic changes in the environment and attention-based control-mechanisms within the algorithms cause dynamic loads.
- Algorithms can be modeled using data flow graphs and have to fulfil real-time constraints.
- Due to different temporal orders of the algorithms, multi-rate computation occurs.
- Algorithms, especially those for high resolution sensors, are computationally expensive and therefore powerful hardware platforms are required.

Thus, software architectures for mobile robots have to offer mechanisms that allow a suitable exploitation of the system resources. Especially mobile systems have to handle limited resources like computation power and battery energy. Therefore, special management mechanisms like load balancing without violating real-time constraints are unavoidable.

3. Hierarchical Agent Based Approach

Here a hierarchical agent based approach for handling dynamic load by migration is presented. Therefore, a load model is defined and a hardware platform is proposed.

3.1. Load Model and Hardware Platform for Mobile Robot Software

Robot application software is normally decomposed into several tasks as shown in figure 2. Depending on the current context, the sequencing and planning units, for simplification called robot control units, map the tasks to the hardware and control it. In order to describe the data and control dependencies of one task, a data flow paradigm is used. Thus, the computation model can be considered as a system that dynamically maps data flow chains to the system hardware. Dynamic load can be caused by outer and inner reasons. That means, currently mapped data flow chains can be manipulated in several ways (outer reasons). For example, data flow chains can be started and stopped or the accuracy of the modeled algorithms can be increased or decreased. Inner reasons are changes of load by the behavior task, e.g. robot velocity increases and as a consequence the cycle rate of an obstacle recognition algorithm.

Furthermore, the approach has to support suitable hardware platforms. The characteristics of used algorithms ranges from simple, computation intensive operations like convolution in vision systems to complex operations used in searching, matching, or planning algorithms. For complex operations, general-purpose processors are appropriate, whereas for computation intensive operations special hardware, e.g. DSP systems, or general multi-processor systems are used. Here embedded cluster systems consisting of off-the-shelf components (e.g. PCs) connected via a fast network offer an attractive solution. These cluster systems have a good price/performance ratio and special hardware is easy to integrate. Thus, for the presented approach these hardware platforms will be assumed.

3.2. Multiagent Environment

As mentioned, an online load balancing approach is presented that handles the resulting imbalances of system load by migration. This implies that migration of data flow nodes is done in a way that real-time constraints are not affected. This can be handled by separating data flow node assignment and scheduling (Krishna, 1997). That means, data flow node assignment and migration is done without real-time constraints. To schedule the allocated data flows, scheduling algorithms offered by the real-time operating system are used. Thus, data flow nodes can be migrated to processing nodes which have enough computation power to fulfil the changed requirements of a data flow. But migration can also be used for compaction, leading to processors that can be switched off (idle mode). For example, a Pentium II 450 MHz has a power consumption of about 30 watts with full load and 2.4 watt in idle mode (0.8 watt in deep sleep mode) (Intel, 1998). Thus, battery power can be saved or a new mapping can be done more easily.

Here, mobile agents are a promising solution to solve the load balancing problem respectively the migration problem. The *mobility* allows an agent to "transport" a data flow node to another processing node. In addition, the mobility can be used to source out tasks, e.g. "long-term" planning tasks, to remote host systems. Due to their a*utonomy,* agents may perform a suitable action by themselves, like reducing the accuracy of their operation. But they may also *cooperate* with other agents to find a solution like finding a target node for a migration. In addition, agents are *pro-active*, and they may perform additional tasks like an administrative service in order to measure computation power consumed by a data flow node.

To handle the data flows by agents, a hierarchical multiagent environment is proposed (figure 3). The environment allows to model reactive behavior of mobile robots and it offers services like obstacle avoidance to the robot control layer. These services are modeled by data flows. The robot control acquires services with certain constraints, e.g. obstacle avoidance with a maximum cycle rate, by requesting a dispatcher agent. The dispatcher agent has to start the services and to guarantee the requested constraints. After a service is started, the robot control layer manipulates and monitors the functional behavior of the services.

If a service violates its constraints or a service cannot be started due to too few hardware resources, the dispatcher agent has to interact with the robot control to find a solution. For example, the robot control could order the dispatcher agent to lower the accuracy or the cycle rate of services. Additionally, the dispatcher agent can be forced to find an own solution. So, the dispatcher agent does an online load balancing in a way that important services (high priorities or hard deadlines) are able to fulfil their constraints. Services with weaker constraints are allowed to violate their deadlines.

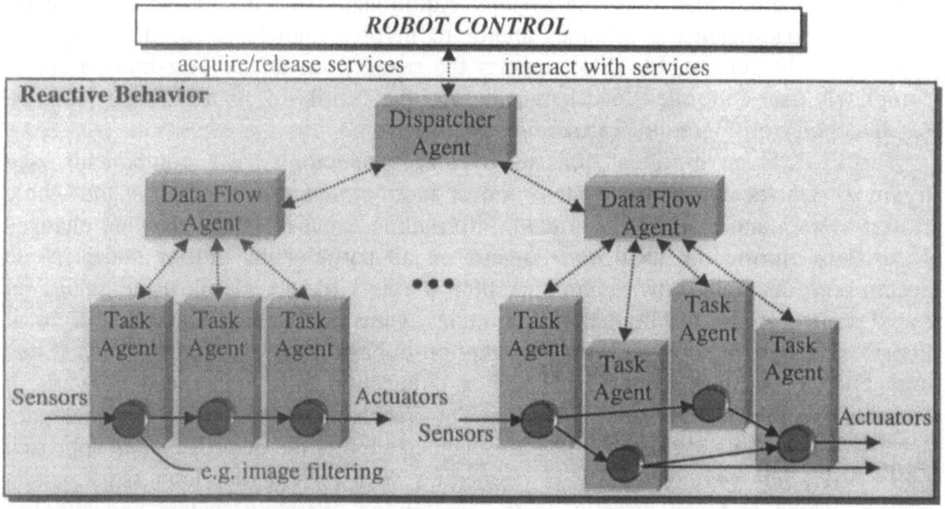

Figure 3. Hierarchical Multiagent Environment.

The dispatcher agent starts a service by ordering a data flow agent. Each data flow agent is responsible for a single service. The data flow agent initiates the mapping of the data flow nodes to the hardware. In addition, it monitors the runtime behavior (deadlines, CPU power consumption, etc.) and interacts with the dispatcher agent if something fails within the service. Data flow agents cooperate among each other to coordinate their actions.

For mapping a service, a data flow agent assigns a task agent to each data flow node. Each task agent is responsible for one data flow node and monitors its runtime behavior. The task agents are mobile and so they can carry or migrate the data flow node to a processing node where the operation is supported.

4. Realization

For a realization of the described approach, a multiagent environment with migration and online load balancing capabilities has to be implemented. As a base, the existing multiagent environment FLASH is used. In this section, the environment and the required extensions are described.

4.1. FLASH

FLASH (Flexible Agent System for Heterogeneous Cluster) is a framework which offers programmers a platform for the creation of distributed, load-balanced applications (Obelöer, et al., 1998) for cluster systems. The user decomposes a problem into several subtasks and assigns each subtask to a mobile FLASH agent. The FLASH agents are responsible for the efficient execution of the given subtasks. Therefore, they travel through a cluster system, e.g. searching for free resources. Without any further information, FLASH uses a simple policy in order to balance the application caused load over the system. Additionally, the user is able to specify alternative load-balancing schemes and/or to involve knowledge about the special application. In general, FLASH supports the range from totally user-transparent to completely user-controlled load balancing and the facility to control single features, e.g. the choice of migration destination.

The FLASH environment consists of four cooperating basic components (see figure 4). On the top of the system one or more *system agents* observe the whole cluster system and maintain up-to-date information about it. If any relevant changes occur, they inform the local *node agents* on all participating cluster nodes. Node agents serve as well-known communication partners for the mobile *user agents* on every visited node. Additionally, the node agents know and maintain all local *interfaces to system services*, which are the fourth basic component of FLASH. If any user agent needs a special service, e.g. a connection to a high-speed network, it contacts the local node agent for help. This mechanism hides the real, machine-specific implementation of a service and hence supports the heterogeneous approach of FLASH. For example, FLASH cooperates with an external load management system, which is based directly on the underlying operating system and supplies system specific load indices. For this purpose the node agents are residing immobile on the nodes. However, for fulfilling dedicated jobs they can create messenger agents. Other important tasks of node agents are the maintenance of up-to-date information about locally residing user agents and support of centralized decisions.

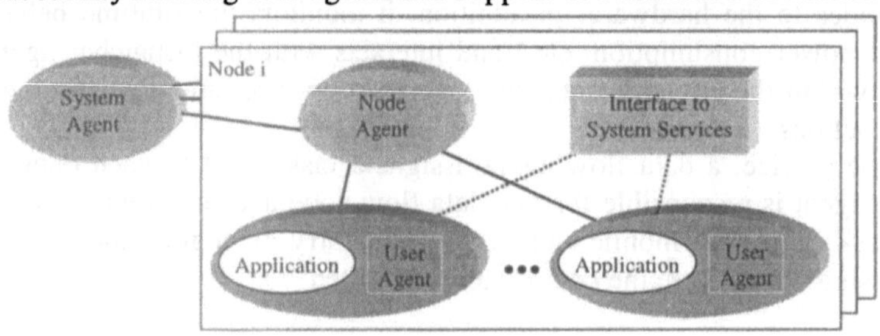

Figure 4. Structure of FLASH.

As shown in figure 4, each user agent contains a single subtask of the application. The agent has to take care for the efficient execution of the subtask. Therefore, it takes into account node capacities, the current load state of the nodes as well as occurring internal and external events, e.g. interactions with other agents or system services. User agents have the possibility to execute the job either directly as a thread in the agent context or to search for a native implementation of the function in the cluster system (accessible via system services). This mechanisms will be explained in the following section.

4.2. Realization of FLASH

Currently, FLASH is mostly written in Java and uses the agent system Voyager (ObjectSpace, 1998) which is completely implemented in Java, too. Voyager offers some unique features (Kiniry, Zimmerman., 1997) and provides the structures and methods for the management and handling of distributed objects. Therefore, it has several kinds of communication types, location transparent handling of remote method invocations, a global name space, and migration facilities. A special Voyager object is the so-called "agent" which is able to cause a migration by itself. On top of this object class the FLASH agents were implemented.

As mentioned, the programmer is able to realize a job in Java or to apply native functions. In FLASH, a native function is accessible via a system service interface. Typically this option is chosen when a node owns special hardware (e.g. a DSP board) or if the computation performance offered by Java is insufficient. Native functions are written in C or C++ and compiled for a specific machine architecture. Thus, Java applications - and consequently FLASH agents - can overcome performance losses resulting from the interpretation of Java Bytecode by the Java Virtual Machine.

4.3. Extension of FLASH

FLASH was originally designed for load balancing of parallel applications without real-time constraints. To use FLASH for mobile robot applications, extensions are required.

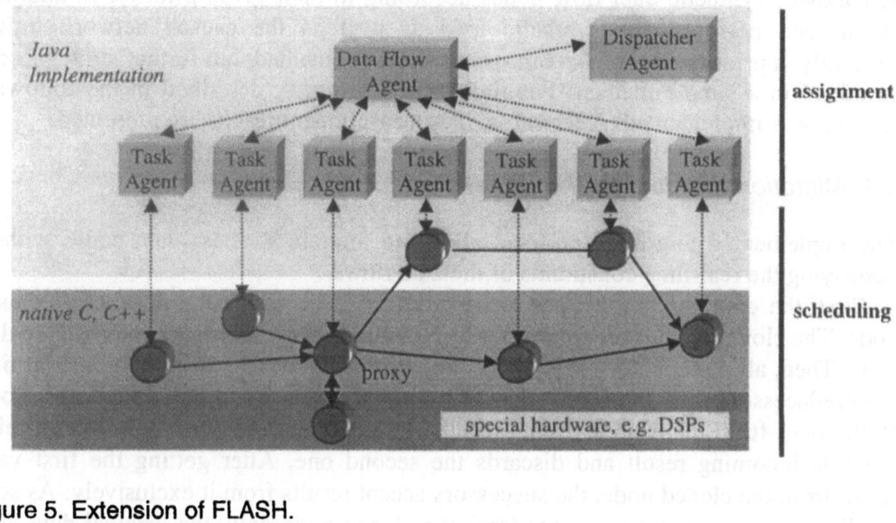

Figure 5. Extension of FLASH.

As mentioned, a separation between data flow node assignment and scheduling is done. Hence, a loosely-coupled mechanism between task agents and data flow nodes is provided (in FLASH, application subtasks are part of the agent, see figure 4). So task agents represent the interface between the agent environment and the real-time algorithms (see figure 5). Real-time scheduling of the data flows is done by the underlying operating system. Thus, agents can run concurrently without directly influencing the data flow.

Due to performance bottlenecks of Java and the absence of needed algorithms, data flow nodes written in native code have to be supported. A data flow node wrapper is introduced, making it possible to combine different implementations within a data flow. The interaction between Java and native code is provided by the Java Native Interface (JNI). Special hardware is supported by a proxy, whose interface is compatible to that of normal data flow nodes. The proxy handles communication between the data flow and the algorithms mapped to the special hardware.

5. Measurements

An efficient realization of the described mobile robot application essentially depends on the appropriate choice of well-suited mechanisms and tools. For this reason, in the first step a distributed emulation environment for the lower C/C++ parts (figure 5) was realized. The prototype helps to explore the feasibility of migrating data nodes without deadline violations. The environment consists of communicating processes (one per cluster node). All data flow nodes of one processor reside in such a process. These processes have a high priority, i.e. they are almost the exclusive users of CPU resources. This allows to implement alternative scheduling strategies independent from the underlying operating system.

The prototype is able to emulate the temporal behavior of several distributed data flows mapped to a cluster system. Therefore, the emulation schedules the CPU demands of synthetic data flow nodes according to their given priority. In addition, the testbed performs the synthetic load as well as the caused network traffic. Currently, a prioritized round-robin strategy is implemented, but further strategies can be added in a simple manner. For migration a protocol, described in the following section, was implemented. Afterwards, first measurement results are presented.

5.1. Migration Protocol for the C/C++ Part

The implemented migration protocol allows to migrate stateless data nodes without destroying the real-time constraints of the data flows.

First, the data node which has to be migrated is cloned at the destination cluster node. The clone rebuilds all connections to the successors and predecessors in the data flow. Then, all participating data nodes are informed about the clone. For a short time the predecessors send their messages to both, the original and the cloned data node. Both nodes fulfil their job and send results to the same successors. A successor takes the first incoming result and discards the second one. After getting the first valid result from the cloned node, the successors accept results from it exclusively. As soon as all successors accept messages from the cloned node only, the original data node stops sending further results. Then the predecessors are informed, which stop sending messages to the original data node. Afterwards the original node is terminated.

5.2. First Measurements

The presented measurements were done on a cluster of dual-processor PCs (Pentium II, 330 MHz) interconnected via Myrinet (Boden, et al., 1995).

For exploration of the described migration scheme two data flows (DF1 and DF2) were configured, which are started periodically (see figure 6). DF1 has a higher priority than DF2. During measurements the time slice in the emulation was adjusted to 10 ms. The medial CPU usage of the single cluster nodes was evaluated for the specified CPU demands. The CPU usage of cluster nodes 0 and 2 is in the range of 35%, the usage of cluster node 1 is about 75%.

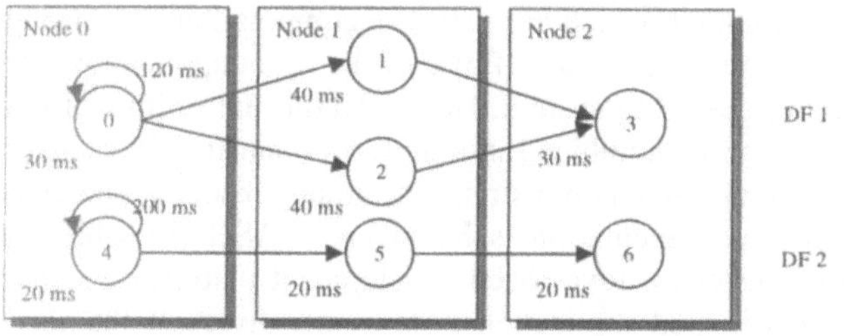

Figure 6. Test Configuration.

For the following measurement it is assumed that the robot aims to increase its velocity. Therefore, it is necessary to reduce the periodicity of DF1 (e.g. to 100 ms). These leads to a higher load on all participating cluster nodes. In addition, the second data flow starves because the higher prior data flow demands more and more CPU resources on cluster node 1. Hence, a migration of a data node is necessary in order to guarantee the functionality of DF2. Here, the migration of data node 1 to cluster node 2 was chosen. Figure 7 shows the CPU usage for time intervals of 0.5 seconds.

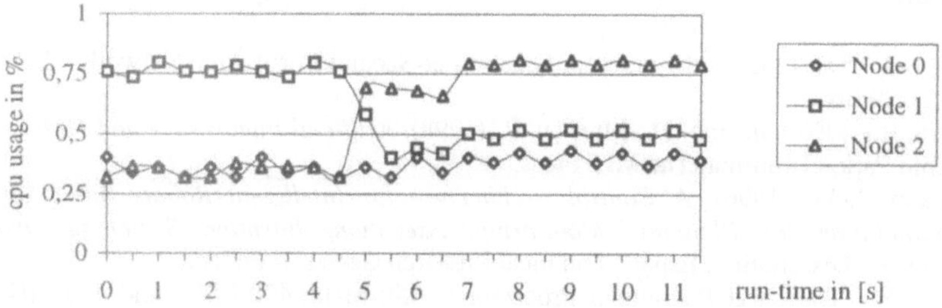

Figure 7. CPU Usage with Migration of a Data Node.

The migration of data node 1 is initiated after 5 seconds and takes 75 ms protocol overhead (without setup-time for a thread or process). As can be seen in figure 7 the load of cluster node 1 decreases (from ca. 75% to 40%) while that of node 2 increases. After seven seconds (two seconds after the migration order) the periodicity of the source data node 0 is reduced to 100 ms which causes an increased load in the system. During the migration as well as afterwards the deadline of DF1 was met.

The migration time of the FLASH agent was measured separately. Here, a migration time of averaged 32 ms was measured for an idle system. The presented measurements are a first confirmation that the proposed agent-based approach is able to fulfil the requirements of real-time applications in the field of service robots.

6. Conclusion

Today high computation power is needed for mobile robot applications, which can only be offered by parallel systems. These applications cause dynamic load fluctuations due to the dynamics of the environment. Hence, a load management has to be applied which considers the special demands of real-time applications.

In this paper a hierarchical multiagent-based management system for robot applications is presented, which consists of a computation and management part. The computation part executes the data flows of the robot application, scheduling is done by the underlying operating system. Here, several realizations of data nodes (e.g. in Java, C, or C++) can be combined in a uniform manner. The management part hides implementation details and administrates the arising resource demands.

Currently, the implementation is based on FLASH (Flexible Agent System for Heterogeneous Cluster), a Java-based development platform which was created as a framework for distributed applications. This paper discusses the necessary extensions of FLASH for combining Java-based and native data nodes. In addition, an emulation environment was realized, which serves as a testbed for the evaluation of distributed and cooperative load management strategies for mobile robot applications. Especially, the possibility of migrating a data node from one computation node to an other was explored.

For the future the evaluation of different load management heuristics as well as the use of the approach in a real mobile robot is planned.

References

Boden, N.J; et al. (1995). "Myrinet: A Gigabit-per-Second Local-Area Network." *IEEE Micro* 15(1), 29-36.

Bonasso, R.P.; Kortenkamp, D.; Murphy, R. (1998). *Artificial Intelligence and Mobile Robots,* Menlo Park, California: The MIT Press.

Hasemann, J.-M. (1996). *A Control Architecture for Intelligent Robots Based on Graph Manipulation for Planning, Monitoring, Execution, Intention Switching, and Fault Recovery,* Dissertation, Espoo: Technical Research Center of Finland.

Intel (1998). "Datasheet Pentium II Processor at 350 MHz, 400 MHz, and 450 MHz." *Intel Corp.,* Ordering Number 243657-002, http://www.intel.com.

Kiniry, J.; Zimmerman, D. (1997). "A Hands-On Look at Java Mobile Agents." *IEEE Internet Computing* 1(4), 21-30.

Krishna, C. M.; Shin, K. G. (1997). *Real-Time Systems.* New York: McGraw-Hill.

Mertsching, B.; Bollmann, M. (1997). "Visual Attention and Gaze Control for an Active Vision System." in *Progress in Connectionist-Based Information Systems* (ed. Kasabov N.; Kozma, R.; et al.), Berlin: Springer, 76-79.

Obelöer, W.; Grewe, C.; Pals, H. (1998). "Load Management with Mobile Agents." in *Proceedings of the 24th EUROMICRO Conference*, Los Alamos: IEEE Computer Society, vol. 2, 1005-1012.

ObjectSpace (1997). *ObjectSpace Voyager Core Package.* Tech. Overview, ObjectSpace, Inc.

Wasson, G.; Bonasso, R. P.; Kortenkamp, D. (1998). "Integrating Active Perception with an Autonomous Robot Architecture." in *Proceedings of the 2nd International Conference on Autonomous Agents*, 325-331.

4 VERIFICATION AND VALIDATION

COMPARING MODEL CHECKING AND TERM REWRITING FOR THE VERIFICATION OF AN EMBEDDED SYSTEM

Klaus Schneider and Michaela Huhn

Institute for Computer Design and Fault Tolerance
(Prof. Dr.-Ing. D. Schmid)
University of Karlsruhe, P.O. Box 6980, 76128 Karlsruhe
Klaus.Schneider@informatik.uni-karlsruhe.de
Michaela.Huhn@informatik.uni-karlsruhe.de
http://goethe.ira.uka.de/people

Abstract: *There are two main streams for the verification of digital systems: Theorem proving methods such as term rewriting are used for the verification of data oriented systems, and model checking of temporal logics is usually used for the verification of control dominated systems. While theorem proving is an inherently interactive verification method, model checking is performed automatically.*
In this paper, we investigate for the verification of algorithms for computing the discrete cosine transform by means of term rewriting and model checking. We show the advantages and disadvantages of both approaches at different abstraction levels of the design.

1 INTRODUCTION

The development of complex concurrent systems is, in general, an error prone task. This holds in particular for the design of parallel embedded systems, as there are still no design flows that are seamlessly supported by appropriate tools. Hence, the integration of formal verification into the design of these systems has been shown fruitful in that (i) more clearly structured designs are obtained and (ii) design errors can be detected early. For this reason, it is on the one hand desirable to integrate formal verification in the first phases of the design. On the other hand, some relevant details e.g. arising from the partitioning of the system into hardware and software components are yet unknown in these early phases. Hence, formal verification must be used in very early design phases, but must then guide the succeeding design when more implementation decisions are added.

Adding verification to the design of embedded systems requires however another expert in the team: Besides the details and requirements of the application under construction, this expert has to be familiar with different verification techniques (see [Gup92] for an overview). For control oriented systems, model checking is one of the favorite techniques which is supported by well developed tools such as SMV [McM93], SPIN [HP96], HSIS [ABC+94] or SVE [FSS+94]. Data oriented systems can be handled by theorem provers as HOL [GM93] or PVS [ORR+96] and in particular by term rewrite systems such as RRL [KZ88]. Since most real world problems contain both, a nontrivial data and a nontrivial control part, verification often needs a combination of different techniques.

To make verification part of the industrial design process, frameworks and tools have to be provided that allow the uniform and convenient access to different verification techniques. In particular, we aim at integrating different verification tools such as the SMV [McM93], SPIN [HP96], RRL [KZ88], and HOL [GM93]. Providing a collection of different techniques, verification can be done efficiently by choosing the technique that is suited best in the sense that the system can be verified with as little human effort as possible.

In this paper, we study the verification of the discrete cosine transform (DCT) which is a significant part of the JPEG or MPEG standard [PM93] for still image data compression. In particular, we compare the application of two different verification techniques, namely model checking and term rewriting. We concentrate on two aspects which are in our opinion crucial for a wide acceptance of formal verification: (i) the appropriateness of the formal description of the system and (ii) the interactive human creativity required for the verification. Appropriateness of the system description is twofold: On the one hand, the formal model must contain enough details to capture the relevant behavior of the system such that all desired properties can be checked. On the other hand, the complexity of the formal description raises the costs of verification in both, human effort and run time. We consider interactive human creativity instead of pure execution runtimes consumed by the verification tools. Usually, the latter grows exponentially with the systems size, such that the automated part is either executed in a matter of seconds, or it is impossible.

Our two approaches to verify the DCT differ substantially with respect to the appropriateness criteria: While the term rewriting solution is based on an abstract data type that partially captures the axiomes the real numbers, the model checking solution is based on bitvectors with a fixed width. For this reason, the term rewriting solution allows a concise straightforward description of the mathematical definition of the DCT as well as different DCT algorithms at an abstract level. The human creativity required to check the correctness of the algorithm against the definition is limited to listing some trigonometric laws that have been used for optimizing the implementations (these can be viewed as the essential design ideas). On the other hand, effects as for instance arithmetic overflows are not captured at this abstract level.

The model checking approach is nearer to real implementations as fixed bit widths must be assumed and therefore problems such as arithmetic overflows or the limited precision are considered. However, the model checking approach suffers in general from a bad scalability, especially for data oriented systems as the DCT. Moreover, symbolic model checking based on BDDs [McM93] seems not to be well suited for the DCT verification since it is well known that BDDs [Bry86] lead to exponentially sized representations of the multiplication function. Multiplication is, however, heavily used in DCT algorithms. For the DCT, the problem can be overcome by abstraction techniques [Lon93] based on the Chinese Remainder Theorem. This however, requires advanced knowledge in model checking and therefore limits the degree of automation of this approach.

2 THE DISCRETE COSINE TRANSFORM

In this section, we briefly present the formal definition of the DCT to be able to explain afterwards what the verification problem is. For a more detailed presentation of the DCT and its application in the JPEG format see [PM93].

2.1 Formal Definition

One has to distinguish between the *one-dimensional* and the *two-dimensional* DCT. Given the input values $x_0, \ldots, x_7 \in \mathbb{R}$, the one-dimensional DCT is defined as the following linear function $\Phi : \mathbb{R}^8 \to \mathbb{R}^8$:

$$\begin{pmatrix} y_0 \\ \vdots \\ y_7 \end{pmatrix} := \underbrace{\begin{pmatrix} a_{0,0} & \cdots & a_{0,7} \\ \vdots & \cdots & \vdots \\ a_{7,0} & \cdots & a_{7,7} \end{pmatrix}}_{=:\mathfrak{A}} \begin{pmatrix} x_0 \\ \vdots \\ x_7 \end{pmatrix}$$

where $a_{i,j} := \frac{1}{2}\cos\left((2j+1)i\frac{\pi}{16}\right)$ for $i > 0$ and $a_{0,j} := \frac{1}{2\sqrt{2}}$. It is important that the matrix $\mathfrak{A}$ is orthonormal, which means that its inverse matrix exists and is obtained by transposition, i.e. the coefficients $b_{i,j}$ of the inverse $\mathfrak{A}^{-1}$ are simply defined as $b_{i,j} := a_{j,i}$. Hence, the *inverse DCT* can be implemented very similar to the DCT.

The *two-dimensional DCT* is a transformation of a 8×8 matrix X of real number to a 8×8 matrix Y of real number. Formally, it is defined with the above matrix $\mathfrak{A}$ as $Y := \mathfrak{A}X\mathfrak{A}^{-1}$. The two-dimensional DCT is separable, i.e. it can be implemented by means of one-dimensional DCTs. Using an intermediate matrix $(u_{j,k})$, this separation is done as follows $u_{j,k} := \sum_{l=0}^{7} x_{k,l}\, a_{j,l}$ and $y_{i,j} := \sum_{k=0}^{7} u_{j,k}\, a_{i,k}$. For this reason, the two-dimensional DCT can be implemented by 16 one-dimensional DCTs (eight for the rows and eight for the columns). Although this does not lead to optimal results (see page 53 in [PM93]), there are very good algorithms for the one-dimensional DCT that lead to almost optimal results for the two-dimensional case. Hence, we completely focus on the one-dimensional DCT in the following.

2.2 Optimizations

The formal definition of the one-dimensional DCT requires 64 multiplications and 56 additions, which would be too much for practical use. However, the DCT can be

Common to all versions:

$$L_{00} := x_0 + x_7 \quad L_{02} := x_2 + x_5 \quad L_{04} := x_3 - x_4 \quad L_{06} := x_1 - x_6$$
$$L_{01} := x_1 + x_6 \quad L_{03} := x_3 + x_4 \quad L_{05} := x_2 - x_5 \quad L_{07} := x_0 - x_7$$

Simple Version (SIMP_DCT): [PM93]

$$\begin{array}{ll}
L_{10} := L_{00} + L_{03} & 2y_0 := c_4(L_{10} + L_{11}) \\
L_{11} := L_{01} + L_{02} & 2y_1 := c_1L_{07} + c_3L_{06} + c_5L_{05} + c_7L_{04} \\
L_{12} := L_{00} - L_{03} & 2y_2 := c_2L_{12} + c_6L_{13} \\
L_{13} := L_{01} - L_{02} & 2y_3 := c_3L_{07} - c_7L_{06} - c_1L_{05} - c_5L_{04} \\
 & 2y_4 := c_4(L_{10} - L_{11}) \\
 & 2y_5 := c_5L_{07} - c_1L_{06} + c_7L_{05} + c_3L_{04} \\
 & 2y_6 := c_6L_{12} - c_2L_{13} \\
 & 2y_7 := c_7L_{07} - c_5L_{06} + c_3L_{05} - c_1L_{04}
\end{array}$$

Loeffler, Ligtenberg and Moschytz (LLM_DCT) [LLM89]:

$$\begin{array}{lll}
L_{10} := L_{00} + L_{03} & L_{20} := L_{10} + L_{11} & z_0 := L_{20} \\
L_{11} := L_{01} + L_{02} & L_{21} := L_{10} - L_{11} & z_1 := L_{24} + L_{27} \\
L_{12} := L_{01} - L_{02} & L_{22} := \mathfrak{Rot}_0(L_{12}, L_{13}, 6) & z_2 := \sqrt{2}\, L_{22} \\
L_{13} := L_{00} - L_{03} & L_{23} := \mathfrak{Rot}_1(L_{12}, L_{13}, 6) & z_3 := \sqrt{2}\, L_{25} \\
L_{14} := \mathfrak{Rot}_0(L_{04}, L_{07}, 3) & L_{24} := L_{14} + L_{16} & z_4 := L_{21} \\
L_{15} := \mathfrak{Rot}_0(L_{05}, L_{06}, 1) & L_{25} := L_{17} - L_{15} & z_5 := \sqrt{2}\, L_{26} \\
L_{16} := \mathfrak{Rot}_1(L_{05}, L_{06}, 1) & L_{26} := L_{14} - L_{16} & z_6 := \sqrt{2}\, L_{23} \\
L_{17} := \mathfrak{Rot}_1(L_{04}, L_{07}, 3) & L_{27} := L_{15} + L_{17} & z_7 := L_{27} - L_{24}
\end{array}$$

Arai, Agui and Nakajiama (AAN_DCT): [PM93]

$$\begin{array}{lll}
L_{10} := L_{00} + L_{03} & L_{20} := c_4(L_{12} + L_{13}) & u_0 := L_{10} + L_{11} \\
L_{11} := L_{01} + L_{02} & & u_1 := L_{31} + L_{24} \\
L_{12} := L_{01} - L_{02} & L_{22} := q_0L_{14} + L_{25} & u_2 := L_{20} + L_{13} \\
L_{13} := L_{00} - L_{03} & L_{23} := c_4L_{15} & u_3 := L_{33} - L_{22} \\
L_{14} := L_{04} + L_{05} & L_{24} := q_1L_{16} + L_{25} & u_4 := L_{10} - L_{11} \\
L_{15} := L_{05} + L_{06} & L_{25} := c_6(L_{14} - L_{16}) & u_5 := L_{33} + L_{22} \\
L_{16} := L_{06} + L_{07} & & u_6 := L_{13} - L_{20} \\
 & L_{31} := L_{07} + L_{23} & u_7 := L_{31} - L_{24} \\
q_0 := c_2 - c_6 & L_{33} := L_{07} - L_{23} & \\
q_1 := c_2 + c_6 & &
\end{array}$$

Figure 1 Optimized DCT algorithms

implemented more efficiently if occurrences of common subterms are exploited: Note first that all trigonometric values that occur in the matrix $\mathfrak{A}$ can be restricted to 8 basic values. To see this, we define the constants $c_k := \cos\left(k\frac{\pi}{16}\right)$ and $s_k := \sin\left(k\frac{\pi}{16}\right)$ for $k \in \mathbb{Z}$ (integer values). Clearly, the following relations hold:

$$\begin{array}{ll} (1)\ c_{-k} = c_k & (2)\ c_k = c_{k \bmod 32} \\ (3)\ c_k = c_{32-k} & (4)\ c_k = -c_{16-k} \end{array}$$

The above equations allow the reduction of the domain of k from $\mathbb{Z}$ to $\{k \mid k \geq 0\}$, $\{0, \ldots, 31\}$, $\{0, \ldots, 16\}$, and $\{0, \ldots, 8\}$, respectively. Moreover, the special cases $c_0 = 1$, $c_4 = \frac{1}{2}\sqrt{2}$, $c_8 = 0$ can be used for optimizations. Clearly, also s_k is only interesting in the interval $\{0, \ldots, 7\}$ and it can be reduced to c_k by the equation $s_k = c_{8-k}$. Considering all this, and computing common subterms only once, we obtain the implementation SIMP_DCT given in figure 1. This implementation requires only 22 multiplications and 28 additions.

Numerous efficient DCT implementations have been presented. The most efficient one, a true two-dimensional approach requires only 54 multiplications, 464 additions and 6 arithmetic shifts [FL90]. Some of the fast DCT algorithms go back to the discrete Fourier transform [CT65], others consider the DCT as a separate field [CSF77]. A survey is given in [DV90].

Figure 1 lists two efficient DCT algorithms, namely the version of Loeffler, Ligtenberg and Moschytz (LLM_DCT) [LLM89] and Arai, Agui and Nakajiama's version (AAN_DCT) [PM93]. The additional optimization obtained by these implementations is based on the following trigonometric addition theorems:

$$\begin{aligned} \cos(x) + \cos(y) &= 2\cos\left(\tfrac{x+y}{2}\right)\cos\left(\tfrac{x-y}{2}\right) \\ \cos(x) - \cos(y) &= 2\sin\left(\tfrac{x+y}{2}\right)\sin\left(\tfrac{x-y}{2}\right) \end{aligned}$$

Using these theorems, additional common subterms can be generated that can then be shared. The LLM_DCT makes additionally use of a rotation operation that is defined with an angle α as follows:

$$\begin{pmatrix} y_0 \\ y_1 \end{pmatrix} = \begin{pmatrix} \cos(\alpha) & \sin(\alpha) \\ -\sin(\alpha) & \cos(\alpha) \end{pmatrix} \begin{pmatrix} x_0 \\ x_1 \end{pmatrix}$$

As written above, the rotation operation would require four multiplications and two additions. Rotations are however computed with an intermediate value ℓ as given in figure 2. This requires three multiplications and three additions. Hence, we decrease the number of multiplications by increasing the number of additions which is reasonable as multiplications are in general more expensive. For figure 1, we define $\mathfrak{Rot}_0(x_0, x_1, \alpha) := x_0 c_\alpha + x_1 s_\alpha$ and $\mathfrak{Rot}_1(x_0, x_1, \alpha) := -x_0 s_\alpha + x_1 c_\alpha$, but we assume that the algorithm of figure 2 is used for the computation. Hence, LLM_DCT requires only 13 multiplications and 29 additions. AAN_DCT does even only require five multi-

$$\begin{aligned} &\ell := \cos(\alpha)(x_0 + x_1) \\ &y_0 := \ell + (\sin(\alpha) - \cos(\alpha))x_1 \\ &y_0 := -(\sin(\alpha) + \cos(\alpha))x_0 + \ell \end{aligned}$$

Figure 2: Rotations with 3 Multiplications

plications and 28 additions.

Both LLM_DCT and AAN_DCT produce scaled results (these are sufficient for a lot of applications as e.g. JPEG): For the variables defined in figure 1, the following equations hold: $z_i = 4c_4y_i = 2\sqrt{2}y_i$, $u_0 = 4c_4y_0 = 2\sqrt{2}y_0$ and $u_{i+1} = 4c_{i+1}y_{i+1}$.

3 VERIFYING DCT ALGORITHMS BY TERM REWRITING

Laws for $\mathbb{R}$
$x + 0 := x$
$x * 1 := x$
$x * 0 := 0$
$x * (y + z) := (x * y) + (x * z)$
$x + -(x) := 0$
$x * -(y) := -(x * y)$
$-(-(x)) := x$
$\sqrt{2} * \sqrt{2} * x := x + x$

Figure 3: Axioms for $\mathbb{R}$

In this section, we show how the correctness of the DCT algorithms of figure 1 is proved with the term rewriting system RRL [KZ88]. For this reason, we establish a canonical term rewrite system that handles real numbers $\mathbb{R}$ and the trigonometric functions. Therefore, some axioms on real numbers and the trigonometric functions have to be added to the definition of the DCTs. The laws for $\mathbb{R}$ are given in figure 3. Moreover, the operators $+$ and $*$ are specified to be associative and commutative. The above laws essentially specify that the real numbers are mathematically speaking a field. Note however, that we do neither need the ordering relation nor the supremum axiom of $\mathbb{R}$ and hence, have not characterized the real numbers completely.

Addition Laws
$\sqrt{2} * c_1 := c_3 + c_5$
$\sqrt{2} * c_3 := c_1 + c_7$
$\sqrt{2} * c_5 := c_1 - c_7$
$\sqrt{2} * c_7 := c_3 - c_5$

Figure 4: Addition Laws

For the verification of LLM_DCT, we also need some instances of the trigonometric addition laws. These are given in figure 4. Moreover, we need the relationship between $\sqrt{2}$ and the trigonometric functions: $c_4 := \frac{1}{2}\sqrt{2}$ and $c_4 * \sqrt{2} := 1$. Using all these equations, the relationship $z_i = 2\sqrt{2}\ y_i$ can be easily proved by means of RRL.

This is done as follows: We first enter all rewrite equations apart from the above addition theorems and establish a confluent rewrite system by means of the Knuth-Bendix completion procedure. After that, we add the above addition theorems and do not invoke a further completion (this does not work with our ordering). Instead the rewrite system is yet powerful enough to make the proofs with simple rewriting (using the boolean ring method).

For the verification of AAN_DCT, we need more instances of the trigonometric addition laws, which are given below. The verification runs then in the same lines as for LLM_DCT: We first enter all rewrite equations apart from the addition theorems and establish a confluent rewrite system by completion. After that, we add the addition theorems below and obtain the proofs with simple rewriting (using the boolean ring method). The proof of the relationship with SIMP_DCT, i.e. the equations $u_0 = 4c_4y_0 = 2\sqrt{2}y_0$ and $u_{i+1} = 4c_{i+1}y_{i+1}$ follows then automatically.

Addition Laws used for AAN_DCT		
$\sqrt{2} * c_6 := c_2 - c_6$	$\sqrt{2} * c_2 := c_2 + c_6$	$c_6 * c_2 := \frac{1}{2}c_4$
$c_1 * c_3 := \frac{1}{2}(c_2 + c_4)$	$c_1 * c_5 := \frac{1}{2}(c_6 + c_4)$	$c_1 * c_7 := \frac{1}{2}c_6$
$c_3 * c_7 := \frac{1}{2}(c_4 - c_6)$	$c_3 * c_5 := \frac{1}{2}c_2$	$c_5 * c_7 := \frac{1}{2}(c_2 - c_4)$
$c_2 * c_2 := \frac{1}{2}(1 + c_4)$	$c_6 * c_6 := \frac{1}{2}(1 - c_4)$	$c_1 * c_1 := \frac{1}{2}(1 + c_2)$
$c_3 * c_3 := \frac{1}{2}(1 + c_6)$	$c_5 * c_5 := \frac{1}{2}(1 - c_6)$	$c_7 * c_7 := \frac{1}{2}(1 - c_2)$

4 VERIFYING INTEGER DCT ALGORITHMS

The definition of the DCT is based on real numbers. However, all implementations, regardless whether they are done in hardware or software, do only work on floating point or fixpoint numbers, i.e. on approximations of the real numbers with a limited precision. For this reason, it might be the case that some of the above optimized DCT algorithms do compute slightly different outputs than others.

Often special fixpoint implementations are used for the DCT that are called integer DCTs: These are obtained by replacing the real valued cosine constants c_i by the integers $\tilde{c}_i := \lfloor 2^n c_i \rfloor$ when n bits are available. As the inputs x_i are also given as integers, only integer operations are then needed.

(1) $qc_1 = c_3 + c_5$
(2) $qc_3 = c_1 + c_7$
(3) $qc_5 = c_1 - c_7$
(4) $qc_7 = c_3 - c_5$

Figure 5: Equation System for LLM_DCT

The verification based on term rewriting presented in the last section did not fix the data domain. The obtained results hold for any data domain with operations $+, -$ and $\cdot$ that has constants $\frac{1}{2}, \sqrt{2}, 0, 1, c_1, c_2, c_3, c_4, c_5, c_6, c_7$ such that the presented equations hold. Hence, if the equations given in figure 5 hold for a specific data domain, then the equivalence between LLM_DCT and SIMP_DCT holds for this domain.

$c_1 = \sqrt{2}c_5 + c_7$	$c_1 = -\sqrt{2}c_5 + c_7$
$c_3 = c_5 + \sqrt{2}c_7$	$c_3 = c_5 - \sqrt{2}c_7$
$q = \sqrt{2}$	$q = -\sqrt{2}$

Figure 6: Solution of the Equations of figure 5

So, let us first consider the solutions of the equation system of figure 5. Apart from the trivial solution where all constants equal to zero, there are infinitely may solutions: c_5 and c_7 can be chosen arbitrarily and the other constants are then determined as given in figure 6. As in particular $q = \pm\sqrt{2}$ holds, there is no integer solution of the equation system. For this reason, the results given in the previous section that are based on term rewriting do not hold for the integer variant of LLM_DCT. The same holds for AAN_DCT.

5 VERIFYING INTEGER DCTS BY MODEL CHECKING

As the proof from the abstract level cannot be transferred to the bitvector level we tried to establish term rewrite systems for integer versions based on bitvector arithmetic. However, this approach turned out to become too complicated such that we dropped this approach.

Instead, we propose to use tautology checking based on BDDs for the verification at the integer level. Our first attempt to this was quite depressing: By a direct invocation of the SMV model checker, we could only handle implementations up to three bits. Even the word-level extension of SMV could not manage implementations with more than four bits.

To circumvent the complexity, we used a reduction technique that is based on the Chinese Remainder Theorem (CRT) that is given below. The CRT is the basis for residue arithmetic that is roughly explained as follows: Given relatively prime numbers $p_1, \ldots, p_n$, i.e. numbers with $\mathsf{GCD}(p_i, p_j) = 1$, each integer x in the interval $[0, \prod_{i=1}^{n} p_i[$ can be uniquely represented as the list of its residues, i.e. $(x \bmod p_1, \ldots, x \bmod p_n)$ (residue number representation). Arithmetic operations are then simply performed by applying the corresponding operation on the residues: Given that x and y have the residue number representations $(x_1, \ldots, x_n)$ and $(y_1, \ldots, y_n)$, then $x + y$, $x - y$, and xy, have the residue number representation $(x_1 + y_1, \ldots, x_n + y_n)$, $(x_1 - y_1, \ldots, x_n - y_n)$, and $(x_1 y_1, \ldots, x_n y_n)$, respectively.

Theorem 1 (Chinese Remainder Theorem) *Given integers $r_1, \ldots, r_n$, b and relatively prime integers $p_1, \ldots, p_n$ with $0 \leq r_i < p_i$ then, there is a unique integer x with $b \leq x < \prod_{i=1}^{n} p_i$ such that $x \bmod p_i = r_i$.*

The advantage of residue arithmetic is that it can be performed in parallel as the arithmetic operations on the single residues are independent of each other. This independence is also useful for the verification as it allows to split the entire problem into a couple of smaller ones: Instead of verifying the equivalence of two b bit implementations, we use some prime numbers $p_1, \ldots, p_n$ such that $2^b < \prod_{i=1}^{n} p_i$ and verify the equivalence of the two versions modulo p_i. As the latter implementation has only $\lfloor log_2(p_i) \rfloor + 1$ bits, it can be checked much faster.

For example, using the prime numbers 7, 11, 13, 17, 19, 23, 25, 27, 29, 31, 32, we can prove for LLM_DCT that $z_i = 4c_4 y_i$ holds for $i = 0, 2, 3, 4, 5, 7$. Also, we can show that $z_1 \neq 4c_4 y_1$ and $z_6 \neq 4c_4 y_6$ holds for some inputs which is due to the limited precision of the integer approximation[1].

The experimental results that we have obtained with the SMV system for proving $z_0 = 4c_4 y_0$ are given in figure 7 (Sun UltraSparc with 128MByte Memory). The runtime given in figure 7 is thereby the sum of the runtimes for checking the equivalence modulo all p_i's. For small bit widths we used however only the necessary prime numbers, e.g. for 8 bits, we only used the prime numbers 7, 11, 13, 17, 19, 23 as $2^{2 \cdot 8+3} = 524288 < 7 \cdot 11 \cdot 13 \cdot 17 \cdot 19 \cdot 23 = 7436429$ (note that the DCT with b bit wide inputs yields in $2^{2 \cdot b+3}$ wide outputs).

6 CONCLUSIONS

We have illustrated the use of term rewriting and model checking for the verification of real number algorithms like the DCT. Some errors in the presentation of algorithms in the literature [PM93] we found prove that the DCT as an embedded system is a non-trivial example that requires formal verification.

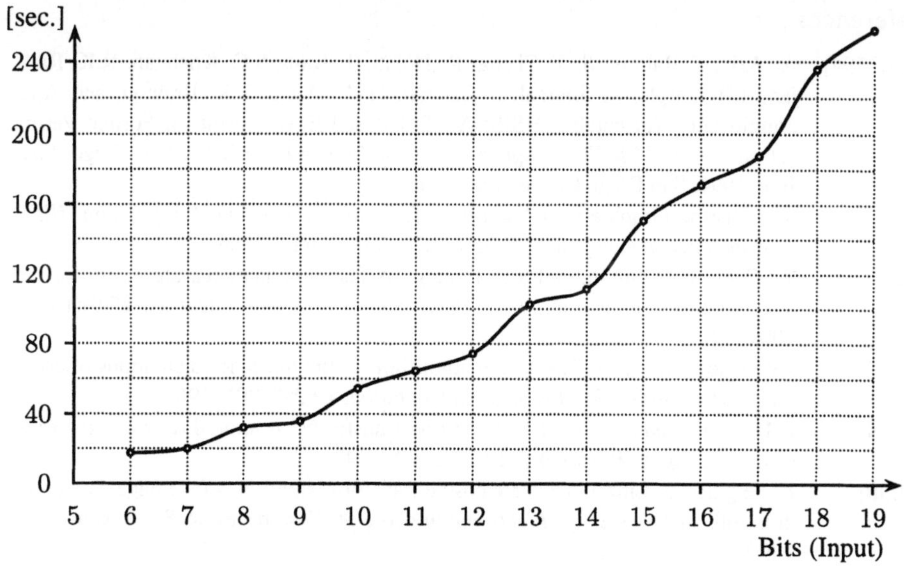

Figure 7 Experimental Results for Model Checking with CRT abstraction

Without doubt, model checking is currently the most popular verification technique for concurrent systems. However, the case study presented in this paper shows that term rewriting is more appropriate for the DCT since it provides a higher degree of abstraction that is often desired in early design phases.

Nevertheless, at the bitvector level where the limited preciseness of the implementation of the real numbers has to be taken into account, model checking seems to be more adequate. But already for small bit widths the systems are far too big to be checked by a direct attempt. To overcome these limits we applied the Chinese Remainder Technique as an appropriate abstraction technique to verify greater bit widths by model checking. The Chinese Remainder Technique is easily applicable by using predefined parameterized modules for residue arithmetic. However, none of the currently available model checkers offers such a feature. Thus, it would be desirable to extend these tools by such abstraction methods.

The Chinese Remainder Abstraction as applied here is only suited for proving or disproving equivalence of two implementations. In particular, it is not possible to verify that certain error bounds hold, since this would require to compare numbers in their residue number representation which is not possible. Our future work will therefore aim at extending the Chinese Remainder Abstraction by an efficient conversion back to the usual radix number representation.

Notes

1. Note that we can only prove that the equations $z_1 = 4c_4y_1$ and $z_6 = 4c_4y_6$ do not hold. It is not possible to prove error bounds $|z_1 - 4c_4y_1| \leq \varepsilon_1$ and $|z_6 - 4c_4y_6| \leq \varepsilon_6$ by the CRT abstraction since it is not possible to compare the size of numbers given in residue number representation.

References

[ABC+94] A. Aziz, F. Balarin, S.-T. Cheng, R. Hojati, T. Kam, S.C. Krishnan, R.K. Ranjan, T.R. Shiple, V. Singhal, S. Tasiran, H.-Y. Wang, R.K. Brayton, and A.L. Sangiovanni-Vincentelli. HSIS: A BDD-Based Environment for Formal Verification. In *ACM/IEEE Design Automation Conference (DAC)*, San Diego, CA, June 1994. San Diego Convention Center.

[Bry86] R.E. Bryant. Graph-Based Algorithms for Boolean Function Manipulation. *IEEE Transactions on Computers*, C-35(8):677–691, August 1986.

[CSF77] W. Chen, C.H. Smith, and S.C. Fralick. A fast computational algorithm for the discrete cosine transform. *IEEE Transactions on Communication*, 25(9):1004–1009, 1977.

[CT65] J.W. Cooley and J.W. Tukey. An algorithm for the machine calculations of complex Fourier series. *Mathemtical Computation*, 19:297–301, 1965.

[DV90] P. Duhamel and M. Vetterli. Fast fourier transforms: A tutorial review and a state of the art. *Signal Processing*, 19:259–299, 1990.

[FL90] E. Feig and E. Linzer. Discrete cosine transform algorithms for image data compression. In *Proceedings Electronic Imaging'90 East*, pages 84–87, Boston, MA, 1990.

[FSS+94] T. Filkorn, H. A. Schneider, A. Scholz, A. Strasser, and P. Warkentin. *SVE User's Guide*. Siemens AG, TR ZFE BT SE 1-SVE-1, Munich, 1994.

[GM93] M.J.C. Gordon and T.F. Melham. *Introduction to HOL: A Theorem Proving Environment for Higher Order Logic*. Cambridge University Press, 1993.

[Gup92] A. Gupta. Formal Hardware Verification Methods: A Survey. *Journal of Formal Methods in System Design*, 1:151–238, 1992.

[HP96] G. J. Holzmann and D. Peled. The state of SPIN. In Rajeev Alur and Thomas A. Henzinger, editors, *Conference on Computer Aided Verification (CAV)*, volume 1102 of *Lecture Notes in Computer Science*, pages 385–389, New Brunswick, NJ, USA, July/August 1996. Springer Verlag.

[KZ88] D. Kapur and H. Zhang. RRL: a rewrite rule laboratory. In Lusk and Overbeek, editors, *Conference on Automated Deduction (CADE)*, pages 768–769. Springer-Verlag, 1988.

[LLM89] C. Loeffler, A. Ligtenberg, and G. Moschytz. Practical fast 1-D DCT algorithms with 11 multiplications. In *International Conference on Acoustics, Speech, and Signal Processing 1989 (ICASSP '89)*, pages 988–99, 1989.

[Lon93] D.E. Long. *Model Checking, Abstraction, and Compositional Verification*. PhD thesis, Carnegie Mellon University, 1993.

[McM93] K.L. McMillan. *Symbolic Model Checking*. Kluwer Academic Publishers, Norwell Massachusetts, 1993.

[ORR+96] S. Owre, S. Rajan, J. M. Rushby, N. Shankar, and M. K. Srivas. PVS: Combining specification, proof checking, and model checking. In Rajeev Alur and Thomas A. Henzinger, editors, *Conference on Computer Aided Verification (CAV)*, volume 1102 of *Lecture Notes in Computer Science*, pages 411–414, New Brunswick, NJ, USA, July/August 1996. Springer Verlag.

[PM93] W.B. Pennebaker and J.L. Mitchell. *JPEG Still Image Data Compression Standard*. Van Nostrand Reinhold, ISBN 0-442-01272-1, 1993.

MICROSCOPIC MODELING OF SUPPORT SYSTEM FOR IN-VEHICLE EMBEDDED SYSTEMS

M. Courrier, F. Simonot-Lion, Y.-Q. Song

This paper deals with the modeling of systems supporting in-vehicle embedded applications. The modeling principle is based on the development of reusable component models with clearly defined interfaces. The design of a whole application model is obtained by using these components and the resulting global model can be simulated for the verification of temporal properties and for the optimization of an implementation.

1. Introduction

The improvement of the safety in a car, the minimization of pollution and the optimization of traffic management are important challenges for automotive industries. A solution of these problems lies in the design of Electronic Control Units, embedded in cars and assuming particular functions as door control, engine control, ... These different units are realized thanks to software applications distributed on computers connected to networks. Therefore the main objectives are, on the one hand, to find the best hardware architecture and the best distribution of functions (**optimization**), in terms of several criteria such as cost, memory size, ... and on the other hand to prove that the result is compliant with safety and real-time requirements (**validation**). The purpose of this paper is to present a method of modeling such applications in terms of queuing networks and of simulation of these models. Principles of modeling are based on the development of reusable component models.

The *optimization* and *validation* process depends on two complementary activities. The first one consists in designing the **Operational Architecture** ; the given data of the problem are a set of functions, their links and their behavior, and a set of hardware component ; the aim of this activity is to define a hardware architecture (computers, networks, ...) and a distribution of the functions. It is not easy to have a deterministic algorithm which calculate the best partitioning of the set of functions. In this paper we don't tackle this problem.

So, we consider that the data of the second activity is a given operational architecture and that the purposes of this second activity are firstly to verify that the operational architecture has the specified properties and, secondly, to determine if it is the best architecture by comparison with other ones. For economic reasons, this optimization and verification process is based on the exploitation of application models. Below (Figure 1) we illustrate this process. The models library contains the models of different hardware components ; this allows a modular approach for the modeling process.

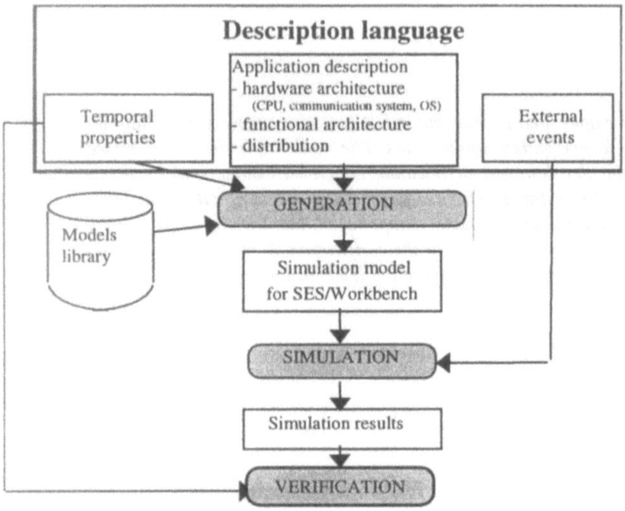

Figure 1 : Validation process

The application model to be simulated is structured in several abstract levels from the functional level (described disregarding the distribution and hardware performance problem) to the hardware level. More precisely, we can identify the following elements :

- **Functional architecture** : it represents the functions, their links and their behavior. In the context of in-vehicle applications, the specification of these functions are closed to programming concepts. That is why we use in this paper terms like "task" (function), "software architecture" (functional architecture) or "message" (data link). The functional architecture specifies the behavior of application in response to external stimuli.

- **Hardware architecture** : it is the model of the execution support of the previous architecture (computers with their operating systems connected on networks with their protocols). In the context of in-vehicle applications, computers are micro-controllers (hardware component) composed of a Central Processing Unit (CPU), a memory and some input/output devices.

- **Operating System** : it manages the computer resources for the tasks. It interfaces hardware and tasks. This concept will allow us to change a hardware component without changing the functional architecture.

- **Central Processing Unit** : it is the heart of a micro-controller. The execution delay of a function depends of it (set of instructions, architecture of the CPU, ...)
- **Communication system** : it supports the messages exchanges. Its Medium Access Protocol and its transmission rate influence the application performances.

Modeling activities of electronic units are usually done thank to the VHDL or VHSIC hardware language description. But this languages are not well-suited to model the functional architecture. Moreover in-vehicle applications are distributed on network such as CAN. Several models of this network are available. Some of them evaluate the performance by analysis of the model. For example [9], [10] and [13] obtain results in the worst case and under strong hypothesis ; [11] proposes an analysis algorithm of a model based on Timed Petri Nets. Finally, some models are based on queuing systems formalism and offer different levels of precision such as in [7], [8], [12]. Note that the same formalism is currently used for the modeling of operating systems and especially the scheduler which has an important impact on the application performances. So this bears out that the validation is processed thanks to the queuing systems formalism. Furthermore we have built a platform based on the SES Workbench [14] in order to assume both modeling and verification activities.

Note that the proposed methodology is suitable to any distributed applications subject to a precise functional architecture description. We have applied it to the in-vehicle embedded systems under some hypothesis : the Operating System is OSEK/VDX [3], [4] and the communication system is CAN [1].

The rest of the paper is organized as following. Section 2 gives the modeling methodology. Section 3 shows an example of the component, illustrates how to build the global model of the application and how to exploit it. Finally, section 4 brings the conclusions on this work.

2. Modeling principles

We present below how to build the interchangeable component models to be included in the models library appeared in Figure 1. These component models should be integrated into the global architecture model, the interface of each of them must be clearly defined. As it has been told above, one of the objectives of this work is to be able to simulate and compare the performance of the operational architecture when different micro-controllers are used, the models of this kind of components must therefore be detailed, this justifies comes the need of the microscopic models.

2.1. Component models

Considering the application processes using the OSEK/VDX operating system running over different micro-controllers [2], [5], [6] interconnected by a CAN network, the components to be modeled are software and hardware as shown by Figure 2. They are: Micro-controllers, CAN controllers, CAN bus, OSEK/VDX,

Application and Environment.

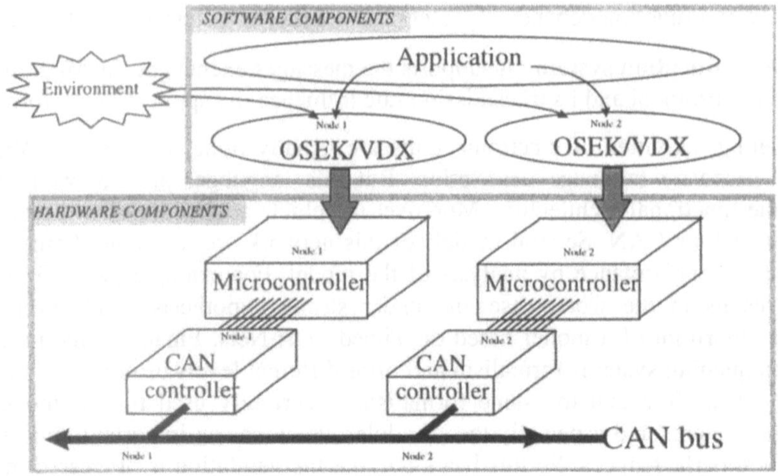

Figure 2 : Software and hardware

In order to provide modularity in the modeling process and interchangeability of hardware component models, we adopt following principles :

- The models of the different micro-controllers (respectively CAN controllers) must be independently developed and have a common interface
- The model of the CAN bus is unique as well as that of OSEK/VDX
- The functional architecture of the application as well as the environment can be considered as the inputs to the model of OSEK/VDX

For the hardware architecture, this leads to four models, each playing an accurate role. The model of the CAN bus represents the message transmission among stations following CAN protocol. The model of the CAN controller, which could be more or less detailed, represents the communication interface of each node. The model of a micro-controller represents the computing capacity of a node, from which the tasks execution times are determined. The model of OSEK/VDX describes the way the resources are handled : processor time sharing (scheduling), inter-tasks communication primitives (messages, event, ...), etc.

2.2. Interface of the component models

The definition of the interaction between the different models consists in on the one hand fixing with accuracy the nature of the exchanged information and on the other hand constructing the necessary interfaces.

Figure 3 clearly shows the need of two interfaces : <OSEK/VDX - micro-controller> and <OSEK/VDX - CAN controller>.

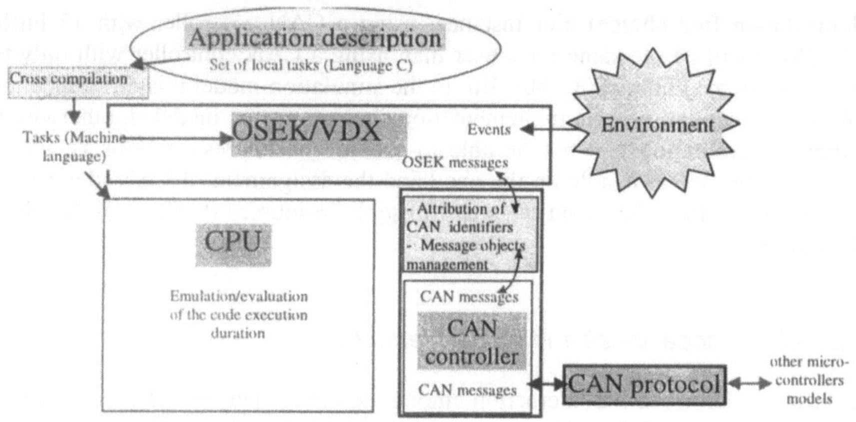

Figure 3 - Interaction definition among component models

2.1.1. Interface between tasks handled by OSEK/VDX and the micro-controller. Two following points should be modeled :

- allocation of the processor to tasks, this relates to the scheduling of OSEK/VDX
- model of the task in terms of instruction executions when the processor is assigned to a task

Two ways can be used to represent the computing load generated by a task. The first consists in estimating the task processing time (the upper bound), the model is thus coarse-grained.

To get a better simulation accuracy, the second way we proposed uses the model of the microscopic micro-controllers model with which we convert a load, represented by a sequence of instructions, to the corresponding exact execution time. The model is thus fine-grained. The problem arisen here is how to describe these sequences. In fact, at the functional architecture level, the nature of the hardware support is masked.

Nevertheless, the model of the micro-controller needs for its input an instruction sequence described in its specific language (machine code) in order to get a good accuracy on the simulation results. We should thus utilize a converter to translate an instruction sequence described in the generic description language at the functional architecture level to its equivalent description in the specific language of the target micro-controller. As we can see in Figure 3, the generic language is the C language while the converter is a cross compiler.

2.2.2. Interface between tasks managed by OSEK/VDX and the CAN controller. The role of the CAN controller is to handle message transmission and message reception according to CAN protocol. OSEK/VDX operating system makes transparency the communication support to users. It allows a task to send messages towards the mailboxes which are addressed using OSEK/VDX identifiers hiding thus the underlying communication controller. Nevertheless for this message exchange mechanism, there is neither priority concept nor reference for mapping a mailbox to one or several buffers of the underlying communication controller (this is left for implementation free choice). For instance, using a CAN controller with 15 buffers (Intel 82527) will be the same for a user than using a CAN controller with only two buffers in tandem (Philips 80C200). But in the simulation model this difference must be taken into account, i.e., the implementation choice must be modeled, otherwise the performance evaluation will not be able to provide useful results. This is why we propose an interface to handle on the one hand the assignment of CAN identifiers to messages and on the other hand the way to use the resources (buffers) of the chosen CAN controller.

2.3. Levels of model detail and model hierarchy

Until now we described the interaction among the component models by considering each of them as a black box. Here we will be interested in the way for modeling the contains of these black boxes. For this we have to choose a good compromise between the level of the model detail and its usability. It is true that a detailed model can gives accurate results but considering the size and the complexity of our whole system, we can not take into account all parameters. Fortunately, in practice not all parameters have the same influence on the system performance. One of the important step for the success of a simulation is then to identify the important parts which will be the object of a detailed modeling.

The use of hierarchical tools like SIM language [14] allows us to model a component with different detail levels, i.e., from a general view to more and more detailed levels. In fact, we can define the different desired detail levels for different units within a component model as well as for different component models according to their importance. Figure 4 shows the four function blocks of the CPU that should be detailed.

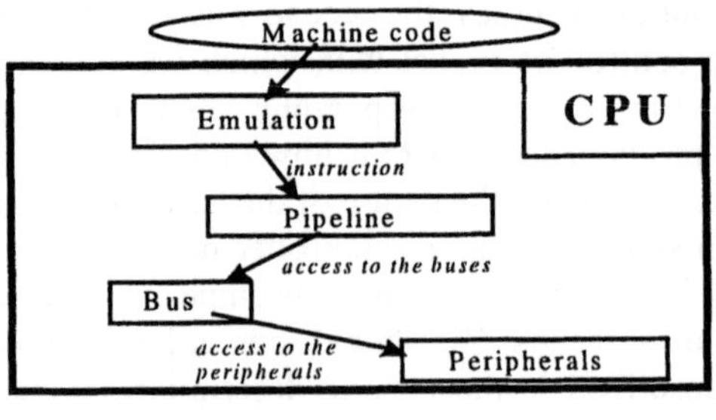

Figure 4 Function blocks of the CPU model

The input to this model is provided by the application processes in terms of a machine code sequence representing the required processing. The code execution is emulated in the first block. This code enters then into the model of the pipeline which allows to evaluate the execution time of the code. This time also depends on the access time to the peripheries, the ROM and the RAM. We model thus these peripherals as well as the busses linking these peripherals to the pipeline. We note that each of the above defined function blocks could be the object of a more or less detailed modeling according to its importance and complexity.

3. Example of component models and model exploitation

We developed different component models representing some hardware components of our in-vehicle applications : OSEK/VDX, CAN bus, CAN controllers and CPUs (Siemens C167 with Intel82527 [5, 6] and Motorola MPC555 with TOUCAN [2]). These models are developed under an industrial contract with PSA Peugeot-Citroën automobile company. Because of the confidentiality, in this section we only describe the component model of OSEK/VDX. An example is also given to illustrate how to exploit the global model by using the proposed framework.

3.1. OSEK/VDX component model

An operating system provides for an application program a framework within which this program runs. The main features of OSEK/VDX are to handle the processor sharing, to provide the communication mechanisms, to synchronize the tasks and to share other resources. The two principal elements are : task scheduler to correctly share the processor and primitives to handle tasks, alarms, messages and events. An application program is described at two levels :

- at the scheduling level, we describe a task by giving all information necessary for its scheduling : task type (basic task or extended one), with or without preemption, priority. Figure 5 shows the model of OSEK/VDX scheduler. Four task states are identified and the transitions between states are specified.
- at the task description level, we describe in the task code the primitive calls such as event waiting, task activation, message sending, ... The model takes into account the execution time of these primitives.

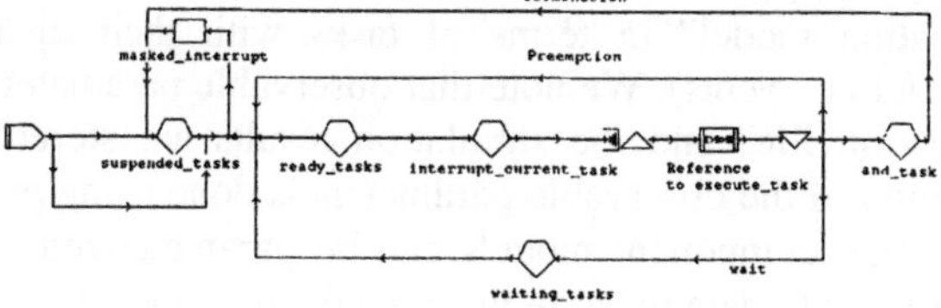

Figure 5 Model of OSEK/VDX scheduler

The execution duration of a primitive depends on the implementation of OSEK/VDX. For each version of OSEK/VDX and for each supporting micro-controller, it is necessary to evaluate the primitive execution time. In some case this time can also be provided by the implementator.

The performance parameters are mainly the response time for a task running request, utilization of the processor, overheads because of the preemption, number of ready tasks, ... We point out that an interrupt is considered as an external event and its corresponding ISR (Interrupt Sub Routine) as a task.

3.2. Model exploitation

The component models described above are included in a library. Figure 6 shows how to build and utilize a model of an operational architecture.

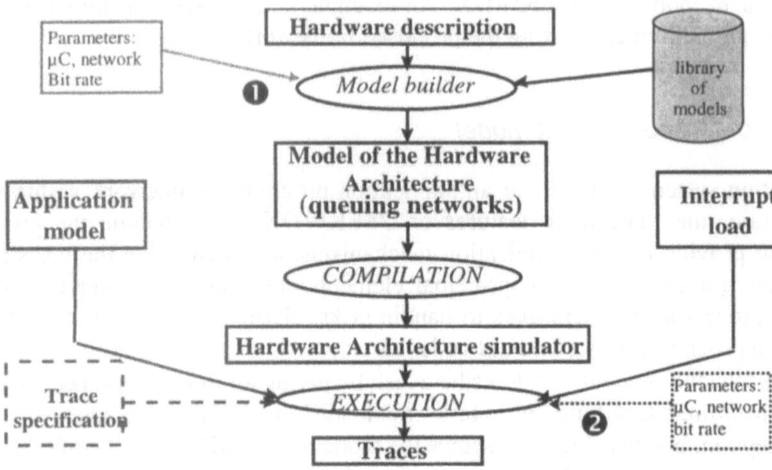

Figure 6 Procedure to build and to use the global model

The first step consists in withdrawing the component models from the "model library" to construct a global hardware architecture model according to the "hardware description file" and "parameters file". The second consists in compiling the model to generate an "executable simulator". And the third consists in the simulation using as inputs the "application model" in terms of tasks with their distribution and the "interrupt load" (external events). We note that observable parameters are specified in the "trace specification file" and the simulation results are stored in "trace files". Actually the definition of the observable parameters is done using probes provided by SES/Workbench. Some component models can be parameterized. In this figure we show two different ways to parameterize the component models :

1. during the building of the global model. In this case the values of these parameters are fixed.

2. before the running of the global model. In fact, SES/Workbench allows a simulator to read a configuration file before each simulation. This second way is more flexible but requires one more configuration file.

Figure 7 shows an example of a global hardware architecture model composed of two nodes using OSEK/VDX as their OS. The executable simulator is generated using the tools furnished by SES/Workbench. In this figure, the role of « initialization » is to read the file describing the functional architecture and the task distribution as well as the interrupts generated by the environment. In this example file, 6 periodic tasks

T_i(*P_i : period, C_i : execution time)* with the same priority are distributed on 2 nodes. Node 1 receives one interrupt every 5000 time units and executes an ISR of duration 500. Node 2 receives two interrupts with ISR of duration = 100 and of period = 5000.

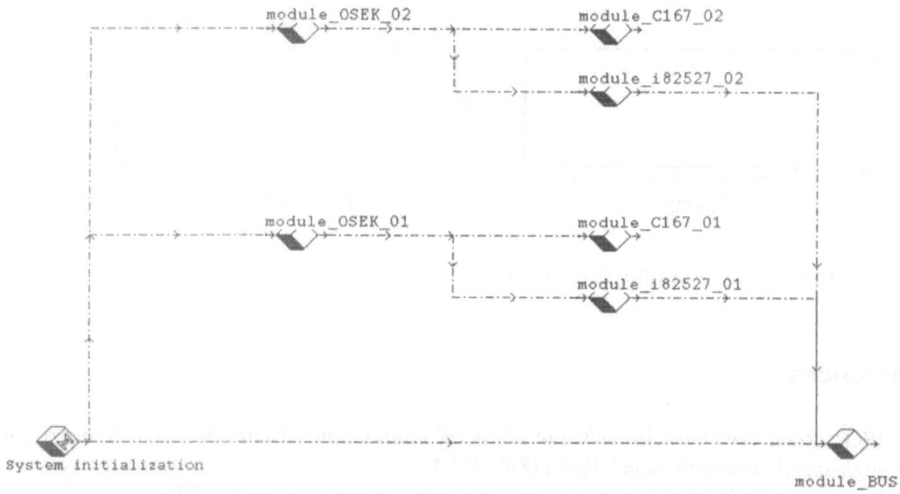

Figure 7 Example of a global hardware architecture model

The table below shows the task set distributed on N1 and N2 according to two configurations :

T_i	P_i	C_i	Configuration 1	Configuration2
1	22000	10000	N1	N1
2	22000	8000	N1	N1
3	*10000*	*300*	*N1*	*N2*
4	10000	300	N2	N2
5	10000	400	N2	N2
6	15000	200	N2	N2

Figure 8 shows one of the simulation results we can obtain. It consists of the inter-activation intervals of the task T3 for the two different configurations. One can see that Configuration 1 can not meet the time constraint on the period of the task T3 while Configuration 2 can meet it.

Conclusion

This paper dealt with the modeling of systems supporting in-vehicle embedded applications. The modeling principle based on the development of reusable component models with clearly defined interfaces is explained and the models of CAN controllers, micro-controllers, OSEK/VDX are developed. An example is provided showing that the design of a whole application model can be obtained by using these components and the resulting global model can be simulated for the verification of temporal properties and for the optimization of an implementation.

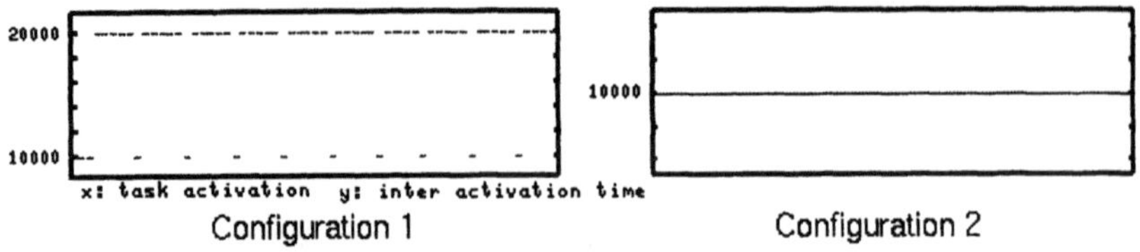

Figure 8 Inter-activation intervals of Task T_3

References

[1] ISO, "*Road vehicles – Interchange of digital information – Controller Area Network for high-speed communication*", ISO 11898, 1994

[2] Motorola, "*RCPU RISC central processing unit, Reference manual*", 1996

[3] OSEK/VDX, "*Communication*", Version 2.1 revision 117, June 1998

[4] OSEK/VDX, "*Operating System*", Version 2.0 revision 115, October 1997

[5] Siemens, "*C167xx,16-Bit CMOS Single-Chip Micro-controllers*", User's manual, 1996

[6] Siemens, "*C16x Family instruction set*", 1996

[7] Simonot-Lion F., Y.Q.Song, J.Raymond, "*Validating real-time applications distributed over CAN : an interoperability verification*", 4th international CAN conference, ICC'97, Berlin (Germany), October 1997

[8] Song Y.Q., F. Simonot-Lion, P. Belissent, "*VACANS - A tool for the validation of CAN-based applications*", Proceedings of IEEE WFCS'97, Barcelona (Spain) October 1998.

[9] Tindell K., A.Burns, "*Guaranteeing messages latencies on control area network (CAN)*", 1st international CAN conference, Maintz (Germany), September 1994

[10] Tindell K., H.Hanson, "*Babbling idiots, the dual-priority protocol and smart CAN controller*", 2nd international CAN conference, September 1995

[11] Toussaint J., C. Philippe, F. Simonot-Lion, "*A model of Can-Based Applications for the Verification of Temporal Properties*", SICICA'97, 3rd IFAC Symposium on Intelligent Components and Instruments for Control Applications, Annecy (France), June 1997.

[12] Upender B.P., A.G.Dean, "*Variability of CAN network performance*" 3rd international CAN conference, pp9.2-9.9, Paris (France), October 1996

[13] Wang Z., H.Lu, G.Hedrick, M.Stone, "*Message delay analysis for CAN based network*", Proceedings of 1992 ACM SIGAPP symposium on applied computing, Kansas city, MO (USA), March 1992

[14] SES, "*Quick start and upgrade guide; creating models; simulating models; technical reference; SIM language reference; using the query language; modeling reference; Cosim reference*", SES/Workbench, 1997

EXTENDED SDL-BASED TOOLS FOR RAPID PROTOTYPING OF APPLICATION SPECIFIC SIGNAL PROCESSORS

Philippe LEBLANC
Jean-Luc ROUX

1. Introduction

This paper presents the use of SDL supported by tools to design, simulate, validate and implement the event-driven command/control part of a typical distributed signal processing software application. SDL, for Specification and Description Language (ITU-Z100, 1996), is a design notation that uses blocks to describe the system structure, those blocks exchange messages through communication channels, and the dynamic behavior in the leaf blocks is described by means of extended finite state machines.

The main objective of the work was to enhance the design of embedded electronic systems, by putting the focus on system level design tools. Thus new capabilities for early prototyping and advanced validation have been developed. Also tool support has been extended along the design cycle in order to automate the design process down to code generation.

The paper is organized as follows: section 2 introduces the SDL notation and associated tool support; this section concludes on the limitations identified in SDL when dealing with HW-SW co-design of embedded systems (Embedsys, 1996) and presents the extensions that have been introduced for this purpose; section 3 describes the context in which the use of SDL has been explored for application-specific signal processors; then the extensions required for a proper application of SDL in this domain are detailed in sections 4 to 6, i.e. introduction of Statecharts in SDL via hierarchical states, distributed simulation and co-execution, non-regression testing of SDL design.

This work has been initiated two years ago within the DARPA-RASSP program (RASSP, 1995), and is being completed within the current ESPRIT-COMITY project (COMITY, 1997).

2. The SDL technology

2.1. SDL, a graphical formalism for real-time system modeling

SDL is a specification and design language (ITU-Z100, 1996) which has been standardized by the ITU (International Telecommunications Union). SDL is based on communicating finite state machines. The latter, called processes in SDL, are extended by data and communicate together by exchanging asynchronous messages, called signals. These signals are stored in FIFO queues, there is one common queue for each process. A complete set of graphical and formal symbols allows the designer to describe all the dynamics of a process. Main constructs available are: sending and receiving of signals, value assignment, timer manipulation, creation and deletion of process instances, function calls.

All these features make SDL well-suited for the design of event-driven, multi-tasking and distributed systems. SDL is largely used for the development of software-intensive applications, for example in Telecom systems. SDL-based tools allow the validation of a system design, and the automatic transformation of SDL descriptions into executable code.

SDL is often used jointly with MSC, Message Sequence Chart (ITU-Z120, 1996), which is also an ITU recommendation. Basically MSC diagrams correspond to chronologies of horizontal arrows, representing exchanged events, drawn on vertical bars, representing system's components. Figure 1 below depicts SDL and the associated MSC formalism. These graphical notations allows for intuitive modeling of systems. Moreover their underlying semantics guarantee the "one diagram, one meaning" postulate, and allow to check the consistency between MSC and SDL diagrams.

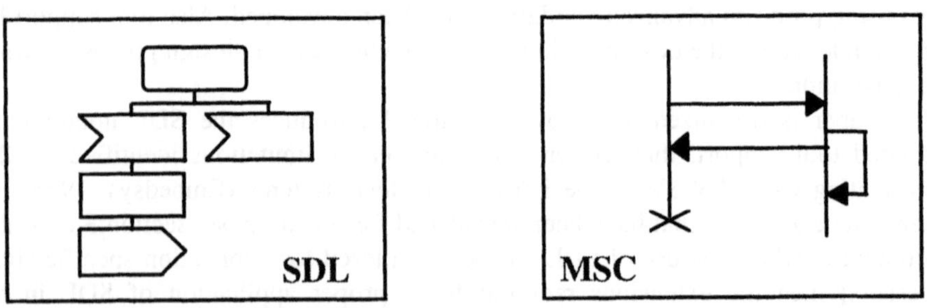

Figure 1. SDL and MSC modeling techniques

2.2. SDL-based tools

SDL has been experimented in RASSP through the application of the *Object*GEODE toolset to a signal processing application. *Object*GEODE (VERILOG, 1997) is an environment that supports the SDL language (Figure 2): it provides a graphical interface to specify in SDL, as well as with associated languages MSC and UML (OMG-UML, 1997), efficient simulation tools, and full C autocoding capability that targets usual real-time operating systems.

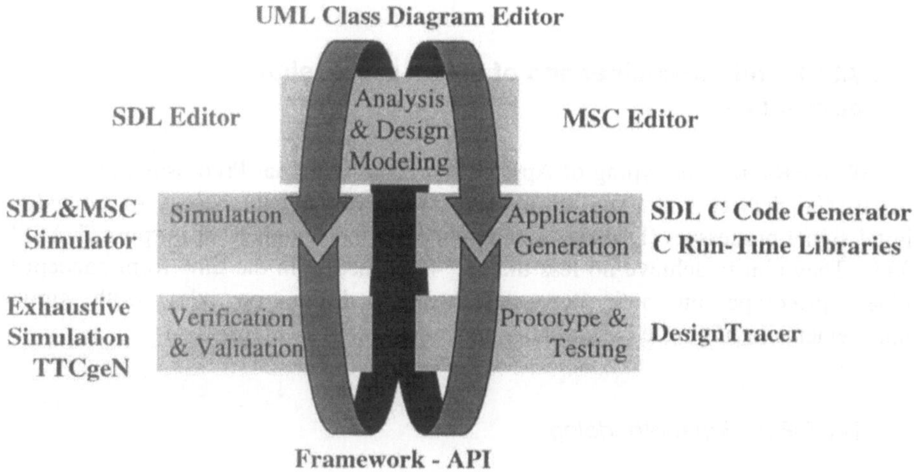

Figure 2. *Object*GEODE toolset

Therefore, the designer with *Object*GEODE can model its system, perform a formal verification by simulation (three modes are available: interactive, random and exhaustive), and generate automatically the code for producing the executable software application.

2.3. Limitations and extensions to SDL for HW-SW co-design

However the SDL notation and tools have two major limitations when dealing with HW-SW co-design and co-simulation:

- Describing the behavior of HW-SW system by means of nested states which represent the system's working modes is natural. Unfortunately SDL does not support a hierarchy of states, and actions cannot be associated to the entry or the exit of a state.
- The command program (SW part) and the signal processor (HW part) must be tested independently. Unfortunately *Object*GEODE simulation is monolithic: the complete model is simulated as a whole and parts cannot be tested separately.

In order to solve these issues, extensions have been specified and developed. The project has started in mid-1997, in the context of a sub-contracting to Lockheed

Martin Advanced Technology Labs (LM-ATL, 1997), to realize a project in the framework of RASSP.

In addition, another extension has been developed to automate non-regression testing: SDL operators are used to model the call to functions driving the signal processor; thus the SDL simulation has been extended to include these functions calls in the generated MSCs, and a semantic comparator has been developed to detect discrepancies in the chronologies of functions calls (including input parameters).

3. RASSP and the engineering of signal processing applications

RASSP, for Rapid Prototyping of Application Specific Signal Processors, is "a major DARPA/Tri-Service initiative to reinvent the development process of embedded digital signal processors (DSPs)", as announced in the statement of purpose (RASSP, 1995). They aim to achieve no less than a "4x reduction in the time from concept to fielded prototype on both new designs and design upgrades, with similar improvements in life cycle cost, quality and supportability".

3.1. RASSP design methodology

A general overview of RASSP methodology for the design of embedded DSPs is represented in Figure 3 below. The system is formally specified and the resulting model can be executed via simulation. New methods for partitioning that enable reuse of existing designs and evaluation of each HW/SW solution are applied. Finally, physical prototypes are automatically generated for both HW and SW parts.

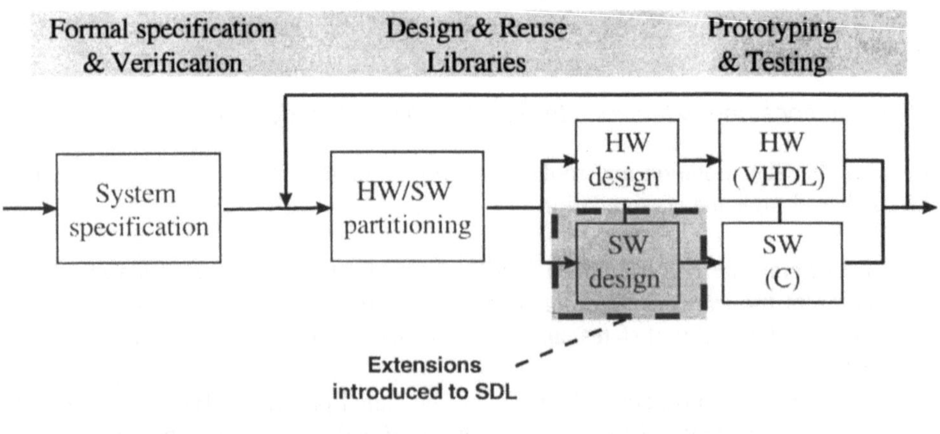

Figure 3. RASSP design methodology

3.2. Autocoding project with Lockheed-Martin ATL

In the RASSP context, Lockheed-Martin Advanced Technology Laboratory has subcontracted Verilog to develop a solution for autocoding from SDL using the *Object*GEODE toolset (LM-ATL, 1997).

A typical large scale architecture consists of a signal processing system which communicates with a command/control system. The signal processing system performs the high-bandwidth encoding/decoding and executes on DSPs. The signal processing system is modeled using a dataflow graph (DFG), and the command program (CP) is represented by a finite state machine. The command program is strongly related to the signal processing system, but it is often designed as part of the command/control system.

The command program (Figure 4) can be seen as an interface between the signal processing system and the rest of the command/control system. It translates system-derived or user inputs into commands accepted by the signal processing system and forwards the results produced.

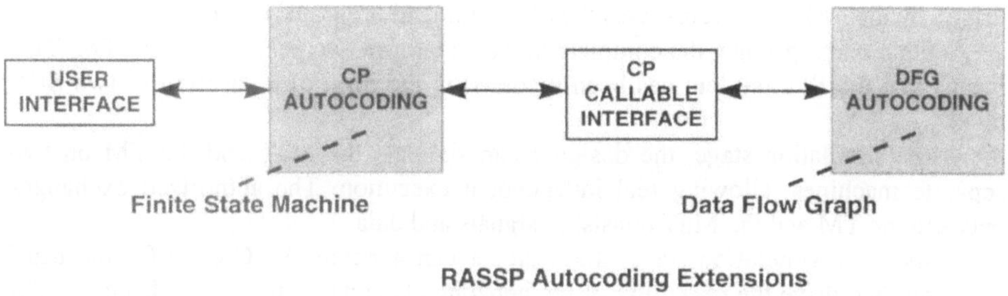

Figure 4. Command Program (CP) autocoding

4. Hierarchical states

SDL users have often expressed the need to describe hierarchical state machines. This is for example the case in the autocoding project (Figure 4), where hierarchical states are used to model the system operational modes monitored by the command program. In addition when handling hierarchical states, we need entering/leaving mechanisms; this can be achieved by entry/exit actions that are used in the autocoding project, to reprogram the signal processor when switching the modes.

Thus based on Harel's Statechart notation (Harel, 1996), we have introduced nested states and entry/exit actions in the SDL language.

Compared to the standardized SDL, the solution has consisted in introducing the concept of macro-state: a macro-state corresponds to an SDL Transition diagram, i.e. a diagram made of transitions starting from sub-states, the latter can themselves be macro-states.

Entry and exit actions have also been introduced in a similar way: two partial transitions, one starting from a label named "Entry", another one starting from a label named "Exit", can be added to a Transition diagram associated to a macro-state. The resulting behavior is that all the transitions starting from this macro-state are enriched at the beginning by the "Exit" transition, and all the transitions ending to this macro-state are enriched at the end by the "Entry" transition.

When building the model, the designer can use macro-states and entry and exit actions in accordance with the rules given above. In order to simulate the model or to produce the executable code from this model, it is necessary to start a utility flattening the nested transitions and introducing the entry and exit actions, in such a way that the resulting model conforms to the SDL notation (ITU-Z100, 1996).

5. Distributed simulation and co-execution

The designer may want to execute the HW and SW parts separately. For this purpose, *Object*GEODE toolset has been enhanced by introducing the concepts of MuT (Model under Test) and TM (Test Model): the MuT represents the signal processor, it is driven by the TM which represents the SW command program (Figure 5).

At the modeling stage, the complete model is built in two parts: MuT and TM. This means that the SDL system has been modeled in the form of a partition of two SDL blocks.

At the simulation stage, the designer can simulate the MuT and the TM on two separate machines, allowing real independent execution. The authorized exchanges between the TM and the MuT consist in signals and data.

At the code generation stage, the designer can generate the C code for the MuT only and then drive the execution of the generated C code on the target, from the TM side which still runs in simulation mode, i.e. the simulated TM plays the role of a User Interface for the MuT.

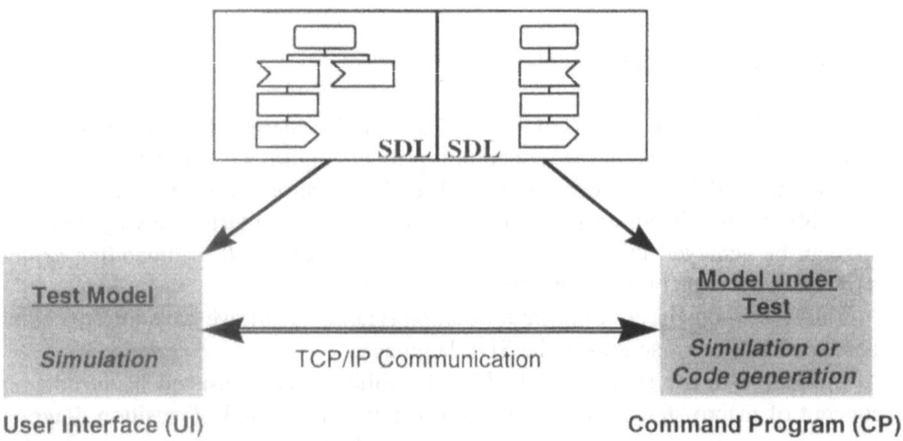

Figure 5. Co-simulation / Co-execution SDL-SDL

6. Non-regression testing

In order to automate non-regression testing, the *Object*GEODE simulator has been enhanced with a semantic comparator of MSCs. The main objective was to perform incremental testing while system design is evolving. During simulation, MSCs are produced reflecting the exchanges observed between the different components of the system (Figure 6).

First of all, the production of MSCs has been enriched by taking into account the calls of functions (in SDL, this corresponds to the call of Abstract Data Types operators). Input parameter values are also taken into account. From the HW-SW co-modeling point of view, the functions represent the lower level signal processor control commands such as *create queue*, *write variable* etc..

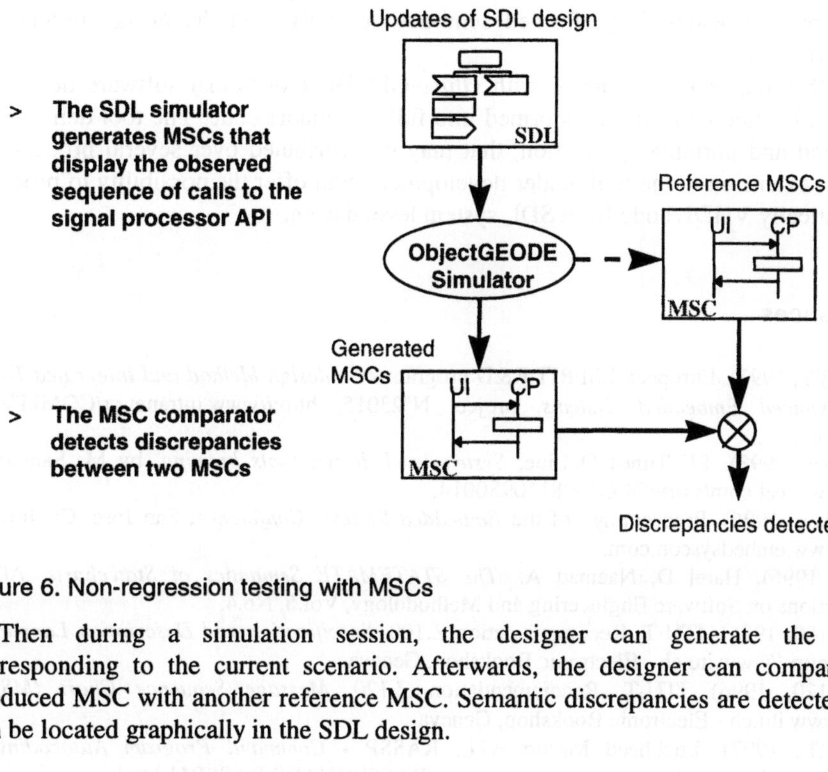

Figure 6. Non-regression testing with MSCs

Then during a simulation session, the designer can generate the MSC corresponding to the current scenario. Afterwards, the designer can compare the produced MSC with another reference MSC. Semantic discrepancies are detected and can be located graphically in the SDL design.

7. Current tool achievements & further work

The previous three extensions have been developed in the context of RASSP. They are now being completed in the COMITY project whose objective is to develop a set of techniques and tools for the design and prototyping of embedded systems, with application to telecommunication, automotive and aerospace domains.

The extension to support hierarchical states is already available in the latest commercial release of *Object*GEODE, as well as an MSC comparator but limited to a syntactical comparison only.

At last, we are currently implementing a new coupling between the *Object*GEODE toolset and a VHDL generator through a partitioning module for HW-SW co-design (EETimes, 1998).

8. Conclusion

The extensions that have been developed in this project, bring highly valuable benefits to the SDL designer in the field of embedded systems. Thus HW-SW system design can be simulated and verified earlier; the designer realizes an abstract modeling and simulation takes place at system level. Behavioral design errors are detected faster, non-regression testing is performed semi-automatically, and the design process is always repeatable.

Another important advantage with *Object*GEODE tool is that software design in SDL can be automatically transformed into full executable code. The tool delivers an optimized and portable application, that may be distributed over several processors. The last extension to the tool, under development, will offer the possibility to produce automatically VHDL code from SDL system level design.

References

(COMITY, 1997). European ESPRIT R&D program - *Co-design Method and Integrated Tools for Advanced Embedded Systems*, project N°23015, http://www.intranet.gr/COMITY - index.html.

(EETimes, 1998). EE Times OnLine, *System-level design tools brewing*, by M. Santarini, http://www.eet.com/story/OEG19981109S0014.

(Embedsys, 1996). Proceedings of the *Embedded Systems Conference*, San Jose, California, http://www.embedsyscon.com.

(Harel, 1996). Harel D, Naamad A., *The STATEMATE Semantics of Statecharts*, ACM Transactions on Software Engineering and Methodology, Vol.5, No.4.

(ITU-Z100, 1996). ITU-T, Recommendation Z.100, *Specification and Description Language (SDL)*, http://www.itu.ch - Electronic Bookshop, Geneva.

(ITU-Z120, 1996). ITU-T, Recommendation Z.120, *Message Sequence Chart (MSC)*, http://www.itu.ch - Electronic Bookshop, Geneva.

(LM-ATL, 1997). Lockheed Martin ATL, RASSP - *Command Program Autocoding* - http://www.atl.external.lmco.com/projects/rassp/RASSPQUADS/RASSP41.html.

(OMG-UML, 1997). Object Management Group (OMG), *UML 1.1 Documentation Set*, ftp.omg.org/pub/docs/ad.

(RASSP, 1995). USA DoD DARPA - *The Rapid prototyping of Application-Specific Signal Processors*, RASSP program, http://rassp.aticorp.org - index.html.

(VERILOG, 1997). VERILOG Products, *ObjectGEODE 3.2 Documentation Set*, http://www.verilogusa.com.

BLOCK DIAGRAM BASED REAL-TIME SIMULATION ON A NETWORK OF ALPHA PROCESSORS AND C40 DSPS

U. Kiffmeier and M. Beine

This contribution describes the inner mechanisms of the so called Real-Time Interface to Simulink for Multiprocessor systems *(RTI-MP). RTI-MP is applied in the area of Rapid Controller Prototyping and Hardware-in-the-Loop simulations, where high-end computing power is required that can not be realized on a single CPU. Typical users are control engineers who are not too familiar with the details of multiprocessor hardware, distributed real-time kernels, and parallel programming. Therefore RTI-MP is based on an intuitive graphical representation of the multiprocessor system in form of a Simulink block diagram, which is well known to control engineers. The simulation model is implemented fully automatical on a network of DEC Alpha processors and Texas Instruments C40 DSPs.*

2. Simulink block diagrams for multiprocessor systems

Ideally, from the user's viewpoint a block diagram for a multiprocessor system should look as much as possible like a block diagram for a single processor. Of course, the implementation on a hardware with distributed computing nodes requires some additional information to be entered graphically in the block diagram:

- the number and type of computing nodes,
- the assignment of different parts of the block diagram to computing nodes, and
- the signals to be communicated between CPUs and the corresponding transfer protocol.

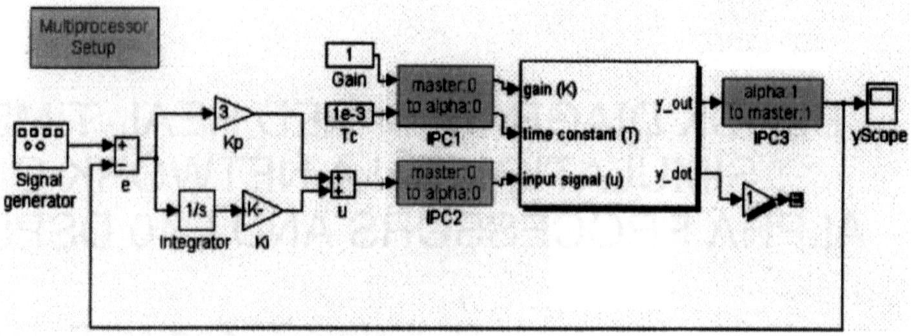

Figure 1. Typical RTI-MP block diagram.

RTI-MP provides the so called *Interprocessor Communication* (IPC) blocks to define this information in a Simulink block diagram. A simple example of a PI controller and a plant model computed on two CPUs is shown in figure 1. The IPC blocks mark the boundaries between CPUs. For example, the block IPC2 transfers the signal `u` from CPU `master` to CPU `alpha` via communication channel `0`. The CPU identity of all other Simulink blocks is determined automatically by RTI-MP from the connected IPC blocks.

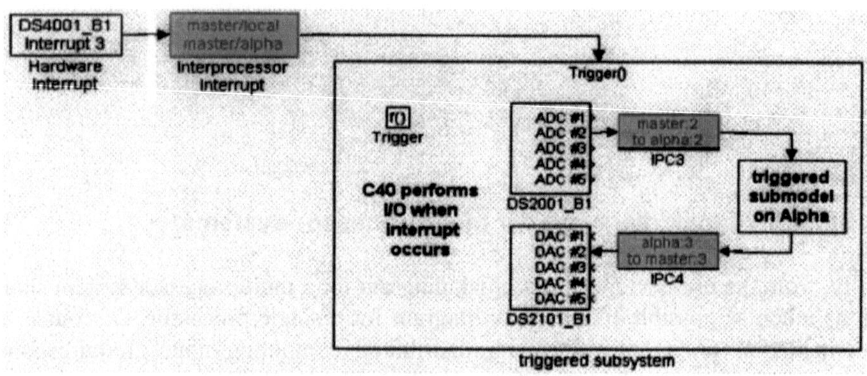

Figure 2. Definition of an interrupt triggered subsystem, which is executed on two CPUs.

Figure 2 shows a triggered subsystem, which is executed each time a trigger event occurs. The trigger event can be an external interrupt from peripheral hardware, or a software interrupt, which is raised when a signal in the block diagram crosses the trigger level. In a distributed system the interrupt source can be located on another computing node than the task to be triggered. It is also possible, that the interrupt task is split over two or more CPUs. For example, the end-of-conversion interrupt from an A/D converter may trigger a task, where the A/D input is read on CPU A and transferred to CPU B, which computes a control algorithm and sends the result back to CPU A for D/A output. RTI-MP supports this with *Interprocessor Interrupt* (IPI) blocks, which define the source and destination CPUs of interrupts. A single interrupt can be sent to multiple destination CPUs, if necessary.

Note, that RTI-MP does not perform an automatic distribution of a Simulink model over a network of processors. It is the user's task to assign submodels to certain CPUs of the hardware system. Experience shows, that the manual partitioning is not too critical in many cases, because

- the assignment of submodels to CPUs often follows directly from physical considerations. For example, in a vehicle dynamics model the front axle is simulated on one CPU and the rear axle on another.
- some submodels require certain I/O resources, which are only available on a specific CPU.

Nevertheless, RTI-MP provides some mechanisms to balance the load in a multiprocessor system, e.g. by allowing to assign individual integration algorithms and step sizes to each CPU (see figure 3). The execution times of all tasks can be monitored in each simulation step. An overload check detects if a task can not be finished before it is triggered the next time.

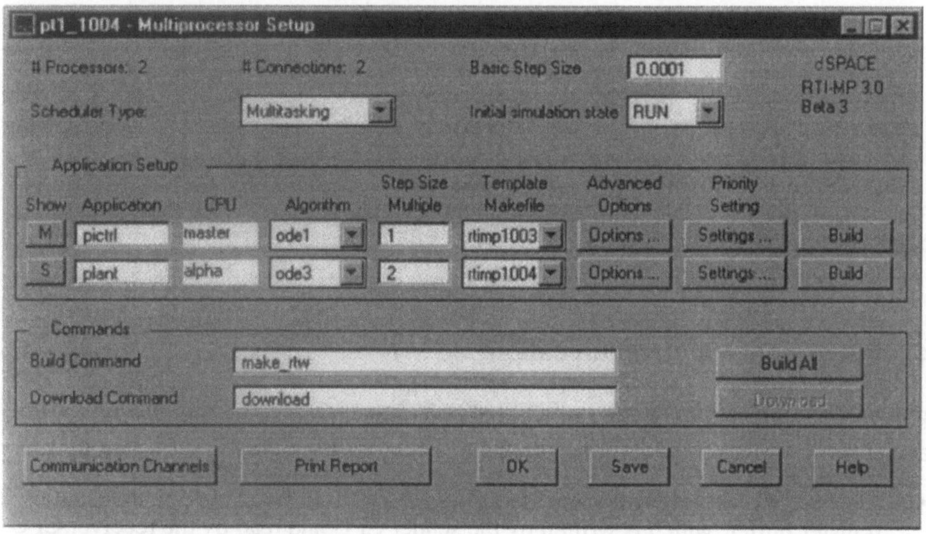

Figure 3. Main dialog window to configure integration algorithms, step sizes, etc.

3. The hardware system

RTI-MP was designed to implement Simulink block diagrams on a hardware system consisting of a network of DEC Alpha processors and Texas Instruments C40 DSPs as shown in figure 4. Due to the tremendous computing power of theoretically 1000 MFlops per CPU the Alpha processors are viewed as the main computing nodes. Each Alpha is connected via a dual-port memory to a dedicated C40 DSP performing I/O tasks and data transfer to other Alpha/C40 combos. Between C40 CPUs data is transferred via 6 high speed communication ports. The physical distance between the Alpha/C40 nodes can be expanded with special ComPort interfaces up to 100 m. All 6 communication ports operate byte-serial with a maximum transfer rate of 20 MBytes per second in both directions.

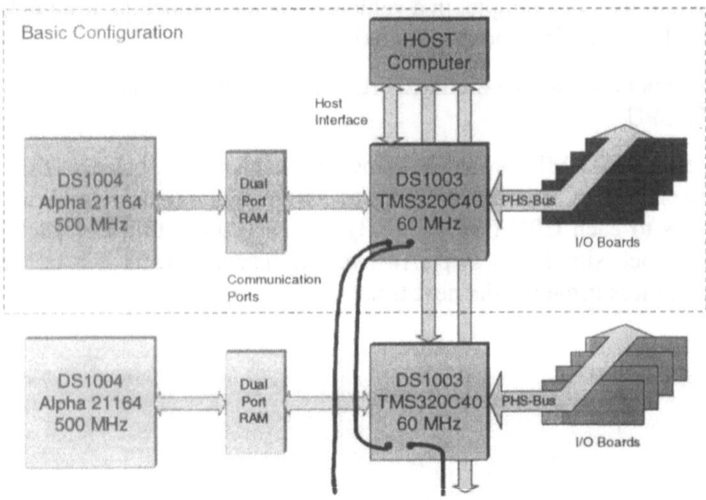

Figure 4. Hardware architecture of the real-time simulator. The PHS bus is used to connect to peripheral I/O boards.

4. Interprocessor communication

For the implementation of Simulink block diagrams on the target hardware described above two transfer protocols are available to send data from one CPU to another:

- The *Virtual Shared Memory* (VSM) protocol (see figure 5) is based on a single transfer buffer, which is written by the sender CPU and read by the receiver CPU independently without synchronization. VSM offers the fastest transfer method by avoiding the overhead for synchronization, but it is well possible that not all data in the transfer buffer results from the same simulation step of the sender at the time it is read by the receiver. It depends on the model dynamics, if this behaviour is acceptable. VSM will mostly be used for slowly changing signals.

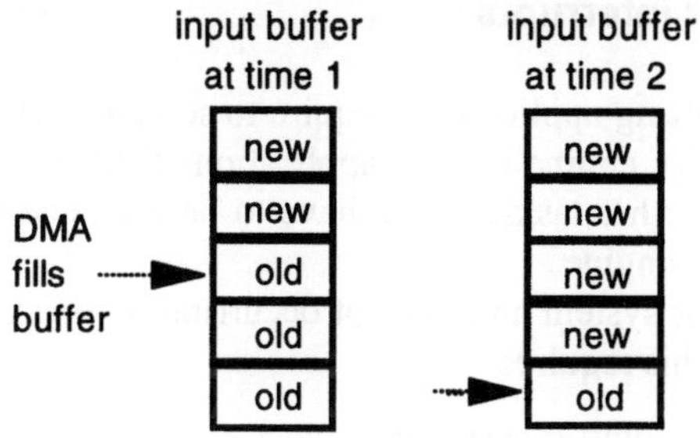

Figure 5. Virtual Shared Memory (VSM) communication protocol.

- The *Swinging Buffer* (SBUF) protocol shown in figure 6 uses a triple buffer system to allow synchronized data transfer and maintain data consistency. When the sender has written all data to one of the buffers, it sets a flag that the data is now available for the receiver CPU. In each simulation step the receiver CPU checks this flag and switches to the latest consistent data buffer available. The sender and receiver CPU never write to / read from the same buffer.

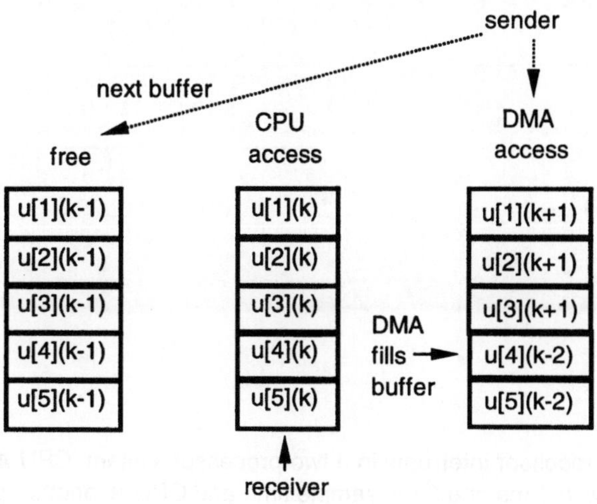

Figure 6. Swinging Buffer (SBUF) communication protocol.

The VSM and SBUF protocols have been implemented for both, the serial data transfer via C40 communication ports and the parallel data transfer via the dual-port memory between C40 and Alpha processors. In the graphical block diagram representation of the simulation model this is fully transparent, i.e. the user needs not to care about the physical type of a communication connection.

5. Interprocessor interrupts

Many control engineering applications require to service asynchronous interrupts. For example, in automotive engine control applications there are typically some periodic time-based tasks and other tasks, which have to be executed based on the crankshaft angle (~ speed) of the engine.

In a multiprocessor system an interrupt occurring on one CPU may trigger actions on other CPUs too. This requires

- the ability to send interprocessor interrupts,
- interruptible, re-entrant communication routines, and
- a priority-based multitasking real-time kernel with low latency running on each CPU.

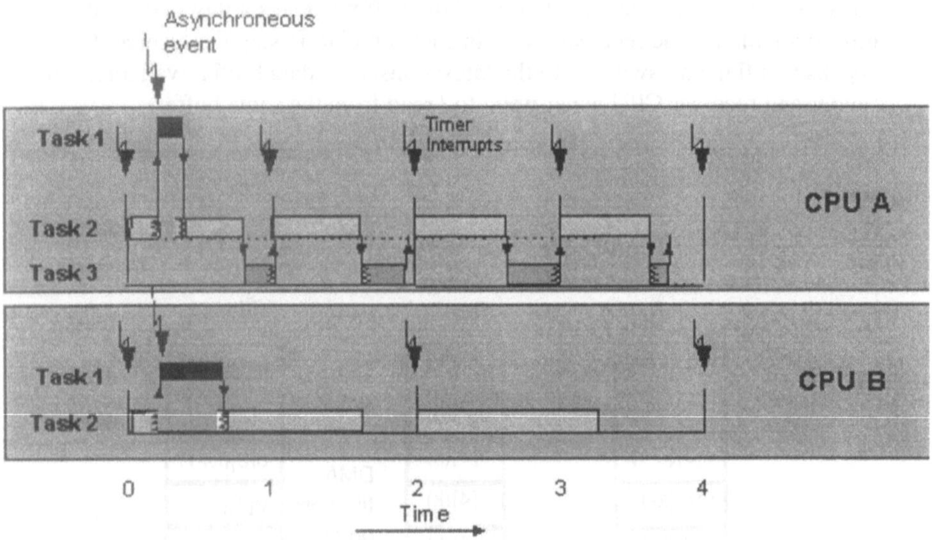

Figure 7. Interprocessor interrupts in a two-processor system. CPU *A* executes two periodic tasks with 1 ms and 2 ms sample time and CPU *B* another periodic task with 2 ms sample time. An asynchronous event interrupts the periodic tasks on both CPUs and schedules another high-priority task.

Hardware interrupts between C40 and Alpha processors can be generated by writing a logical interrupt number to a certain memory location in the dual-port memory. When an interrupt occurs, the real-time kernel checks this logical interrupt number and schedules (or queues) the corresponding task depending on the selected priority (see figure 7).

To exchange interrupts between C40 processors a separate communication port line is used. This allows to send interrupts at any time, even if the interrupted task writes a large data block to another communication port at the same time. The DMA coprocessor of the C40 generates an interrupt each time a data word (= logical interrupt number) is received via the interrupt line and the corresponding interrupt handler calls the scheduler to activate the desired task.

6. Real-time simulation frame

In a multiprocessor environment it is especially difficult to perform a coordinated *start* and *stop* of the simulation. Upon simulation start all CPUs must (re-)initialize their internal state variables. If the applications running on each CPU are automatically generated and external I/O is involved, it is very difficult to predict how much time the initialization process will need on each CPU, but for control applications all CPUs in a multiprocessor system must start the simulation *exactly* at the same point in time.

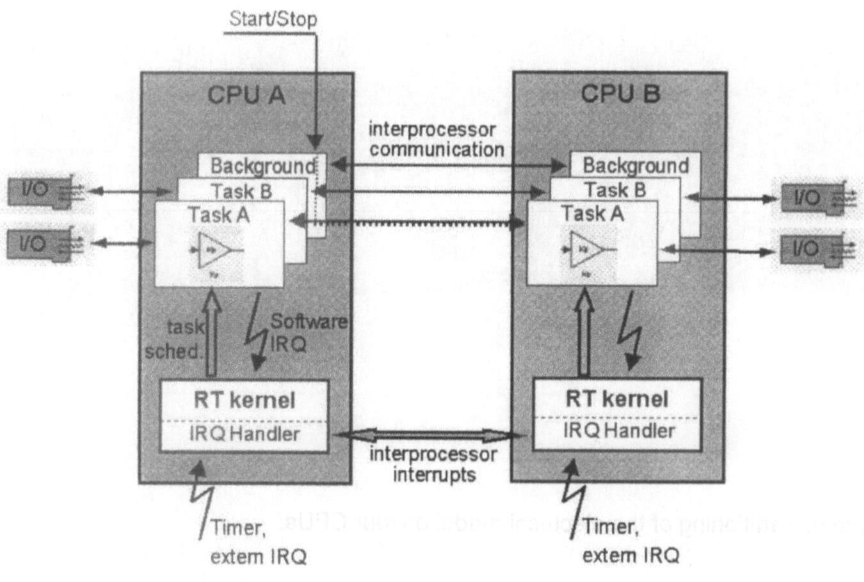

Figure 8. Software architecture of the real-time simulation frame.

With RTI-MP one of the processors is selected as the so called *master CPU*. Only the master CPU can send the signal to start and stop the simulation to other CPUs. In each simulation cycle the desired execution state (= `RUN`, `PAUSE`, or `STOP`) is sent from the master to the slave CPUs. One cycle before the simulation state is actually switched from `STOP` to `RUN`, the master CPU sends a command to all slaves to re-initialize their states. This allows to perform a coordinated simulation start in the next step.

Note, that RTI-MP maintains the interprocessor communication even if the simulation is stopped. This is necessary if the user wants to adjust simulation parameters on a distant CPU during `STOP` state *before* the next simulation run is started. To transfer the new parameter settings to a CPU, which can not be reached from the host directly, interprocessor communication must always be available.

7. Application example

The following industrial application example describes a Hardware-in-the-Loop (HIL) simulation running on two C40 DSPs and two Alpha processors. This simulator was developed by the locomotive manufacturer Adtranz to perform a system integration test of the controller equipment of electric locomotives (Keller et al, 1997). For this purpose all power electronic devices, two asynchronous motors, and a mechanical model of the locomotive had to be simulated.

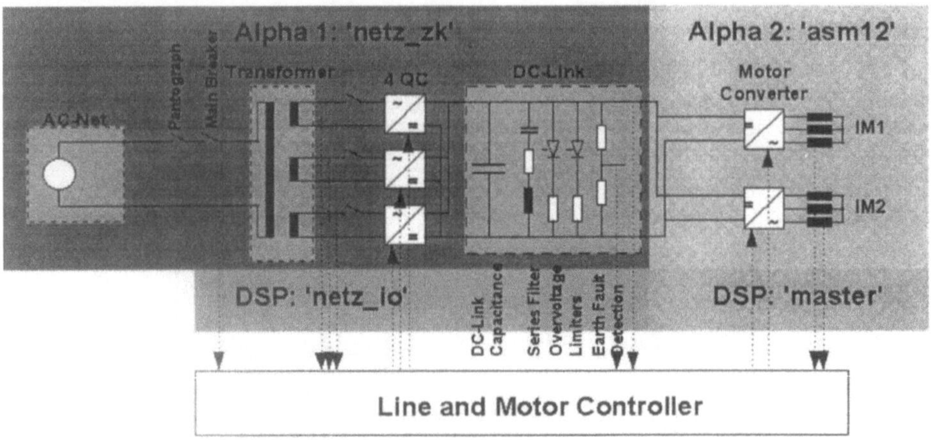

Figure 9. Partitioning of the electrical model on four CPUs.

Modern power electronic switches, like GTOs and IGBTs, which are applied in the line and motor converters of electric locomotives can switch currents with rise times of up to 2 A/µs. To keep the error in the simulated currents minimal, the computational dead-time of the HIL simulator must be as small as possible. Off-line simulations have shown that step sizes of 40 µs or less are required to achieve acceptable simulation results. Even with such small step sizes the error in the simulated currents can be up to 80 A in the worst case, which is about 4 percent of the whole range. Since the desired performance could not be achieved on a single processor, Adtranz decided to implement the HIL simulator on a multiprocessor system with RTI-MP.

Figure 9 shows the partitioning of the electrical model on two C40 DSPs and two Alpha processors. The corresponding RTI-MP block diagram is given in figure 10. The first Alpha computes the line side of the model including three rectifiers and the intermediate DC link. The second Alpha simulates the two motor converters and asynchronous motor models.

Both C40s are completely dedicated to the necessary I/O operations, while the Alphas compute the main simulation model. Not all 84 I/O signals need to be sampled with a step size of 40 µs. To save execution time in the 40 µs task some of the I/O signals are serviced in the background process. The corresponding non-time-critical I/O blocks are placed into the subsystem *background I/O tasks* on the top level of the Simulink block diagram in figure 10.

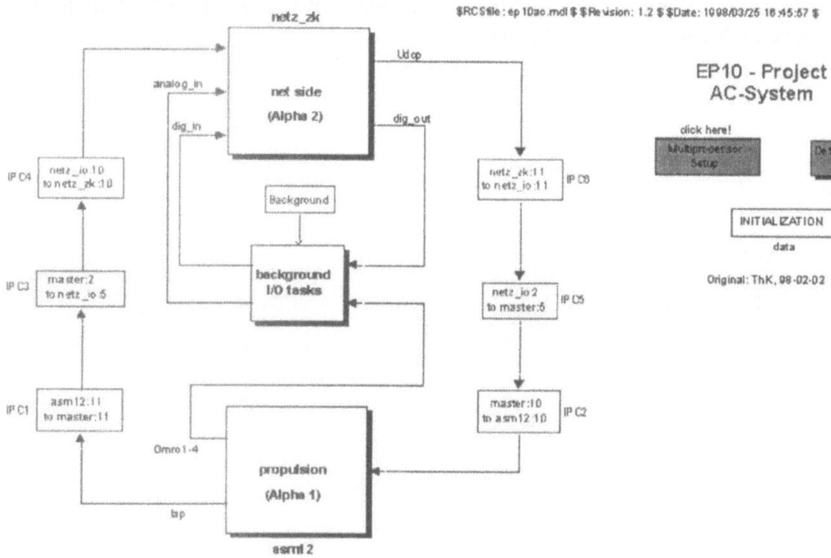

Figure 10. RTI-MP model of the HIL Simulator.

Adtranz has applied the described multiprocessor system successfully to a number of HIL simulation projects. Meanwhile there exist 5 copies of the simulator in different departments of Adtranz. Thus system integration tests by HIL simulation have become a standard part of the development process.

8. Conclusions

RTI-MP provides an intuitive graphical programming of multiprocessor systems based on Simulink block diagrams. All code for I/O operations, communication between CPUs, interprocessor interrupts, and the underlying real-time frame is generated fully automatical. This enables control engineers to apply multiprocessor simulators to very practical problems in domains where big mainframe or expensive analog computers were required before. The distribution of a control application over the available processors is still a remaining task for the user.

References

Kiffmeier, U. (1995). Automatic Code Generation for Multi-DSP Networks on the Basis of Simulink Block Diagrams. EUROSIM Congress '95, Wien, Austria, Sep. 11-15, 1995

Otterbach, R. and Kiffmeier U. (1996). Eine neue Generation hochleistungsfähiger Echtzeitsimulatoren auf der Basis des DEC Alpha Prozessors" ASIM '96, Dresden, Germany, 1996

Kiffmeier, U. (1997). Real-Time Simulation of a 3-D Vehicle Dynamics Model on the DEC Alpha Processor." 15th IMACS World Congress, Berlin, Germany, August 24-29, 1997

Keller, Th., Scheiben, E., and Terwiesch, P. (1997). Digital Real-Time Hardware-in-the-Loop Simulation for Rail Vehicles: A Case Study." European Power Electronics Conference EPE '97, Trondheim, Norwegen. Sep. 7-9, 1997.

5 DESIGN ENVIRONMENTS

THE DASE TOOL: AN ENVIRONMENT FOR THE DEVELOPMENT OF REAL-TIME APPLICATIONS[1]

M. Di Natale and A. Domenici
Università di Pisa - Scuola Superiore S. Anna
Dipt. Ing. dell'Informazione
Pisa

In this paper we discuss some design issues related to the handling of timing constraints in embedded systems and present a tool for the analysis of timing constraints at the architectural design level. Most design tools for real-time applications do not perform any kind of real-time analysis and do not allow the definition of explicit timing constraints. Our tool is aimed at real-time schedulability and performance analysis. It guides the decomposition of the application architecture into a set of hierarchical abstractions representing the active components and the cooperation among them (messages and/or use of shared resources). Deadlines can be specified between any couple of events. The real-time schedulability analysis requires a sufficiently accurate description of the (hardware) architecture, the mapping of the software components on the application nodes and the choice of the resource management algorithms.

1. Introduction

The growing complexity of today's embedded applications and the methodologies for the development of complex hardware and software systems strongly affect the way embedded systems are designed. An automated tool for the design of embedded systems should assist the developer in making decisions, estimating and verifying the functional and timing behavior of the system as early as possible and possibly automatically synthesizing some of the system components for him. If we examine the available design tools for embedded systems, only a few are able to support a rea-

[1] This work has been supported by the Ministero dell'Università e della Ricerca Scientifica e Tecnologica of Italy (MURST) in the framework of the MOSAICO project.

sonably extended portion of the development cycle (usually with no guarantees on its efficiency or the timing constraints).

Reactive embedded systems belong to a special application domain. First, in most such systems (known as real-time systems), responses to external events must be bounded in time (control loops, for example, are very sensitive to time delays). Second, the development process of most embedded system requires a performance evaluation phase, a major factor in deciding the partitioning of functionality between hardware and software. These particular requirements generally make the development of real-time embedded software much more difficult than the development of non-real-time software. In real-time systems the application asks for time constraints or deadlines. These deadlines can be critical (or hard), that is if the results are produced after the deadline, the system is not going to work properly (or maybe is not working at all). Time constraints are neglected by most development tools which are often focused on functional properties and do not allow designers to specify deadlines, nor to check their feasibility after the completion of the design stage. Deadlines are imposed by the environment and bound the response of the system to the external stimula. These (end-to-end) deadlines span the execution of several tasks hosted by the same or different machines and are very complex to manage. In fact most research results show how to handle (and guarantee) a different type of problem: tasks and messages having individual deadlines. Single-task deadlines can be obtained only by overconstraining the original requirements. In this case the design tool should guide the decomposition of end-to-end deadlines to produce an analysable configuration. Finally, while it is relatively easy to mantain functional properties when changing the implementation or the host architecture, the same is not true for real-time properties. The latter are strongly dependent on the implementation and the host architecture which needs to be described with enough detail to afford a first order analysis of the timing behavior.

In our view these are the desirable features for a RT Software Engineering toolset:

- RT SWE tools should support at least the whole design phase and the early coding phase. Support for analysis and requirements specification and for testing is highly desirable. Obviously, support for the whole coding phase is also desirable, but that can be delegated to standard programming environments. The notations used should be easily understandable and yet precise enough to express all the necessary information, at the different levels of detail needed at different stages of development. Ideally, the notation should make it possible to employ formal analysis techniques wherever applicable.
- RT properties and constraints should be dealt with explicitly throughout development. Verification and simulation tools should be integrated in the development environment.
- RT SWE tools should model both SW and HW. HW should be modeled in sufficient detail and yet in a sufficiently abstract manner.

We designed and implemented a toolset composed of a design editor, a schedulability analyser, an emulator and an estimator of the WCET (worst case execution time) of the code. Its main features are:

- The tool contains a design editor that allows the hierarchical description of the active components and their functional relationships. The user can specify real-time constraints between any pair of events.
- It guides the decomposition of end-to-end deadlines (where necessary) and the choice of the most suitable scheduling and resource management algorithm in order to optimize (and check) the schedulability of the application tasks (i.e. the feasibility of the time constraints) as early as possible.
- The real-time schedulability analysis not only guides the assignment of the CPU time, but tells beforehand which tasks are going to make their deadlines and why the others are going to be late. In alternative, the tool can assist the designer in the construction of a cyclic schedule (or generate it automatically) that satisfies all the timing constraints.
- In order to perform the timing analysis the toolset requires an accurate description of the hardware architecture and a description of the mapping of the software into the processing elements.
- The worst case running time of the application tasks can be estimated using another tool which could be useful not only for checking the schedulability of the SW components but also to decide which components are to be implemented in hardware and which ones by software.

The DASE tool can perform schedulability analysis in a fairly general way but it still lacks a lot of the features that would make it a complete design environment. In order to extend it we are considering Object Oriented (OO) methodologies, which are are becoming very common in the development of general purpose software. Objects orientation improves scalability, software reuse and management of complexity. OO techniques can prove significantly efficient in modeling embedded systems as well.

The *Unified Modeling Language* (UML) is gaining acceptance as a standard notation for Object-Oriented software development. It draws from earlier well-known notations and brings them together into a consistent framework, aiming to be a general and flexible means of expressing the concepts needed in software design. UML designers realized that timing constraints have not received enough attention from researchers and software developers. Therefore UML claims to be a notation suitable to the description and the validation of timing constraints. However, neither in [3] nor in [9] there is a proper analysis of the real-time constraints. The second reference proposes a good number of stereotypes (extensions to the base language) and notations (a real-time logic) in order to enhance the expressiveness of the base language.

1.1. State of the Art

Software engineering tools are now in widespread use by developers. Typically, they are centered around an interface that the designer uses to draw diagrams representing the application's architecture in a supported notation. The abstraction level of the representation corresponds to the development process phase addressed by the tool: currently, many tools assist developers from the requirements analysis phase (requiring the highest level of abstraction) to the coding phase (requiring the finest level of detail). The best tools, however, do not just produce and store diagrams, but maintain a *design database*, or *repository*, where the logical structure underlying the diagrams is kept, along with all the information that must or can be associated to the structure, such as constraints, comments, source code (tool- or user-generated), version control data, and the diagrams themselves. This information is used to check designs for syntactic correctness and consistency, and can be accessed by the designer for reference. Source code and documentation can be produced automatically from the information stored in the repository.

Real-time tools came into life in the last decade, prompted by the increasing use of electronic control systems and the first results in real-time software analysis (which started in the late 70s, prompted by the well known result by Liu and Leyland [6]). Among the most notable examples of real-time tools or methodologies we have:

RT-HOOD: developed at the University of York [2] as an extension to HOOD (Hierarchical Object Oriented Design), adopted by the European Space Agency (ESA) as a design standard. The methodology consists in the description of the application according to a hierarchical OO scheme. Active elements eventually belong to a few stereotyped classes, including hard and soft real time processes and periodic, aperiodic and sporadic processes. The analysis considers the case of a single processor application and is based on Rate or Deadline Monotonic analysis.

PERTS: Allows the modeling of the tasking and resource graph in a real-time application [4]. It analyses the schedulability of the application against the deadlines. The tool performs a limited form of end-to-end analysis for distributed applications. PERTS asks for a description of all the tasks and resources in the application and performs the schedulability analysis on computation nodes. (The end-to-end analysis is obtained by composing the analysis at the node level without considering the communication between nodes).

Both tools ask the user for an estimate of the worst case execution time of the application tasks. The user is free to give figures based on his experience, testing or whatever he likes. The tools rely on these timing assumptions heavily and yet provide no help in figuring them out.

OBJECTIME-ROOM: The Objectime toolset, based on the ROOM (Real-time Object Oriented Modeling) methodology is perhaps the best known commercial solution for the design of RT applications. Although the ROOM methodology and the toolset automate most of the production phases and establish a clear, effective and understandable design paradigm, Objectime does not provide any feature for analysing and verifying the timing constraints (which are not even part of the system description). Without being OO, our design abstractions are very close to those used in ROOM.

The main limitations of the current tools and methodologies are the following:

- A restricted process model: most of the tools are based on the concept of periodic activity; aperiodic tasks are an unpleasant exception that is made to fit into the picture by means of periodic servers. Deadline constraints are attached to tasks. Since application deadlines are often end-to-end, the user has to figure out how to partition the application deadlines into task deadlines. Sometimes, the user must translate the deadlines into priorities.

- No support for checking the schedulability of distributed computations (i.e. end-to-end deadlines). Most tools assume a single processor architecture. Only a very small number consider end-to-end deadlines. Network links are simply neglected.
- No architectural modeling, no tools for estimating the worst case computation time. All these tools assume knowledge of the worst case computation time of the tasks. These figures are essential for embedded systems since they guide the software/hardware partitioning process.

Our tools make use of a number of algorithms and theorems developed by researchers on real-time systems. These results can be used to predict the execution times of tasks and predictably schedule the application tasks. The number of results that can be applied to special cases is very large, ranging from algorithms that produce a static ordering of tasks and messages to those that perform dynamic scheduling. Among the latter some require standard mechanisms (priority scheduling) while others make use of sophisticated procedures. These results make it possible to check the schedulability in a wide range of system configurations, from single CPUs [6,10,1] running periodic tasks to pipelines of tasks running on different nodes and exchanging messages over a network [11].

2 Uml as a standard notation

According to UML, a system is seen under different views, each corresponding to one or more types of diagrams: *use case diagrams* describe the interaction of the system with external agents; *class diagrams* are an Object-Oriented description of the entities composing the system, and of their static properties and relationships; *behavior diagrams* describe the dynamic properties of the entities composing the system, using various notations; and *implementation diagrams* show the physical structure of the software and hardware components. Not all designs require the full array of UML diagrams. For Real-Time applications, the class diagram, some of the behavior diagrams, and the implementation diagrams are particularly useful.

The *class diagram* is the core of a UML specification, as it shows the logical structure of the system. For each class, *attributes* and *operations* are specified. The information associated with relationships between classes may include *role* names for the participants in the association, their *multiplicity*, association *attributes*, and other items. All diagram elements can be annotated with *constraints* of various kinds and *comments*. *Behavior diagrams* comprise *statechart diagrams*, *sequence diagram*, and *collaboration diagrams*. Statecharts [5] describe the evolution in time of an object or an interaction between objects by means of a *hierarchical* state machine. *Sequence diagrams* show the possible message exchanges among objects, ordered along a time axis. The timepoints corresponding to message related events can be labeled and referred to in constraint annotations. *Collaboration diagrams* also show message exchanges among objects, but they emphasize structural reationships among objects rather than time sequences of messages. *Implementation diagrams* are either *component diagrams* or *deployment diagrams*. Component diagrams describe the physical structure of the software in terms of software *components* (modules). Deployment diagrams describe the hardware architecture in term of processing or data storage *nodes* connected by communication associations, and show the placement of software components onto the hardware nodes. Normally a UML specification consists of several diagrams of each kind, giving several levels of detail. The UML notation includes a few extension mechanisms. In particular, *stereotypes* can be used to tailor the notation to different application domains or design techniques. A stereotype is basically a way to classify and label some recurring uses of modeling elements such as classes or associations.

1.2.1 Real-Time requirements and UML

Real-Time systems specification and design have been prospected as a very promising application of UML since its earliest definition. Recently, the ROOM (*Real-Time Object-Oriented Modeling*) methodology [8] has been shown [9] to be expressible in terms of the UML notation: the ROOM modeling concepts (such as *actors*, communication *ports*, and *messages*) can be seen as stereotyped usages of UML classes and associations. Both ROOM and UML use sequence diagrams where timing constraints can be expressed using annotations in a language chosen by the designer, however neither notation offers any specific, easily identifiable notation for such constraints. Further, sequence diagrams may not be the most appropriate means to specify them, as they can only represent *scenarios*, that are specific instances of interactions. It has been proposed [7] that timing constraints should be expressed in terms of *transactions*, i.e., end-to-end computations that can be extracted (or abstracted) from sequence diagrams.

2 The DASE tool

A designer using the DASE tool describes a RT system by means of a *software* and a *hardware* architecture. A *mapping* between the two architectures associates software modules to processing nodes.

2.1 Software architecture

The basic elements of a software architecture are *tasks*, *resources*, and *messages*. Tasks are active entities that *use* resources, resources provide *services*, and messages are exchanged between tasks. The designer specifies timing properties of the three kinds of basic elements, such as period for tasks and messages, and execution time for services offered by resources. Timing properties for tasks and messages may also be described by statistical distributions used in simulations. Other properties relevant to RT design include criticalness (*hard* vs. *soft*) and periodicity (*periodic*, *sporadic*. *aperiodic*) for tasks and messages, and synchronization semantics (*synchronous*. *asynchronous*, ...) for messages. Messages are characterized also by their data format.

Tasks and resources are grouped into higher-level constructs: *task containers* group tasks and resources, *module containers* group task containers and (recursively module containers. The term *module* refers to module containers, task containers tasks, or resources. Modules are represented by various icons, and messages are represented as lines between modules. Figure 1 shows part of a software architecture model. The larger icons are module containers and the small rectangles are mess

Different types of arrows denote different communication semantics. The lower part of the picture shows data about the top level module.

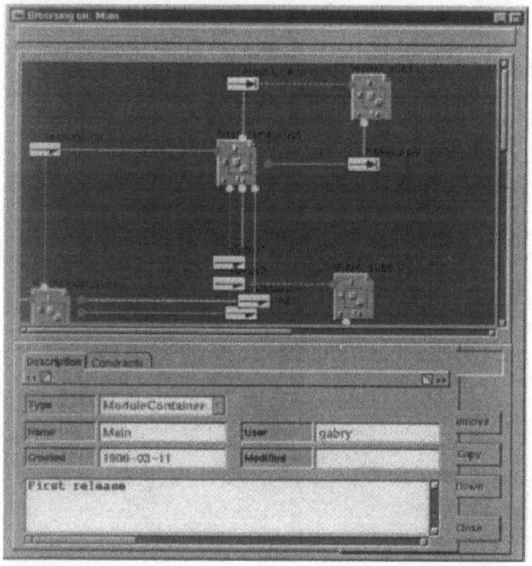

Figure 1: Part of a software architecture

The DASE tool enforces top-down development. Design starts from two top-level modules representing the system and its environment: first, the interaction between system and environment is modeled as a set of messages, then the system module is expanded into submodules, until the software architecture is entirely specified in terms of tasks, resources, and messages. A module's expansion is represented graphically as a new diagram showing the module's internals. We observe that with this approach we specify messages that are exchanged between modules rather than between tasks. This is required in order to describe the interaction between two subsystems (modules) before they have been decomposed to the level of detail where the tasks originating and using the messages are defined. To maintain consistency across levels of detail, *ports* representing a message's endpoints in the sending and receiving modules are used. Figure 2 shows part of the expansion of module **Real_Time_subs** from Figure 1. The icons at the top are the output and input ports for messages **Model_request** and **Model_reply**, respectively. The other large icons are tasks. The lower part of the screen shows the characteristics of message **do_mng_msg**.

Ports are a convenient way to refer to a message within a module, but, more important, they are also the means whereby a designer can express timing constraints.

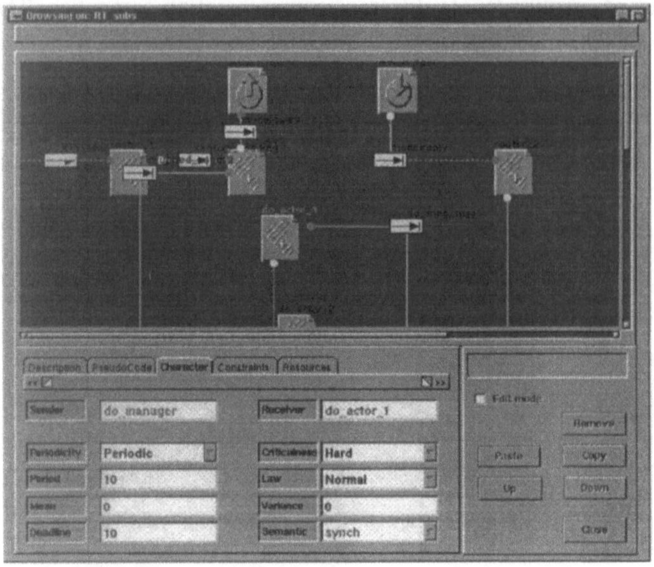

Figure 2: Tasks and ports

A *constraint* on an input port **I** and an output port **O** in the same module is the maximum time interval allowed to elapse between the arrival of a message at **I** and the issue of a message at **O**. A constraint *C* on a pair of ports implies that the module containing the ports is supposed to react to a stimulus at the input port with a response at the output port. The behavior between these two events will usually consist in the exchange of a series of messages between submodules. These messages in turn will have constraints associated with the respective ports, and these constraints will have to be consistent with the original constraint *C*. The set of messages generated in response to a stimulus and leading to its response (excluding the response itself) is the *message chain* of the constraint. A message defined on a path between a constrained pair of ports can be added to the message chain of the constraint together with the task originating it. The constraints on the new message and task can then be checked for compatibility against the chain's constraint. Further, the tool can list all the messages associated with a given constraint.

2.2 Hardware architecture and mapping

The building blocks of a hardware architecture are *nodes*, *buses*, *interfaces*, and *nets*. Nodes are the processing elements, that are connected to buses. Buses, in turn, are connected to nets through interfaces. Several parameters are specified for these elements, such as clock frequency, transmission speed, bandwidth, and communication protocol. Figure 3 shows part of a hardware architecture. Several hardware architectures can be defined for the same system. For each hardware architecture, the designer specifies which modules are allocated to each node. The minimum allocable unit is the task container. The tool checks if a physical path exists between communicating modules placed on different nodes. If more than one path exist, they are higlighted and the designer can select one of them. Figure 4 shows a mapping. The left-hand pane displays the list of nodes existing in a selected hardware architecture, and the list of tasks allocated to node **RTS**. The rest of the screen shows the software architecture.

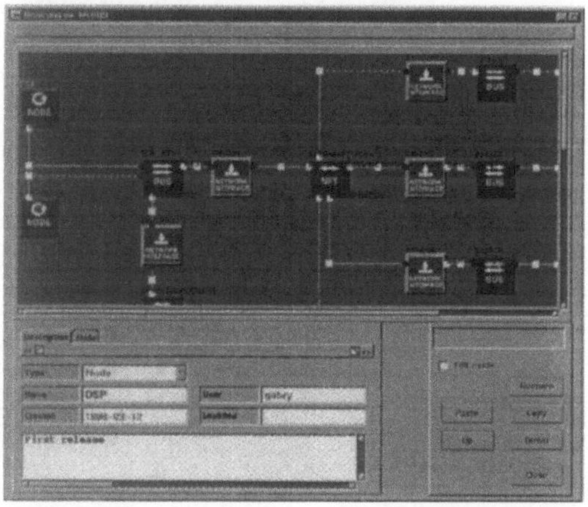

Figure 3: Part of a hardware architecture

2.3 Scheduling analysis

Among the abstractions that compose the logical design there are the managers of the system resources: processor schedulers for nodes, network protocols and resource access protocols for shared resources. The process of mapping the software architecture onto the hardware involves selecting a set of resource managers for each node and network. The designer selects a set of predefined resource management algorithms and maps it to a node. The DASE tool checks the tasks already allocated to the node for schedulability with respect to the selected algorithm and the messages with respect to the network scheduling protocol.

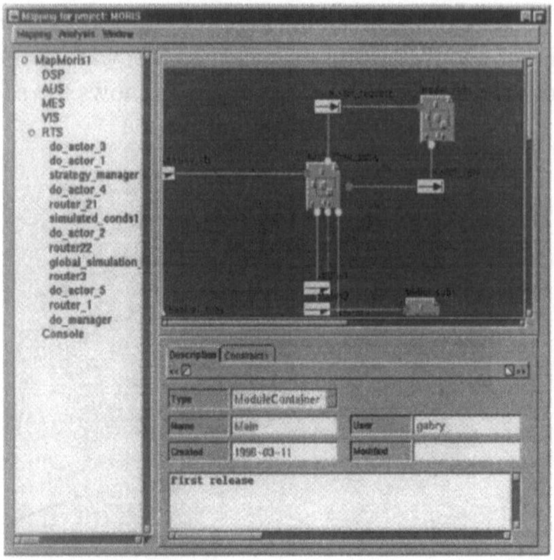

Figure 4: Module mapping

3 Beyond DASE

If we compare the DASE tool to the tools currently available for general (non RT) applications we notice a few limitations. Most notably, DASE does not support the basic object-oriented concepts, such as classes and inheritanceand has no facilities to specify interfaces and encapsulated data. Another significant limitation lies in its restricted scope across the development process. The tool is tailored to the architectural design phase, and should be extended to analysis and to detailed design.

The DASE tool compares better in the area of RT tools, but still we must point out a few drawbacks. First, it enforces a top-down approach. While this is often desirable for various reasons, including work planning and distribution, it is considered impractical for co-design efforts, where performance evaluation may lead to extensive redesign, including software/hardware repartitioning. Then, the set of modeling concepts is perhaps too restrictive. Finally, there is no way to specify dynamic behavior (states and transitions). Again, we are led to reconsider our choices concerning the modeling language adopted in DASE. The original decision of making a limited number of fundamental abstractions (such as *task* or *resource*) available to designers is useful in the early (architectural) stage of a RT design process where focus is on timing properties, but it is unsatisfactory in the later design and coding phases, where an accurate definition of the software architecture requires greater expressive power.

The modeling language should conform to a standard as far as possible. UML is currently the most promising candidate, and its controlled extension capabilities can be used to provide those specialized abstractions we deem useful in RT design. The modeling approach adopted in DASE is compatible with the UML approach, but establishing a correspondence between them is not immediate. The DASE language deals with objects rather than classes, so a DASE software architecture diagram is a form of a UML collaboration diagram rather than a class diagram. A further discrepancy is in the modeling of messages. UML associates messages only to events and to data exchanged between objects, while DASE associates them with more parameters, such as period or criticalness. In order to map DASE messages into UML modeling elements, we have the choice of representing them as full-fledged objects or as associations with attributes. In any case, a designer should be aware of the semantic difference between DASE and UML messages. Further, the tool should be able to extract the timing information associated with DASE messages and use it to create sequence diagrams that show object interactions in terms of UML messages. Ports are another DASE modeling element that can be expressed in different ways in UML. They could be expressed as attributes of messages, or tasks, or modules. They could be seen as independent objects, and this would make it possible to map them explicitly to hardware interfaces. Constraints between ports could be expressed as standard UML constraints or as stereotyped associations between ports. We may notice that the concepts of constrained ports and their associated message chains have some similarity to the transactions proposed in [7]. The information DASE associates with hardware nodes and communication links is much richer than the information mentioned in published examples of UML specifications, but in UML these modeling elements are actually stereotypes of classes or objects and of associations. Therefore the hardware modeling elements envisioned in DASE can be easily made to fit the UML framework.

References

[1] T.P. Baker. (1991) "Stack-based scheduling of real-time processes." *The Journal of Real-Time Systems*, (3):67--99.

[2] A. Burns. (1991). "Scheduling hard real-time systems: a review." *Software Engineering Journal*, pages 116--128.

[3] Bruce Powel Douglass. (1998) *Real-time UML: Developing Efficient Objects for Embedded Systems*. Addison-Wesley.

[4] J.W.S. Liu et al. (1993) PERTS: a prototyping environment for real-time systems. In Proc. 1993 IEEE Real-Time Systems Symposium.

[5] D. Harel. Statecharts: a visual formalism for complex systems. Science of Computer Programming, 8:231--274, 1987.

[6] C.L. Liu and J.W. Layland. Scheduling algorithms for multiprogramming in a hard-real-time environment. Journal of the ACM, 20(1):46--61, Jan. 1973.

[7] M. Saksena, P. Freedman, and P. Rodziewicz. Guidelines for automated implementation of executable object oriented models for real-time embedded control systems. In Proc. IEEE Real-Time Systems Symposium, 1997.

[8] B. Selic, G. Gullekson, and P.T. Ward. *Real-Time Object-Oriented Modeling*. John Wiley and sons, 1994.

[9] B. Selic and J. Rumbaugh. *Using UML for Modeling Complex Real-Time Systems*. ObjecTime, March 1998. (av. from www.objectime.com).

[10] L. Sha, R. Rajkumar, and J.P. Lehoczky. Priority inheritance protocol: An approach to real-time synchronization. IEEE Transactions on Computers, 39(9):1175--1185, Sept. 1990.

[11] K. Tindell and J. Clark. Holistic schedulability analysis for distributed hard real-time systems. Microprocessing & Microprogramming, 40(2--3):117--134, April 1994.

PARADISE: *Design Environment for **Para**llel & **Dis**tributed, **E**mbedded Real-Time Systems*

W.Hardt, P. Altenbernd, C. Böke, G. Del Castillo, C. Ditze, E.Erpenbach, U. Glässer, B. Kleinjohann, G. Lehrenfeld, F.J. Rammig, C. Rust, F. Stappert, J. Stroop and J. Tacken

Today's embedded systems (ES) are characterized by more and more parallelism, distribution over different locations and hard real-time (RT) requirements. Consequently, the modern, structured design process has to deal with heterogeneous requirements and restrictions. The integration of several core competencies is essential for establishing a methodological structured design process for parallel distributed embedded real-time systems. In this paper we present an overall structuring of the design process as well as the Paradise Design Environment reflecting the design process structure. Our activities are based on wide, theoretically well-founded concepts and tool support is built upon these theoretically foundations.

1 Introduction

Today's embedded systems (ES) are characterized by more and more parallelism, distribution over different locations and hard real-time (RT) requirements. Consequently, the modern, structured design process has to deal with heterogeneous requirements and restrictions. Especially the integration of HW-design tasks with SW-design tasks and operating system functionality with respect to RT requirements is a main challenge. The integration leads to systems with enormous overall complexity because the complexity of each design partition itself has been doubled nearly every three years. This explains the need of well-founded theoretically paradigms, automation tools, and a globally applicable design methodology.
Traditionally several design domains are known and existing beside each other. Knowledge, algorithms and techniques used in a special design domain may be called

core competence. Core competencies needed for establishing a design methodology for today's ES are:

- specification and modeling
- analysis and verification
- RT SW-synthesis and RT operating systems
- HW-synthesis and rapid prototyping.

A core competence should cover all levels of abstraction within one design domain. A very good structuring of the HW-design domain has been suggested by Gajski. This structure is called Y-chart and distinguishes a behavioral, structural, and a geometry design-view. All three design-views are additionally divided into five different hierarchical layers, namely: the algorithmic, register-transfer, gate, symbolic-layout, and the electrical-layout-layer. Under security and productivity aspects a test-view has to be introduced as fourth design-view leading to the X-chart [Ra89]. The X-chart extends the Y-chart by the test-view. If this abstract structure is generalized for the design of today's ES a global applicable design methodology can be established.

In our approach the X-structure is applied to each design domain separately. Once the abstract structure is found domain specific interpretations can be brought together. This new abstract structuring of the design process of today's ES is illustrated in Figure 1. The five different layers of abstraction (algorithm to layout) of Gajski's Y-chart are depicted for each of the eight core competencies and each one is structured by Rammig's X-chart.

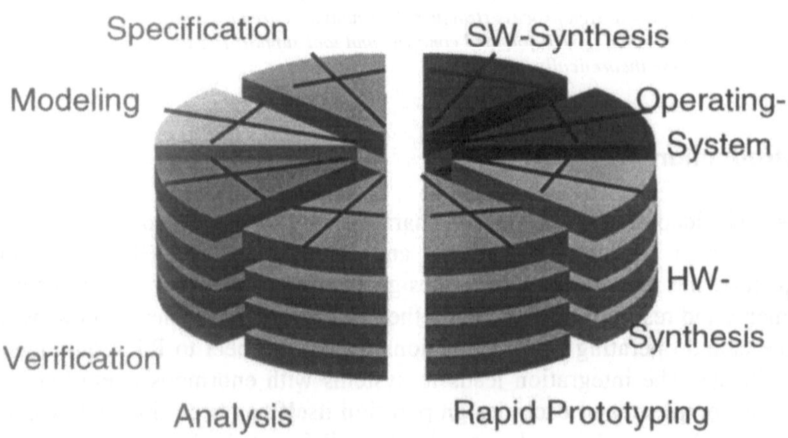

Figure 1. **Abstract structuring of today's ES design.**

Based on this concept a variety of automation tools for different design domains have been integrated within the PARADISE Design Environment. The PARADISE Design

Environment is understood as an approach towards an implementation of a globally applicable, integrated design methodology. In this paper we give an overview over the concept and the integrated tools. Next the theoretical concepts structured by the core competencies are explained. Then a summery of the tools integrated in the PARADISE Design Environment is given. Finally, the benefits resulting from the PARADISE design methodology are illustrated.

2 Concepts

Our core competencies are founded on the following theoretical concepts:

- abstract state machines (ASM)
- predicate transition nets (PrT-net)
- control-data flow graph (CDFG)
- state-charts (SC).

Abstract State Machines - formerly called Evolving Algebras [Gur95] - combine declarative concepts of first-order logic with the abstract operational view of transition systems in a unifying framework for mathematical modeling of discrete dynamic systems. The underlying computation model constitutes a simple yet powerful semantic basis to deal with concurrent and reactive behavior in a direct and intuitive way; it naturally enables operational interpretations of high-level system specifications and thereby facilitates machine-supported analysis and validation (e.g. through simulation) of the resulting models. Numerous ASM applications (see for instance the annotated ASM) to real-life systems engineering problems - in particular, formal semantics of programming languages, modeling languages and protocols - contributed to establish general abstraction principles needed to cope with the complexity of large systems. In contrast to many traditional formal methods with a monolithic character, the ASM method is open to be combined with other (e.g. application domain specific) modeling techniques, thus providing additional flexibility

The second concept, extended predicate transition nets (Pr/T-Nets), has been developed from petri nets. We choose a high level form of petri nets, since pure petri net models tend to become very large and therefore rather incomprehensible when modeling realistic systems. We extended the basic definition of Pr/T-Nets with hierarchy and timing concepts. Our timing concept supports the specification of real-time restrictions as well as execution and idle times for the actions assigned to transitions in a Pr/T-Net. Hierarchical Pr/T-Nets support a modular specification and allow the reuse of predefined nets in several models. The definition of hierarchical Pr/T-Nets within our formalism is closely coupled with a mechanism for graphical abstraction of Pr/T-subnets. Based on this graphical abstraction a domain specific representation of the internal model is possible.

The third concept, the control/data flow graph (CDFG), brings together control flow oriented information with data flow. During the history of research in HW-design automation both aspects have been evaluated intensively. As one result may be stated, that both aspects have valuable advantages. This has been realized by the definition of

the CDFG representing both and provide references in between. CDFGs are used by the core competencies HW-synthesis and rapid prototyping.
Last, the state-chart concept is well suited for the specification of reactive embedded systems. Closely related to the paradigm of synchronous languages, state-charts offer ideal abstraction primitives for a deterministic specification of a system's behavior. Work is going on to automatically transform such specification into software realizations not only for rapid prototyping but also for target systems.

3 Tool support

The previous section summarizes the conceptional base on which the core competencies have been implemented. All core competencies are supported by specialized tools. In this section we give an overview over the tools available in PARADISE Design Environment. Ongoing extensions ensure the adoptions to new algorithms, requirements or usability aspects. The modeling core competence is based on ASMs. This concept was implemented in the ASM-Workbench. This includes simulation and comfortable debugging of ASM-models (Figure 2). It has been found that ASM-model execution is much faster than traditionally used co-simulation. This is because the simulation granularity of traditional co-simulation is fixed.

ASM-SL: Specification Language for the tools of the ASM Workbench
ASM AST: Abstract syntax tree representation of ASM-SL
ASM runs: Representation of ASM simulation traces
MONTAGES: Methodology for the specification of programming languages: extends abstract state machines by a visual formalism for static semantics.

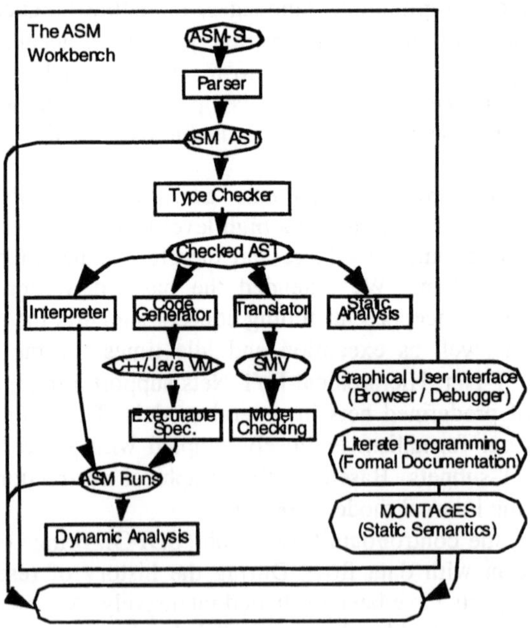

Figure 2. ASM Workbench

The specification and analysis tasks are based on extended Pr/T-Nets and are supported by the tool SEA. In addition to Pr/T-Nets, SEA allows the integration of other design domain specific languages due to the mechanism of graphical abstraction (Figure 3). For the resulting common extended Pr/T-Net, SEA provides powerful simulation and visualization facilities [KlKlTa96]. In order to analyze and verify the model, some methods known from petri nets have been applied to Pr/T-Nets. The analysis results are used for optimization of the model. For further processing by other components of the PARADISE Design Environment a description in a 'Meta Language' containing both, the model as well as the analysis results, may be generated.

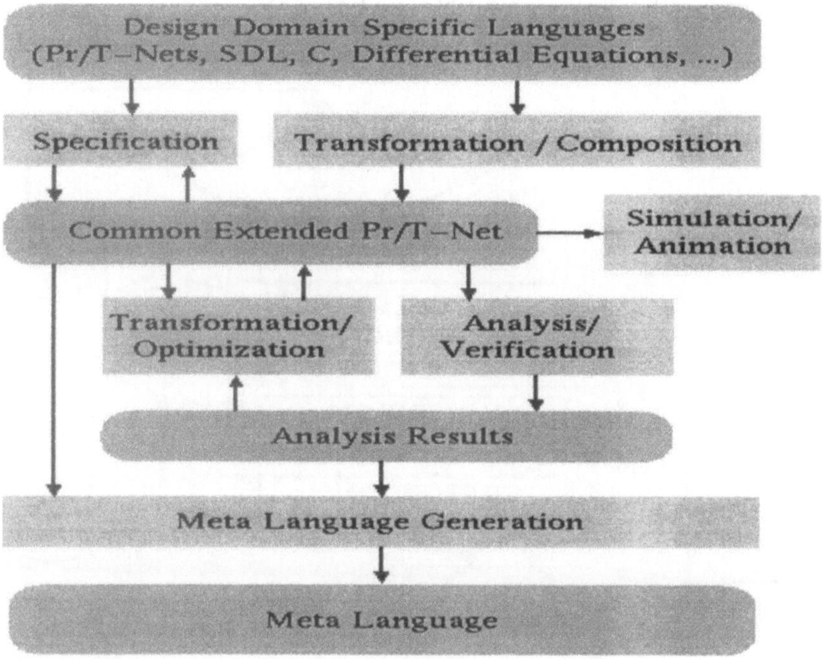

Figure 3. Concept of specification and analysis tool SEA

HW/SW-codesign partitions the specification extracted from SEA. Consequently the design tasks HW-synthesis, RT-SW-synthesis and RT-operating system design can start wherefore the PARADISE Design Environment provides automation tools:

PMOSS (HW-synthesis)
CHaRy (RT-SW-synthesis
TEReCS (RT-communication
DReaMS (RT-operating system design).

The main features of PMOSS are HW/SW partitioning, high-level transformation for early design optimization and high-level synthesis [HaRo97]. For implementation a modular concept has been chosen, i.e. classes of algorithms for all tasks have been implemented. Thus each task can be adapted to the primer optimization goal by choosing the best algorithm. The main tasks are depicted in Figure 4. Several frontends read from tools within the PARADISE Design Environment, results are visualized by graphic editors and brought back by backends.

RT-SW-synthesis for parallel distributed systems can be performed by the CHaRy tool. As CHaRy processes deterministic C-code descriptions this toolset can ideally be combined with a state-chart language compiler currently under development. This compiler automatically transforms state-chart models into a software implementation based on C code. In order to generate production quality code, e.g. for microcontroller targets, analysis results of CHaRy will be considered during the automatic transformation. Several tasks for the guaranty of real-time behavior within a heterogeneous architecture are available (see Figure 5).

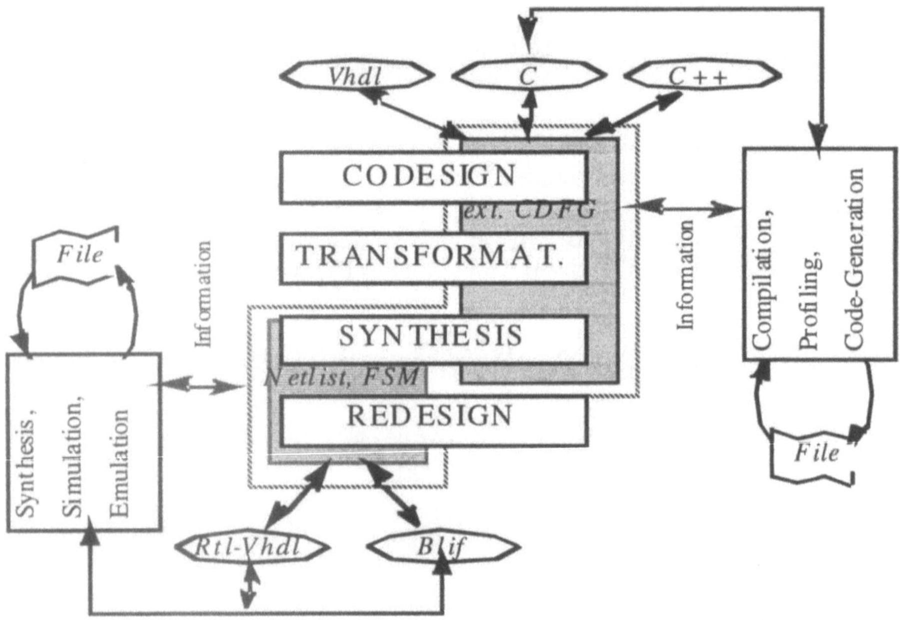

Figure 4. Main tasks of design tool PMOSS

The operating system design within the PARADISE Design Environment is driven by the today's ES's requirements. Experiences gained from the design of micro-kernel related to either high-performance or hard real-time computing have shown that customization plays a major role to enhance the performance of applications while maintaining a reusable and flexible software architecture.

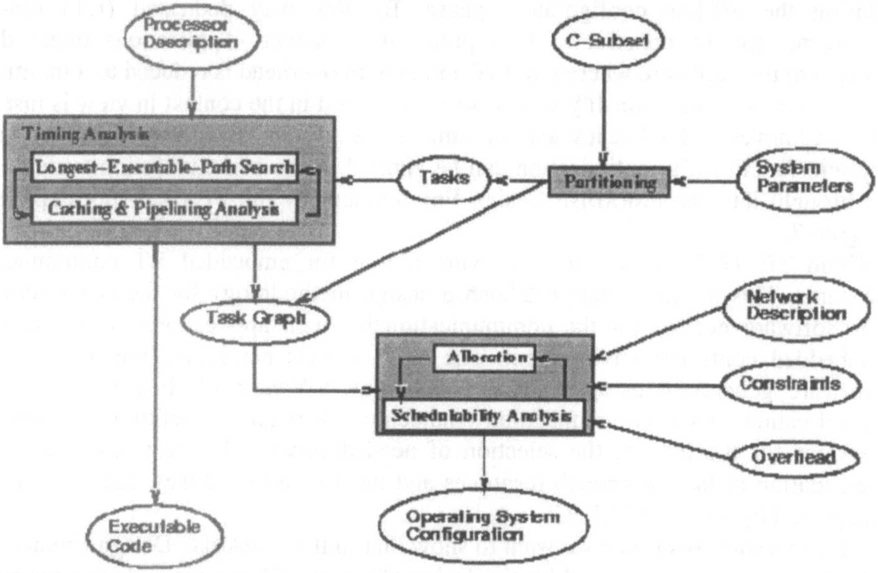

Figure 5. Conception of CHaRy

DReaMS [Di98] is a customizable library operating system intended to be used as a basis for the synthesis of either application-specific run-time platforms or operating system kernel in both fields (see Figure 6). Zero-DReaMS, the minimal core set of the system software implements only functions necessary to start application code on a native processor. All other services (including mechanisms for dynamic re-configuration and extensions) are optional features which can be integrated a priori

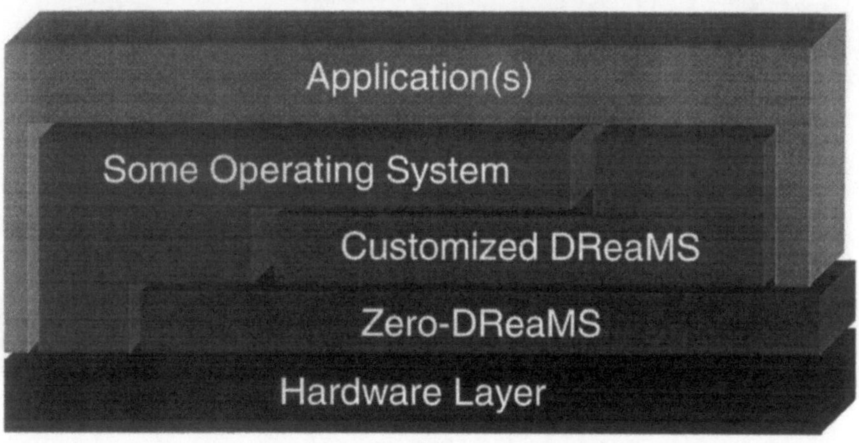

Figure 6. DReaMS overview

during the off-line configuration phase. By this way dedicated (RT) run-time platforms can be constructed in a predictable manner. Applications retain direct access to the hardware where required and system overhead is reduced to a minimum.

That is, only functionality which is really needed in the context in view is inserted. This removes redundancies and minimizes the system size. Beside the operating system functionality optimization can be applied to the communication system. This is brought into the PARADISE Design Environment by the TEReCS tool depicted in Figure 7.

Within TEReCS we intend to provide a tool for embedded RT communication systems. This toolkit should establish a design methodology for the construction of the software needed for the communication between applications on a distributed embedded controller environment. The main aspects persecuted are the automatic software generation using a library containing SW-services. Beginning from the specification of the communication connections through the definition of the SW-services for the library, the selection of needed services for each node, up to the verification of having enough resources and meeting all deadlines, each step will be supported by a task of TEReCS.

By this short overview we want to show that in the PARADISE Design Environment all core competencies needed for the design of today's ES are available in concept and automation tools. Table 1 gives a relation between a given core competence and the

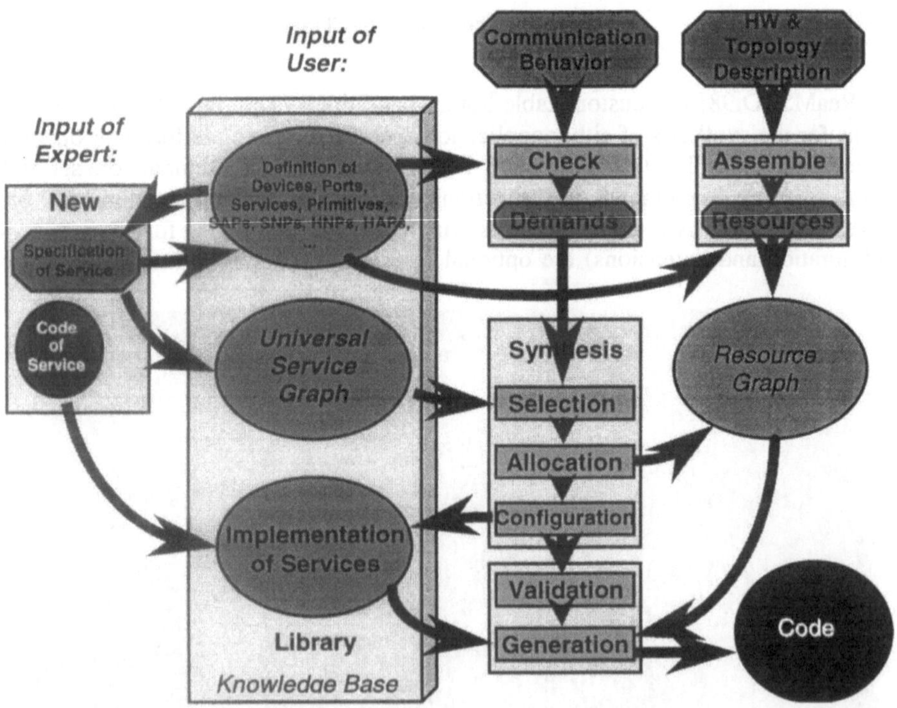

Figure 7. Conception of communication system design tool TEReCS

corresponding automation tool. It points out that different tools may be used within the same core competence, e.g. for analysis. This is due to the different levels of abstraction a core competence is structured by. The integration of tools is by now based on file-exchange.

	specification	modeling	SW-synthesis	operating system	HW-synthesis	rapid prototyping	verification	analysis
ASM-WB		X						X
SEA	X						X	X
PMOSS					X	X		
ChaRy			X					X
DreaMS				X				
TEReCS				X				

Table 1. Tools related to core competencies in the PARADISE DESIGN ENVIRONMENT

4 Integration

The mentioned tools are available within the PARADISE Design Environment. For an automated design path the question of integration comes up. We decided not to build up a tightly coupled framework because of the overhead caused by consistency checks, data base reaction time etc. Within PARADISE three types of integration with different degrees of coupling are distinguished:

1. **Shared data structures**: This is the strongest coupling. All algorithms are implemented on the same data structure which provides a very fast data exchange between algorithms. All tools within PARADISE use for their own algorithms unique data structures.
2. **Standardized exchange formats**: The definition of data exchange formats is a very commonly used manner to couple tools together. The complexity and expressiveness of such formats differ in wide ranges. We have found that data exchange formats must be adapted to the level of abstraction they refer to. On algorithmic level, e.g. after HW/SW-partitioning, the programming language 'C' has been found a very good formalism. Within the PARADISE Design Environment SEA and PMOSS are using this format for data exchange.
3. **Propagation**: On each design level and within each design step the design can be described by it's characteristics. The next task can be specified by

the requirements the design has to meet after performing the design task. This information has to be shared by several tools. Therefore we suggest to provide propagation mechanisms for design characteristics as well as for design rewirements.

Based on these integration concept a powerful design path can be provided. Each tool can be used autonomously as well as in combination with the other tools involved in PARADISE.

5 Conclusion

The integration of several core competencies is essential for establishing a methodological design process for parallel distributed embedded RT systems. in this paper we presented a overall structuring of the design process as well as an overview over the PARADISE Design Environment. Our activities are based on wide, theoretically well-founded concepts and tool support is built upon these theoretically foundations.

Further tasks needed within the PARADISE Design Environment should deal with visualization of results obtained from the different core competencies as well as from different levels of abstractions. This will help the designer to get a more global view of the design process because all results are brought together. Also a direct integration of the used concepts could be helpful for optimizing data exchange and tool performance.

6 References

[Di98] C. Ditze. Constructing a customizable library to support software synthesis for embedded applications and micro-kernel operating systems. In *Proc. of the 8. ACM SIGOPS European Workshop*, Sintra, Portugal, September 1998.

[Gur95] Y. Gurevich. Evolving Algebras 1993: Lipari Guide. Börger, Editor, *Specification and Validation Methods*. Oxford University Press, 1995.

[HaRo97] W. Hardt, W. Rosenstiel. Prototyping of Tightly Coupled Hardware/Software-Systems. *Design Automation for Embedded Systems*, vol. 2, no. 1 (1997).

[KlKlTa96] B. Kleinjohann, E. Kleinjohann, J. Tacken. "The SEA Language for System Engineering and Animation", *In Applications and Theory of Petri Nets*, LNCS 1091, Springer Verlag, 1996.

[Ra89] Franz J. Rammig. *Systematischer Entwurf digitaler Systeme*. B. G. Teubner, Stuttgart, 1989.

MCI – MULTILANGUAGE DISTRIBUTED CO-SIMULATION TOOL

F.Hessel, P.Le Marrec, C.A.Valderrama, M.Romdhani, A.A.Jerraya

System-Level Synthesis Group
TIMA Laboratory
Grenoble, France

Nowadays the design of complex systems requires the cooperation of several teams belonging to different cultures and using different languages. It is necessary to dispose of new design and verification methods to handle multilanguage approaches. This paper presents a multilanguage co-simulation tool that allows co-simulation of multilanguage specifications for complex systems. The main idea of our approach is to allow validation of the functional completeness of the system at a behavioral level. MCI starts with a configuration file that describes the interconnection between modules written in different languages. It generates automatically a software co-simulation bus and the interfaces required to connect the different simulators in a distributed way. The proposed tool is used to assist the design of an adaptive speed control system that was described in three different languages (VHDL, SDL and MatLab).

1. Introduction

The design of complex electronic systems such as those embedded in a modern car or aircraft may require the cooperation of several design groups belonging to different companies with different cultures. Of course, different parts of the design may require different concepts such as hardware/software, control/data, continuous/discrete, synchronous/asynchronous and etc.

The specification of each part of the system is usually made by cooperating groups using different languages. Of course, a natural question arouses. Is it possible to find a specification language that may accommodate all kinds of applications at different abstraction levels?

Experiments with system specification language [2,3,6] show that there is not a unique universal specification language to support the whole life cycle (specification, design and implementation) for all kind of applications. New specification and design methods are necessary to handle these cases where different languages and methods need to be used within the same design. These are multilanguage specification design and verification tools.

The concept of multilanguage specification aims at coordinating the different cultures through the unification of the languages, formalisms and notations. Nowadays, the use of more than one language correspond to current need in embedded system design. In most system houses, software design groups are separated from hardware design groups. Multilanguage specification is driven by needs of modular and evolutive design because of the increasing complexity of designs. Modularity helps in mastering this complexity, promotes design re-use and more generally encourages concurrent engineering development.

The basic idea behind multilanguage design is to allow modular specification. The communication scheme is described separately from the rest of the system. This allows hiding the details related to the inter-processes communication. All accesses to the interface of a communication unit is made through specific communication procedures that fix the protocol of exchanging parameters between the subsystems. Specific communication units may be necessary when complex protocols are used for exchanging data.

The goal of this work is to show a multilanguage distributed co-simulation environment, called MCI (**M**ultilanguage **C**osimulation **I**nterface). The objective of the environment is to run concurrently simulators for the simulation of the different subsystems. The inter-simulators communication is automatically generated starting from of a configuration model. This approach is based on a multilanguage co-simulation backplane.

The next section introduces the state of the art. In section 3, we give a brief overview of automatic generation of co-simulation interfaces. The section 4 describes the MCI tool. The above mentioned concepts will be clarified by a real example in section 5. And finally, in section 6, we conclude with perspectives and directions of future work.

2. Multilanguage Co-Simulation

Multilanguage co-simulation is a key issue of codesign methodology. Through co-simulation it is possible to validate the functional correctness of the system specification. Co-simulation can also be used to gain information about an embedded system before the prototype is actually build [7,9]. Furthermore, co-simulation allows designers to perform experiments that could be impractical in a prototyping environment.

As codesign proceeds, the level of co-simulation evolves from the behavioral level to the implementation level in which timed co-simulation would be necessary to validate timing requirements. In the behavioral level, the functional completeness of an implementation can be effectively verified with untimed simulation [10].

Co-simulation aims at using several simulators concurrently. The key issue for the definition of a co-simulation environment is the communication between the different simulators.

Several researchers have described frameworks and methodologies for the co-simulation of heterogeneous system specifications, typically C-VHDL co-simulation model [1,4,8,13]. Few recent works addressed the problem of multilanguage co-simulation [5].

Coware [15] and Siera [16] are typical environments supporting such codesign scheme. They start from a mixed description given in VHDL or VERILOG for hardware and C for software. All of them allow for co-simulation. These approaches restrict the specification for hardware and software by using specific languages.

A general multilanguage approach requires the combination of any kind of languages for the specification of modules. Only few systems in the literature allow such codesign model. These include the PTOLEMY and the RAPID systems [5] and the work described in [6]. As in the case of heterogeneous specification, the problem of interfacing and multilanguage validation need to be solved.

The main problems of multilanguage specification are:

(1) How to decide the most appropriated paradigm for each part of global specification,

(2) How to compose these subsystem specifications in a unified format suitable for codesign,

(3) How to verify if the subsystem specifications and the unified format correspond to the requirements and constraints of global specification.

The co-simulation approach (Figure 2.1) consists in interconnecting the simulation environments associated to each of the partial specifications. Co-simulation is an engineering solution to multilanguage validation that performs just a shallow integration of partial specifications [4].

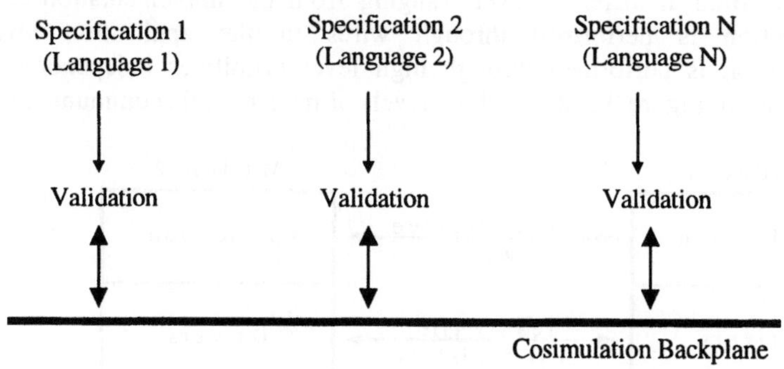

Figure 2.1: Validation through co-simulation

3. Automatic Generation of Co-simulation Interfaces

When dealing with co-simulation, the most tedious error-prone procedure is the generation of the link between different simulation environments. In order to overcome this problem automatic co-simulation interface generation tools are needed. This kind of tools take as input a user defined configuration file, which specifies the desired configuration characteristics (I/O interface, interconnection modules debugging tools) and produces a ready-to-use multilanguage co-simulation interface [13].

Figure 3.1 shows a generic inter-simulator interface generation scheme.

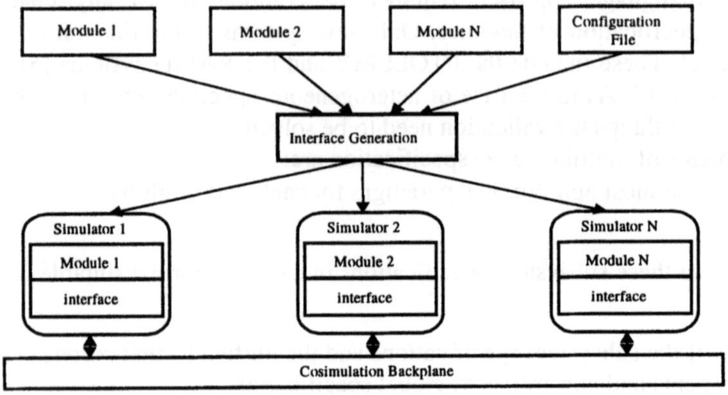

Figure 3.1: Inter-simulator interface generation

Based on the information provided by the configuration file, the interface generation process produces automatically the interface between the modules and the co-simulation bus.

The configuration file specifies the inter-module interactions. These interactions may be specified at different levels ranging from the implementation level where communication is performed through wires to the application level where communication is performed through high level primitives independent from the implementation. Figure 3.2 shows three levels of inter-module communication [14].

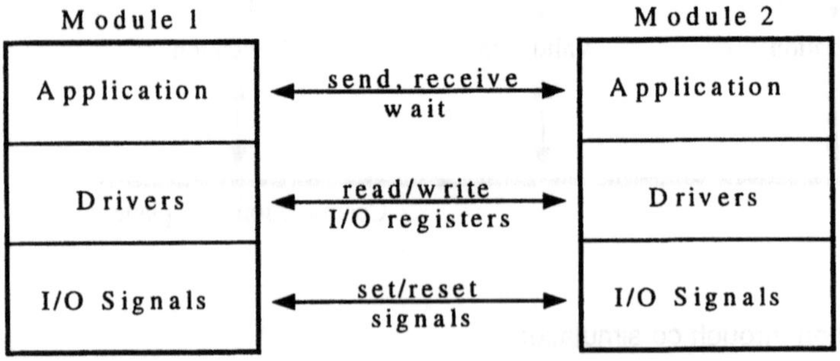

Figure 3.2: Abstraction levels of inter-module communication

4. MCI: A Multilanguage Co-simulation Interface

The figure 4.1 shows the global view of MCI. The proposed approach starts from a multilanguage specification of the system and a user defined configuration file. This file specifies the desired configuration characteristics, as a list of the subsystem specifications, a list of interconnections between subsystems, a list of properties concerning the machine that will execute each subsystem specification and the language of each subsystem was described. The simulator names are included into the subsystem characteristics for to give information about what simulator to use for the model debugging tools during the co-simulation process.

The MCI tool (figure 4.1) takes the configuration file to produces a ready to use multilanguage co-simulation environment. The environment is composed of a cosimulation backplane and a simulation interface for each simulator that will be run. The co-simulation backplane is based on a communication network protocol that is used as a co-simulation bus. All simulators communicate with one another by means of this cosimulation bus. The cosimulation bus is in charge of transferring data between the different simulators via the router process.

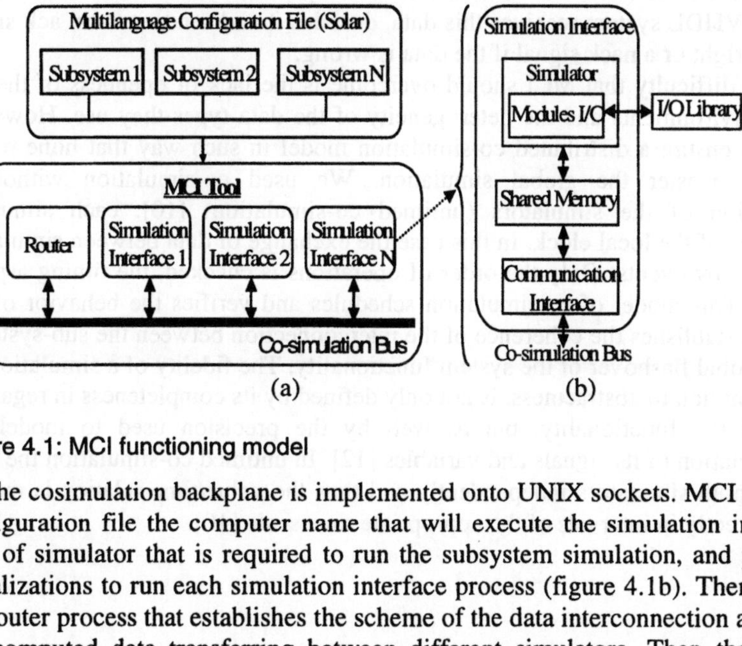

Figure 4.1: MCI functioning model

The cosimulation backplane is implemented onto UNIX sockets. MCI reads on the configuration file the computer name that will execute the simulation interface, the type of simulator that is required to run the subsystem simulation, and performs all initializations to run each simulation interface process (figure 4.1b). Then MCI loads the router process that establishes the scheme of the data interconnection and manages the computed data transferring between different simulators. Then the simulation interfaces are automatically loaded by remote connections with the local host name where MCI is running as parameter. This allows to connect each communication interface to the router by means of sockets. When the simulation interface is in the running mode, it loads the associated simulator.

Before starting the simulation processes, each subsystem specification is linked to a specific library that allows to send/receive data to/from the external world. The computed data that are sent to the external world are stored in a shared memory. This shared memory is dynamically created by the first external port computed by the simulator. After the creation of the shared memory all external ports write the values in this memory and change an update flag (data modified or data not modified). The communication interfaces extract out of the shared memory the modified data only specific flag is setting has been modified. Then it sends the new data to the router via the connected socket. The router receives this modified data and, respecting the data interconnection schema, sends the new data to the right communication interface. The communication interface receives the new data, stores it into the shared memory of the simulation interface and changes the flag of the data as modified. Finally the simulator, via the external input, receives the new data and changes the flag for not modified data.

Once the system is loaded, the designer may interact with any simulator, setting breakpoints, examining registers, change parameters, etc. This can be done during the simulation, so it can be easy to parameterize a complete system. In its current version MCI makes use of four simulators (VHDL, C, SDL, and Matlab).

Figure 4.2 shows a configuration file. We used a SOLAR intermediate form [11], an EDIF like format for the specification of configuration files. In this configuration, we can view two modules: send and receive. The send module is a SDL system and the receive module is a VHDL system. The SDL system sends a data to the VHDL system. The VHDL system receives this data, decodes it and sends it to an ack signal if the data is right or a nack signal if the data is wrong.

The main difficulty that MCI should overcome is the lack of openness of the co-simulation environments and the heterogeneity of the data types they use. However, MCI aims to ensure a distributed co-simulation model in such way that none of the tools should master the global simulation. We used co-simulation without a synchronization of the simulators (untimed co-simulation) [10], each simulator running under of the local clock. In this case the exchange of data between simulators are controlled by events. Only the order of operations is checked, the timing aspects are ignored. This model of co-simulation schedules and verifies the behavior of the system, and establishes the coherence of the interconnection between the sub-systems, showing a global flashover of the system functionality. The fidelity of a simulation, as the contrary notion to abstractness, is not only defined by its completeness in regard to modeling of the functionality, but as well by the precision used to model the value/time relation of its signals and variables [12]. In untimed co-simulation the time proceeds in both simulators independently and thus the value/time relation is merely modeled correctly in intervals of the appropriate time scale [10].

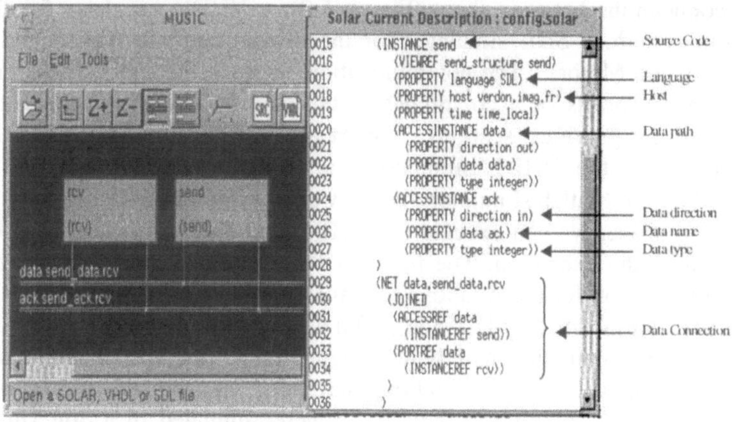

Figure 4.2: Solar Configuration File

5. Application Example

This section describes an experiment performed with the MCI tool. In this example, we modeled an Adaptive Motor Speed Control system. The system manages the motion of the set of motors in order to adjust their actual trajectory. For example, the control in a 2-D space needs a motor for each axis (X and Y) and an associated control system for a continuous movement. The system can handle up to 18 motors. However, in order to simplify the presentation, we will explain a single motor application.

As figure 5.1 shows, the Adaptive Motor Speed Control is composed of two sub-systems, Distribution and Speed Control. The Distribution sub-system provides the travelling distance to the Speed Control. The Speed Control sub-system computes the number of speed control pulses, using the specified final position and the current state of a motor, and translates them into motor control signals. This computation uses a regulation algorithm.

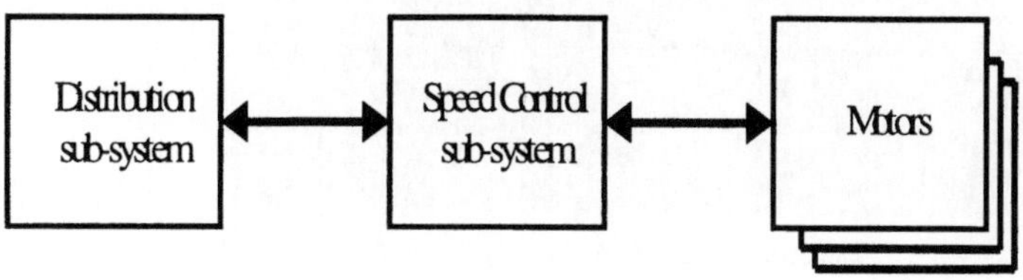

Figure 5.1: Adaptive Motor Speed Control system

The system is modeled into three sub-systems. The Distribution sub-system is modeled in SDL; the Speed Control sub-system is modeled in VHDL and the Motors are modeled in Matlab.

The entire system was simulated at the behavioral level using the MCI tool. For this purpose, we used a configuration file that describes the interfaces of each subsystem and the connections between them (Figure 5.2), a VHDL simulator for the Speed Control sub-system, a SDL simulator for the distribution sub-system and a Matlab simulator for the Motors. The communication between the sub-systems and the motors is made by means of a co-simulation bus and the simulation interface processes, described in previous sections. The results of co-simulation are the waveforms generated by the VHDL simulator, the SDL execution traces and a graphical generated by the Matlab simulator that shows the evolution of the motors.

During the debug phase, we can execute the VHDL and SDL simulators step by step in order to follow the execution. The figure 5.3 is a screen capture showing a simple co-simulation session for the Adaptive Control Speed system consisting of the execution of the SDL simulator (top-left side), VHDL simulator (top-right side) and Matlab simulator (bottom-left side and bottom-right side). The Distribution sub-system was simulated in a Sun Sparc station, the speed control sub-system was simulated in a Sun Sparc-5 station and the motors were simulated in a Sun Ultra-Sparc station.

After co-simulation, the next steps of the codesign (partitioning, communication synthesis) can be made by means of the existing tools, as MUSIC framework, and a second co-simulation can be performed to verify the time constraints.

The main advantages of this approach are the flexibility and modularity of specifications, as well as the verification of the functional completeness. The execution of appropriates symbolic or high level debuggers can be used to debug each sub-system specification. The limitations of this approach are related to the real-time applications, when the timed co-simulation is necessary. In this case, the capability of synchronizing the execution of simulators must be added in the MCI tool.

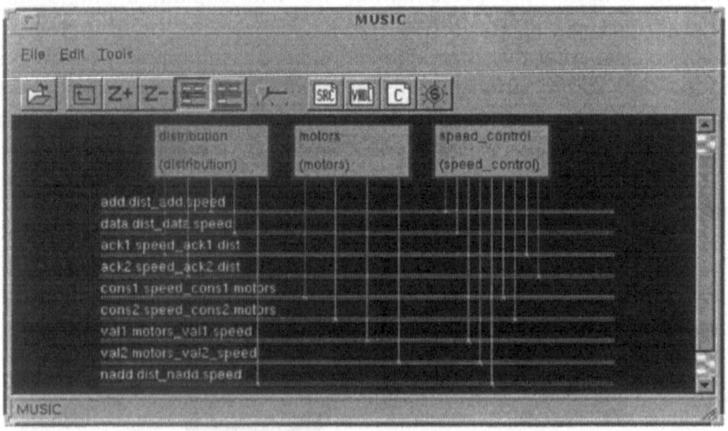

Figure 5.2: Solar configuration file

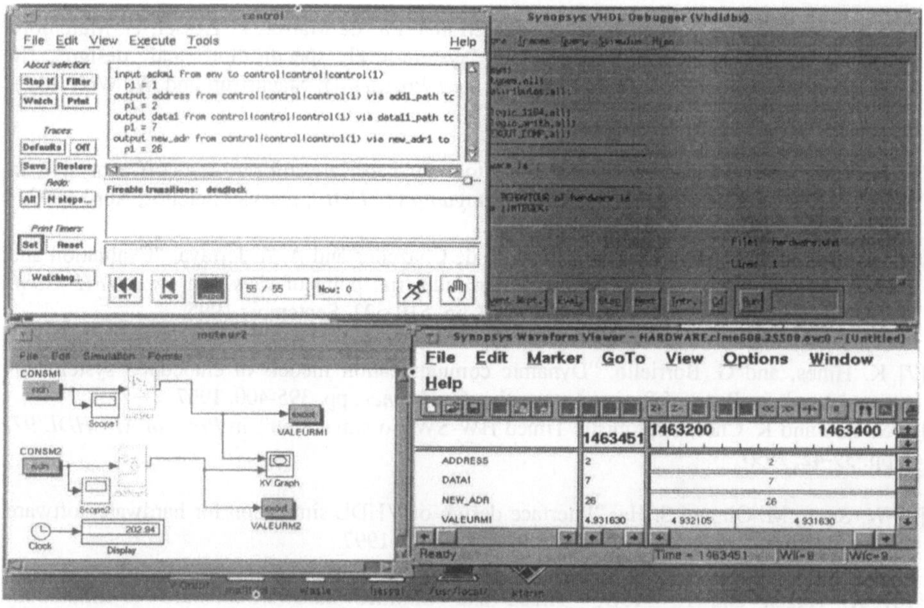

5.3: Adaptive Speed Control System co-simulation

6. Conclusions and Future work

This work presented a multilanguage distributed co-simulation tool, called MCI. It allows to co-simulating multilanguage specifications, starting with a Solar configuration file. The current version of MCI allows parallel-execution of SDL-C-Matlab-VHDL simulators and it is possible to run on a single CPU or across networks on different platforms without any additional implementation effort. Other languages can be plugged in MCI.

References

[1] D. Hermann, J. Henkel, and R. Ernst, "An approach to the adaptation of estimated cost parameters in the Cosyma system", in *Proc. Third Int'l Workshop on Hardware/Software codesign*, pp. 100-107, IEEE CS Press, 1994.

[2] W. Wolf, "Hardware-software co-design of embedded systems", *Proceedings of the IEEE*, vol. 82, pp. 967-989, July 1994.

[3] L. Lavagno, A. Sangiovanni-Vicentelli, and H. Hsieh, "Embedded system co-design: Synthesis and verification", in *Hardware/Software Co-Design* (G. DeMicheli and M. Sami, eds.), pp. 213-242, Kluwer, 1996.

[4] A. A. Jerraya, M. Romdhani, C. A. Valderrama, Ph. Le Marrec, F. Hessel, G. Marchioro and J. M. Daveau, "Languages for system-level specification and design", in *Hardware/Software Co-design: Principles and Practice* (J. Staunstrup and W. Wolf eds.), pp. 307-357, Kluwer, 1997.

[5] N. Rethman and P. Wilsey, "RAPID: A tool for hardware/software tradeoff analysis", in *Proc. IFIP Conf. Hardware Description Languages (CHDL)*, Elsevier Science, April 1993.

[6] M. Romdhani, R. Hautbois, A. Jeffroy, P. de Chazelles and A. A. Jerraya, "Evaluation and composition of specification languages, an industrial point of view", in *Proc. IFIP Conf. Hardware Description Languages (CHDL)*, pp. 519-523, September 1995.

[7] K. Hines, and G. Borriello, "Dynamic communication models in embedded system co-simulation", in *Proc. of Design Automation Conference*, pp. 395-400, 1997.

[8] S. Yoo and K. Choi, "Optimistic Timed HW-SW Co-simulation", in *Proc. of APCHDL'97*, pp. 39-42, 1997.

[9] W. Sung, M. Oh and S. Ha, "Interface design of VHDL simulation for hardware-software co-simulation", in *Proc. of APCHDL'97*, pp. 43-49, 1997.

[10] K. Hagen and H. Meyr, "Timed and Untimed hardware/software co-simulation: application and efficient implementation", in *CODES'93*, 1993.

[11] A. A. Jerraya and K. O'Brien, "Solar: An intermediate format for system-level design and specification", in *IFIP Inter. Workshop on Hardware/Software codesign*, Grassau, Germany, May 1992.

[12] K. Hagen and H. Meyer, "Modeling at different levels of abstraction within an ASIC design project", in *Modeling and Simulation (ESM)*, pp. 95-99, June 1993.

[13] C.A. Valderrama, A. Changuel, P.V. Raghavan, M. Adib, T. Ben Ismail and A.A. Jerraya, "A unified model for co-simulation and co-synthesis of mixed hardware/software systems", in *Proc. European Design and Test Conference (EDAC-EDTC-EuroASIC)*, IEEE CS Press, March 1995.

[14] D.E. Thomas, J.K. Adams and H. Schmit, "Model and methodology for hardware-software codesign", in *IEEE Design and Test of Computers*, 10(3):6-15, September 1993.

[15] H. DeMan, I. Bolsens, B. Lin, K. Van-Rompaey, S. Vercauteren, D. Verkest, "Codesign for DSP systems", in *NATO ASI Hardware/Software Codesign*, Tremezzo, June 1995.

[16] M. Srivastava, R. Brodersen, "Sierra: A unified framework for rapid-prototyping of system-level hardware and software", in *IEEE Transactions on Computer-Aided Design of Integrated Circuits and Systems*, pp. 676-693, June 1995.

6 OBJECT ORIENTED APPROACHES

RAPID PROTOTYPING OF DISTRIBUTED MECHATRONIC APPLICATIONS

Markus Deppe, Carsten Homburg

This paper presents a unified approach to optimize the information-processing structure of a distributed mechatronic system with respect to the inherent physical structure. It is based on a process-oriented model representation by means of Mechatronic Processing Objects. Hierarchical clustering mechanisms allow the treatment of parallel and distributed system architectures. The possibilities of employing a specialized dataflow processor for the rapid prototyping of distributed mechatronic applications are discussed. As an example, the design of an active vehicle suspension is presented.

1. Introduction

Mechatronic systems are complex, modern technical systems comprising mechanical, hydraulic, and electric parts that are integrated by means of information processing in order to convey optimal functionality. A typical mechatronic system consists of hierarchically organized functional units with control structures on each level.

The design process of a mechatronic system typically starts with a topological, hierarchically organized model of the system, describing the significant phenomena on a sufficiently abstract level. Based on this hierarchical, physical model of the mechatronic system, a hierarchical, partitioned information-processing structure has to be found which reflects the inherent physical structure of the system and meets real-time requirements. As a result of this process of restructuring the model and designing the information structure, the mechatronic engineer obtains a distributed model of the mechatronic system, including model partitioning, task allocation, and communication structure. Distributed hardware-in-the-loop simulations of this parallel model on a rapid prototyping hardware allow a fast and flexible validation of the control and the communication structure. The requirements and structure of the controller network in the final mechatronic product can be directly derived from this parallel model.

The approach presented is based on a process-oriented model representation by means of *Mechatronic Processing Objects*. A Mechatronic Processing Object (MPO) is a uniform model representation active at all stages from modeling to controller realization, perfectly suited for off-line and on-line numerical evaluation of the behavior of the system. Hierarchical clustering mechanisms allow the treatment of parallel and distributed system architectures. Software tools for manual or automatic model partitioning and restructuring, code generation, distributed off-line simulation, and hardware-in-the-loop simulation can work on this process-oriented model representation efficiently at short turn-around times.

Since the behavior of the system on the process-oriented representation level is described as a calculation graph, a dataflow architecture is an ideal hardware platform for the rapid prototyping of mechatronic information-processing structures. The possibilities of employing a specialized dataflow processor for the rapid prototyping of distributed mechatronic applications will be discussed in the following.

Finally, the approach presented is applied step by step to the information-processing design of an active car suspension with a distributed and hierarchical controller structure and a test implementation on a transputer network.

2. Mechatronic Processing Objects

In order to simplify modeling and to keep it apart from numerical processing, three different levels of model description languages for mechatronic systems were defined at MLaP (Hahn and Richert, 1994): O-DSS (Objective-Dynamic System Structure) on the structural level to specify the system topology by descriptions proper to the various technical disciplines, DSL (Dynamic System Language) to represent system dynamics on the mathematical level, and DSC (Dynamic System Code) as a compact, process-oriented, yet hardware-independent description of the system behavior. Each of these descriptions can automatically be transferred to the lower levels.

The efficient design and evaluation of a distributed, mechatronic information-processing structure requires very flexible facilities for model partitioning and scheduling of communication, along with short turn-around times for the derivation and download of the distributed model. Additionally, hardware-in-the-loop simulations require fast code to realize cycle rates of 1 kHz and above. To meet these demands, the *Mechatronic Processing Objects* were introduced at MLaP (Homburg, 1998).

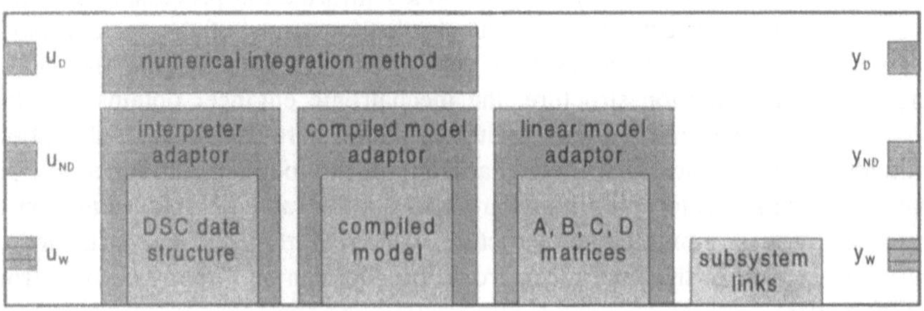

Figure 1. Mechatronic Processing Object (MPO).

A Mechatronic Processing Object (MPO) is a modular model representation on the process-oriented level based on DSC. It is an executable instance of a particular model component active at all design stages from modeling up to controller realization. The schematic architecture of a MPO is shown in Figure 1. An MPO contains the directed input-output behavior of a mechatronic system component in form of an interpretable DSC data structure, compiled machine code, or a linear matrix representation. All of these representations can be loaded and exchanged dynamically. Access to the different model representations is encapsulated in specific adaptors that can also be loaded dynamically. This allows a lean implementation that is especially necessary for hardware-in-the-loop simulations. Multiple MPOs can be interlinked to make up a complex system, and the different model representations can be mixed.

A special feature of an MPO is its ability to adapt the order of evaluating the inner equations to the coupling context; this is even possible with previously compiled model components. One system type has to be compiled just once and can then be used in any coupling context. The time-consuming task of recompilation after each modification of the coupling structure is no longer necessary. This is achieved by dividing the model code into three code classes in conjunction with black-box and white-box communication described in the next section. Regarding the input-output dependencies, the code to calculate the behavior of the system can be classified as follows (Schröer, 1994):

- *Indirect link code (ND code).* This code contains the computations of the output quantities y_{ND} that depend exclusively on the current state quantities. An immediate computation of this code is possible because no current input values are required. Multiple MPOs can execute this code class in parallel.

- *Direct link code (D code).* This code contains the computations of output quantities y_D that directly depend on the current values of the input quantities u_D. The current input values u_D must be available before computation of this code class can start. Multiple MPOs have to execute this code class sequentially.

- *State code (S code).* This code contains the computation of the state derivatives *dx/dt* and the new system state by numerical integration. The current values of all input quantities u_D and u_{ND} must be available. Multiple MPOs can again execute this code class in parallel.

For distributed, coupled MPOs a correct evaluation order of the direct link code is computed throughout the network in an initialization phase. Dynamic computation of the evaluation order at runtime is also possible.

The modular architecture of an MPO guarantees high portability of the concept presented. Each MPO as a stand-alone, active program object can be implemented by a co-routine, a thread, a process, or a process network. Minimum requirement is an ANSI-C compiler; the non-preemptive co-routine solution does not need any support by the operating system.

3. Distributed Information Processing

In order to structure the information processing of a mechatronic system, three levels of mechatronic systems were introduced at MLaP (Honekamp et. al., 1997). The lowest level is represented by *Mechatronic Function Modules* (MFMs), which encapsulate mechanical, hydraulic, or electric system components with embedded local control, each performing a very specific task. On the next level, individual Mechatronic Function Modules are coupled to make up an *Autonomous Mechatronic System* (AMS). On this level, there are mainly two different kinds of couplings. First of all, you have mechanical couplings resulting from the MFMs interacting and the passive mechanical frame of the system. Additionally, there are many information-processing interconnections to convey optimum functionality. *Cross-linked Mechatronic Systems* (CMS) represent the top level of this hierarchy. They are made up of groups of AMSs, coupled exclusively via exchange of information data.

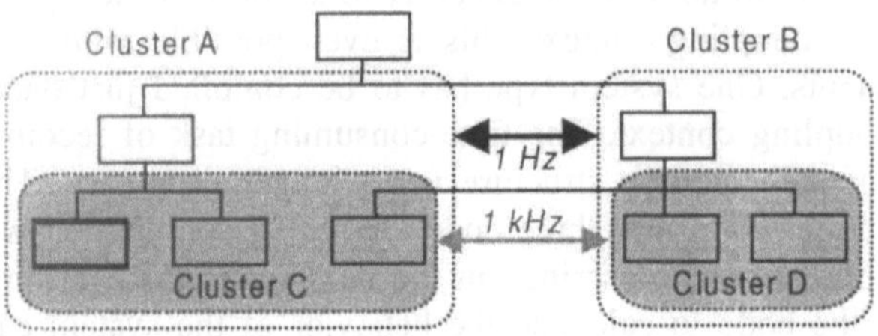

Figure 2. Structuring of the distributed information processing with clusters.

To support hierarchical, distributed information-processing structures, MPOs can be grouped to form hierarchical clusters (Figure 2). A cluster is a processing unit containing a part of the model. It can be mapped to a thread, process, processor, or even a processor network. Clusters can be hierarchically organized with possibly different communication rates on each level. In early design stages, the hierarchical model of the physical structure of the system, specified by the mechatronic engineer, typically does not map to an optimal distributed information-processing structure. The cluster concept provides additional structuring mechanisms to organize the entire system in a very efficient way as regards communication aspects and timing restrictions. In order to optimize the information-processing structure of the system and to find an efficient arrangement of MFMs, AMSs, and CMSs, the original hierarchical model of the physical structure of the system has to be restructured to map the cluster structure. Adaption of the physical model to a given cluster structure can be executed automatically by means of software tools.

Hierarchical communication at possibly different rates on each level require special consideration. MPOs provide two types of communication: The *black-box* communication contains two input operations per cluster and cycle for u_D and u_{ND} as well as two output operations for y_{ND} and y_D. This type of communication forces the MPO to act like a black box that reads inputs and writes outputs in two large steps. Intermediate input or output operations of input or output values that are already valid are not possible. With increasing cluster size, exclusive use of black-box communication will result in unnecessary deadlocks because of algebraic loops. In order to solve this problem, an MPO provides a mechanism for *white-box* communication. This mechanism allows multiple, partial input and output operations of u_D and y_D via the white-box communication variables u_W and y_w. The scheduling of input and output operations can be mastered on subcluster levels across cluster boundaries. This allows calculation of a valid evaluation order according to the coupling context on cluster level. High-level communication at typically lower communication rates is performed by black-box communication. White-box communication is especially necessary for the processing of high-frequency mechanical interactions caused by the mechanical frame of a mechatronic system. These interactions are typically handled on the lower cluster levels.

Optimization of the information-processing structure is supported by several tools. Given a specific processor network and a fixed communication rate, the DSC-based LoDiT (Homburg and Naumann, 1996) calculates a flat cluster structure with nearly optimal speedup. The result can be used as a basis for further manual structure optimizations. For the analysis of real-time properties, CHaRy (Altenbernd, 1996) can be used. It provides an input interface for DSC model descriptions. Visualization tools present partitioning results, schedules, and code dependencies according to the engineer's needs.

4. Rapid Prototyping with Dataflow Architectures

Rapid prototyping of a mechatronic system is impossible without hardware-in-the-loop simulations. The design of the distributed control and information-processing structure has to be evaluated with regard to real mechanical, hydraulic, or electric components. A suitable hardware has to provide a flexible and scalable network of processors. The simulation of complicated mechanical components with their interactions via the passive mechanical frame requires high computation and communication rates of the same order. High data throughput must be provided for the connection to the physical process. Additionally, the processing of floating-point values is necessary because in early hardware-in-the-loop simulations the engineer does not possess detailed information on the ranges of each system variable.

Dataflow processors are a promising rapid-prototyping hardware architecture that meets these requirements. A dataflow graph can be directly derived from the DSC model representation of a MPO and mapped to a dataflow processor, exploiting the inherent parallelism of the model. Dataflow subgraphs can be interpreted as parallel model partitions, representing MPO clusters. Connectivity without certain links or buses brings about easy scalability. Parallel working operators ensure low latencies.

For means of hardware-in-the-loop simulations, a specialized dataflow processor (FLYSIG) is currently under way at C-Lab (Hardt and Kleinjohann, 1997). In order to increase runtime performance the FLYSIG processor is statically configured during an initialization phase. In order to find an appropriate quantity of operators, we had a close look at several typical mechatronic systems. The example of a vehicle model is shown in Figure 3. Note the frequent occurrence of trigonometric functions, such as sine, cosine, etc., that have to be supported efficiently by the processor.

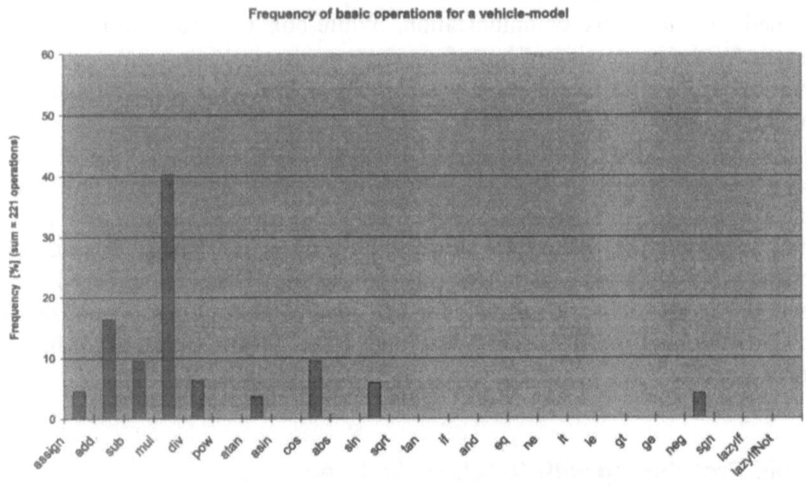

Figure 3. Frequencies of basic operations for a vehicle model.

5. Example

The approach presented here is applied to the design of an active vehicle suspension (Figure 4). The active vehicle suspension provides several advantages, such as improved riding comfort, enhanced driving safety and automatic leveling (Gillespie, 1992).

In addition to passive spring and damper elements, each suspension strut is equipped with a controlled hydraulic actuator. A main car controller computes the force setpoints for each local strut controller. The local setpoints are depending on the vertical position and velocity of the half-vehicle at each side of the car body. By this, less vertical acceleration and rolling of the car body can be achieved.

Therefore, we apply a hierarchical control concept. The local struts are typical Mechatronic Function Modules (*MFMs*) consisting of passive mechanical elements, actuators, sensors, and a local information-processing unit (controller).

For distributed simulation, it is important to partition the model appropriately. The physical topology of the model as well as its suitability for parallel computation have to be taken into account.

Models often include inherent parallel structures. The latter may help to find suitable partitions. Because of the complexity of mechatronic systems, it is necessary to apply the right granularity to partitioning. It is not useful to consider each and every equation of a model. We use the code classes of the basic systems as the smallest units.

The interdependencies of the code classes *ND*, *D*, and *S* of each basic model component make up an acyclic directed graph. The tool *DSCBIND* is able to generate such a graph automatically from the *DSC* model-description language (Figure 5).

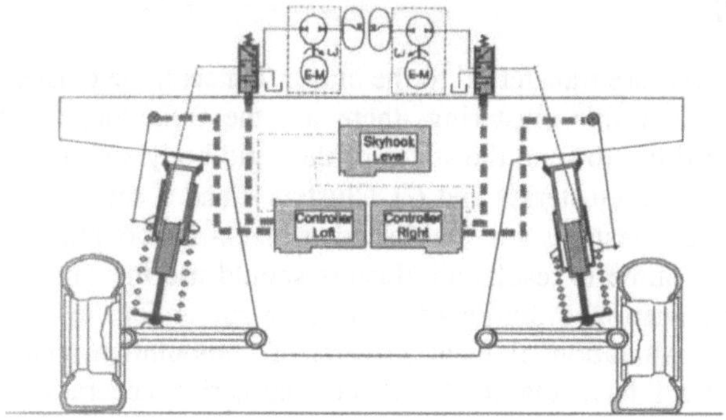

Figure 4. Half-vehicle with active suspension.

5.1 Code Structure of the Model of the Half-vehicle

The two struts are coupled to the rigid body (*RigidBody_ND, RigidBody_S*) and the main vehicle controllers (*Level_D, Skyhook_D*) by *D* code of the spring and damper basic systems (*SpringLeft_D, SpringRight_D, DamperLeft_D, and DamperRight_D*). The code relating to the struts can be entirely executed in parallel.

This inherent parallel structure leads directly to one partition of the main controllers comprising the rigid body and one partition per strut comprising the local controllers. These partitions take into account the *MFMs* of the model and allow efficient parallel computing.

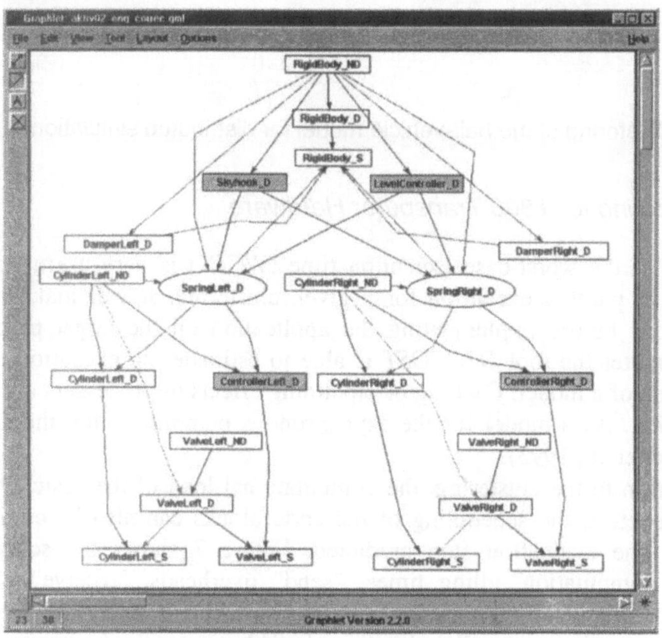

Figure 5. Code graph of the active suspension model of the half-vehicle.

5.2 Clustering

When the partitions are transferred to the cluster concept, the clusters *A*, *B*, and *C* will arise (Figure 6). For this clustering, there are the following demands on communication: cluster *B* has to send the states of the rigid body and the controller setpoints to either of the struts (clusters *A* and *C*). Clusters *A* and *C* send back the strut forces to cluster *B*. These connections are established as black-box couplings.

To gain exact numeric results all clusters should use the same rates for computation and communication. Additionally, the same solver for the differential equations should be used. Alteration of local solvers, of computation and/or communication rates (multirate) will have a large effect on the numerical accuracy.

In this example the eigenfrequencies of the rigid body ($\approx 1\ Hz$) in cluster *B* are more than ten times lower than the eigenfrequencies (wheel eigenfrequencies) of the struts in clusters *A* and *C*. Due to this, a distributed multirate simulation is also compared with the standard simulation results.

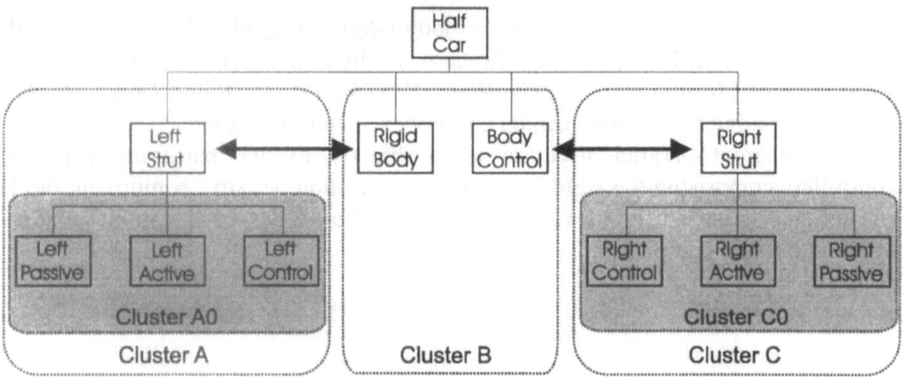

Figure 6. Clustering of the half-vehicle model for distributed simulation.

5.3 Scheduling for T800 Transputer Hardware

Prediction of the worst-case execution time (*WCET*) is very useful to evaluate the efficiency of parallel execution for a given clustering. It will make possible to do optimizations before implementing the application on the target platform. For the T800 transputer the tool *DSCCOST* is able to estimate the execution times of every basic system of a model. Caching or pipelining effects of processors are not taken into consideration. As a model for the asynchronous communication the *LogP* model is used (Culler et al., 1993).

In addition to the clustering, the computational load of the basic systems and the *LogP* parameters, the scheduling of the code blocks can also be computed and the *WCET* of one evaluation step predicted. Figure 7 shows the scheduling of our example. Computation, idling times, "send" overheads, "receive" overheads, and latencies are graphically represented.

For this example, a parallel *WCET* of *812 microseconds* in comparison with sequential *1343 microseconds* is predicted (Figure 7).

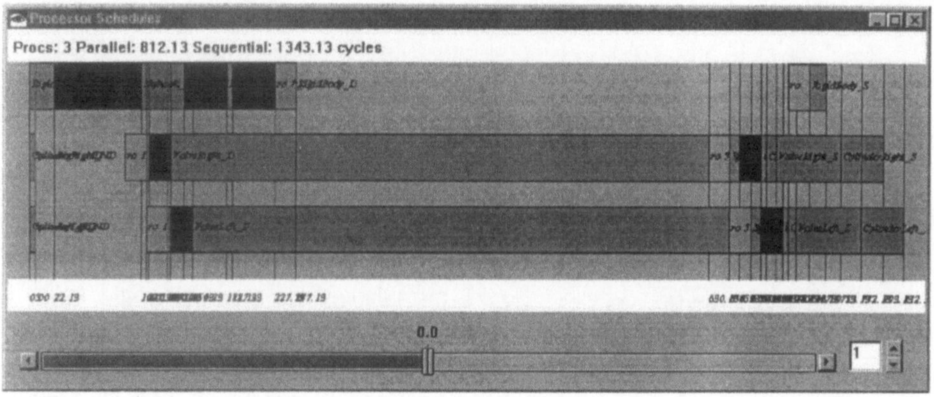

Figure 7. Graphical view of the code-block scheduling for three T800 transputers.

5.4 Simulation Results

The model described can be simulated by means of the runtime platform *IPANEMA* (Honekamp, 1998; Stolpe and Zanella, 1998)). Distributed off-line simulations on *WindowsNT* or *UNIX* hosts as well as on-line simulations on a transputer network are supported.

As an external excitation to the model, we chose a harmonic lateral body acceleration. It serves to examine cornering effects on the vehicle body. The vertical position on the outer body side and the roll angle are compared in active and in passive mode.

To simulate the model a Runge-Kutta solver of 4th order with constant stepsize was used. The simulation stepsize was *1 millisecond*. Four communication steps per major integration step are necessary. Simulation with an Euler solver at a stepsize of *0.5 millisecond* produces the same results in active and passive modes.

For the multirate simulation the solver type for the vehicle body is Euler and for the strut, Runge-Kutta of 4th order. This brought about one communication step per major integration step. Inputs during intermediate integration steps of the Runge-Kutta solver are set to the major integration step inputs. The simulation stepsize has then to be reduced to *0.5 millisecond* to bring about accurate results (Figure 8). This means about four times more calculations and the same number of communications as compared to the previous simulation.

The simulation results show the increased damping of the vehicle body during cornering in the active mode. The maximum roll angle in the active mode is less than half that of the passive mode for the chosen excitation. The model and the distributed simulation can easily be extended to a whole vehicle application with two or more axles. Then active damping for the pitch motion can also be taken into consideration.

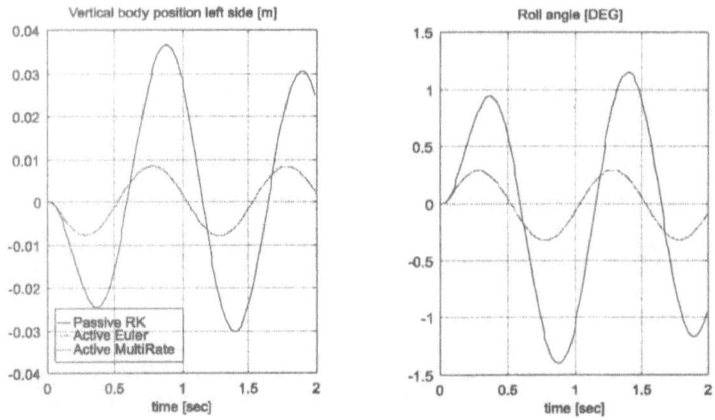

Figure 8. Simulation results for harmonic excitation with lateral acceleration of 1 Hz frequency and 1 g amplitude (cornering).

References

Altenbernd P. (1996). "On the False Path Problem in Hard Real-Time Programs." 8th *Euromicro Workshop on Real Time Systems (WRTS)*, L'Acquila, Italy.

Culler D., Karp R., Patterson D., Sahay A., Schauser K. E., Santos E., Subramonian R., Eicken T. (1993). "LogP: Towards a Realistic Model of Parallel Computation." 4th *ACM SIGPLAN Symposium on Principles and Practice of Parallel Programming*, San Diego, CA.

Gillespie T. D. (1992). *Fundamentals of Vehicle Dynamics*, Society of Automotive Engineers, Inc., Warrendale, PA.

Hahn M., Richert J. (1994). "DSS - DSL – DSC. The Three Levels of a Model Description Language for Mechatronic Systems." *Proceedings of the ICMA'94 "Mechatronics Spells Profitability"*, 777-794, Tampere, Finland.

Hardt W., Kleinjohann B. (1997). *Eine asynchrone Datenflußarchitektur für eingebettete Systeme*, Technical report 09/97, C-Lab, Paderborn, Germany.

Honekamp U. (1998). *IPANEMA - Verteilte Echtzeit-Informationsverarbeitung in mechatronischen Systemen,* Fortschr.-Ber. VDI, Reihe 20, Nr. 267. VDI-Verlag, Düsseldorf, Germany.

Honekamp U., Stolpe R., Naumann R., Lückel J. (1997). "Structuring Approach for Complex Mechatronic Systems." 30th *International Symposium on Automotive Technology & Automation – Mechatronics/Automative Electronics*, 165-172, Florence, Italy.

Homburg C., Naumann R. (1996). "LoDiT – Automatisches Partitionieren von mechatronischen Systemen für die verteilte Simulation." *10. Symposium Simulationstechnik*, 279-284, Dresden, Germany.

Homburg C. (1998). "Mechatronic Processing Objects." *12. ASIM-Symposium Simulationstechnik*, Posterband, ARGESIM Report Nr. 13, 53-60, Zurich, Switzerland.

Schröer J. (1994). *Eine Modellbeschreibungssprache zur Unterstützung der Simulation und Optimierung von nichtlinearen und linearisierten hierarchischen Systemen.* Fortschr.-Ber. VDI, Reihe 20, Nr. 128. VDI-Verlag, Düsseldorf, Germany.

Stolpe R.; Zanella M. (1998). "A Distributed Hardware-in-the-Loop Simulation Environment in Use on a Testbed of a Series Hybrid Drive." *ESM'98 – 12th European Simulation Multiconference*, Manchester, UK.

AN OO BASED METHODOLOGY FOR REAL-TIME HW/SW SYSTEMS MODELING

O.P. Dias[1], I.M. Teixeira[2], J.P. Teixeira[2], C.E. Pereira[3]

The purpose of this paper is to present a methodology for modeling, at system level, complex real-time hw/sw systems. The methodology makes use of an object-oriented modeling technique. A method is proposed to integrate the time dimension at system level specification. The method adapts some concepts of UML. The quality of the architectural solution is assessed in terms of timing constraints, performance, testability and diagnosability. The main features of the methodology are ascertained through an example.

1. Introduction

Specification and design of hardware/software systems, supported on heterogeneous technologies within the hardware (hw) and software (sw) domains, pose difficult challenges [1,2]. If the time dimension is considered, at system level, those difficulties further increase. The need of formal methodologies for hw/sw system description at architectural level, as well as the adequacy of Object-Oriented (OO) paradigm [3] and of CASE-like tools for accomplishing such needs is pointed out in [4]. It is also pointed out as desirable that "architecture performance evaluators will evolve to general evaluators of system performance". The authors in [5] and [6] have also pointed out those aspects, and proposed solutions for the raised problems.

A significant R&D effort is being undertaken in the last decade, both from academia and vendors, in the area of hw/sw systems specification, design, and simulation. The inclusion of the *time* variable, at system level specification of hw/sw systems, is not a trivial task [7,8]. In fact, most of the available literature on real-time systems specification refers, mainly, to sw systems [9-13]. For instance, some useful

[1] Escola Superior de Tecnologia/Instituto Politécnico de Setúbal, INESC, Portugal
[2] Instituto Superior Técnico (IST), Universidade Técnica de Lisboa, INESC, Portugal
[3] Universidade Federal do Rio Grande do Sul, Porto Alegre, Brasil

guidelines for such inclusion are provided in [12,13] making use of data flow analysis techniques [14] and of object-oriented models [13].
The purpose of this paper is to introduce a methodology for modeling, at system level, complex real-time hw/sw systems. The paper is organized a follows. In section 2, the methodology is presented. Section 3 describes the proposed technique to introduce the time variable, at system level. Section 4 details the metrics used for the assessment of the quality of the architectural solution. Section 5 describes a case study, which demonstrates the usefulness of the proposed methodology. Finally, section 6 summarizes the conclusions.

2.Methodology

Referring to OO paradigm, which is the basic modeling technique in our methodology, guidelines provided in [13] assume that objects and corresponding scenarios of behavior are already identified. However, UML points out *use-case diagrams*, identifying the main system functionalities and the corresponding responsible actors, as crucial tools to the design and the development processes. In this work, we follow this approach, and start the design process with use-case diagrams. This approach allows system architects to start at higher levels of abstraction, searching for a near-optimum object definition. That is, instead of starting, directly, with the static view of an OO model, we decompose high-level use-case diagrams in lower-level use-case diagrams, which allow us to identify functionality that is not immediately assigned to the already identified objects. This functional description of the problem under analysis corresponds, in fact, to its DFD[1] (Data Flow Diagram) representation [15]. In this context, a DFD corresponds to a use-case functional description. This is the approach proposed in this work. Thus, the DFD representation of use-case diagrams is a basic construct of the proposed methodology for architectural design and quality assessment. In fact, as it will be shown in section 3, it allows us to introduce *functionality* and *time* at system level specification. In fig 1 (a) and (b) an abstract example is depicted to highlight this approach.

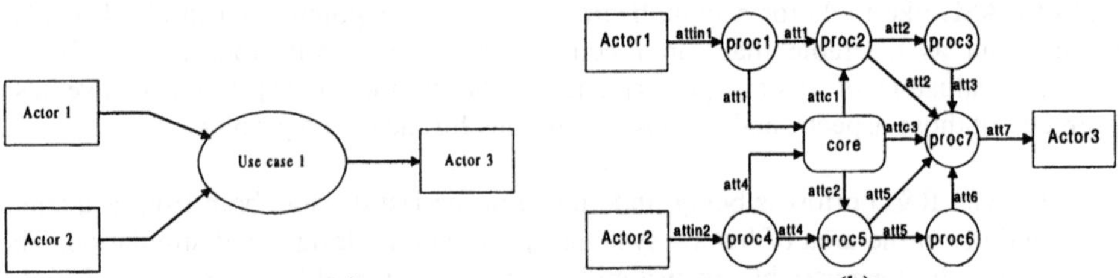

(a) (b)

Fig 1 (a) Abstract use-case diagram; (b) Processes within use-case

The proposed methodology aims at: (1) the inclusion of the time dimension at system-level specification, in order to encompass real-time hw/sw systems; (2) the generation of hw/sw system architectures that meet pre-defined functional, performance and test requirements [8,18]. As referred, the first step of the proposed methodology is applied to the DFD description of a given problem. Based on this DFD, a first directed graph (PAG, Process and Attributes Graph) is derived, in which vertices are attributes and/or processes (Fig. 2 (a), corresponding to example in fig.1). In PAG, edges represent either attribute update through a process, or a necessary input of an attribute to a process. In order to use powerful graph partitioning tools, like `Chaco` [16], a second graph (TOG, Task-Oriented Graph) is built. In TOG, vertices are *tasks.* A task is defined as the association of a process and the attribute updated by it. Hence, atomic processes are assumed [15]. `Chaco` analyses the graph (e.g., Fig. 2 (b)), in order to achieve a *task clustering* that satisfies a minimal-cut criterion. Such criterion guarantees that the resulting objects exhibit moderate cohesion, coupling and autonomy[3], which are, as will be shown, key features, both from the design and test points of view. According to a pre-specified number of graph partitions, clustering result is mapped into objects. `Chaco` is embedded in `SysObj` [6], a CASHE (Computer Aided Software Hardware Engineering) tool under development. As a result, for each number of pre-specified objects, an OO model, which is, in fact, a possible solution for system architecture, is obtained. Criteria and *quality metrics* have been formalized (section 4), and are, then, used, through `SysObj`, for assessing architecture quality.

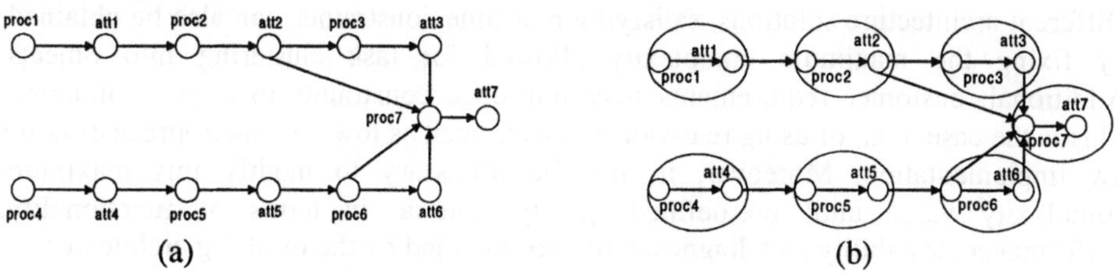

Fig. 2 (a) PAG Graph; (b) TOG Graph

3. Inclusion of Real Time Constraints

In order to include the *time* dimension, at system level specification, we assume that *task complexity* [8] may be expressed in terms of the time required to its execution. At this stage, complexity is formally quantified by assigning *weights* to the tasks. The partitioning algorithm of `Chaco` allows task weighting, which can be user's defined. Moreover, we propose that the unit of time may correspond to **delay** units, to **clock** units or to **real-time** units. By doing so, it is possible to model different types of systems.

Task execution ends when the corresponding attribute is up-dated. Two different mechanisms are introduced to assign weights to tasks. In the first mechanism, a weight is attributed to the *process* within a task, reflecting the intrinsic complexity of the process. The second mechanism consists of introducing time constraints to the *attributes* [8], thus simulating sequences, or interrupts of task execution. To achieve this purpose, we sequence the attribute update, either by associating the attribute to a number that represents its position in the sequence rank, or by describing the attribute in connection with a condition (or a guard, in OO technology).

At this phase of the hw/sw design process, weights can only be predicted, as implementation (either in hw and/or in sw) is yet to be defined. If it is not possible to reach an architectural solution that complies with real-time requirements, then the design task is restarted. The initial DFD is, hence, modified, by assigning the required functionality to other task distribution. Atomic processes are, as referred, assumed, which eases process testability and diagnosability.

An extension of the methodology proposed in [18,19] is used to derive architectural solutions. *Now*, the methodology *carries out task clustering according to the weights assigned to the tasks*. Task clustering is carried out in order to obtain a *balanced* (of equivalent complexity) aggregation of tasks. Aggregated tasks are mapped into objects leading to an architectural solution. The association to each task of the time required to its execution, thus constrains the resulting architecture. Attribute and task sequencing determines the time schedule for object activation, thus modeling real-time systems process. As the min-cut algorithm of `Chaco` is used, concurrent features are obtained, namely moderate cohesion, coupling and autonomy, for system objects. Consequently, balanced dynamic performance is achieved, thus allowing the exploitation of parallelism both in normal operation and during test sessions.

Different architecture solutions, satisfying real-time constraints, can also be obtained, by fixing the maximum complexity allowed for task clustering into objects. Additional, customer requirements may introduce constraints to object autonomy. This is the case, e.g., of using real-world objects such as low-cost microprocessors for hw implementation. Moreover, it may be necessary to modify this maximum complexity value until pre-defined quality criteria, in terms of functionality, performance, testability and diagnosability are satisfied by the resulting architecture.

4. Quality Metrics

For evaluating the quality of each solution three quality metrics are proposed, namely, object *autonomy*, object *cohesion* and *coupling* among objects [19]. Object autonomy, defined as the ratio between the number of edges inside an object, and the number of PAG edges reaching or leaving an object is an indicator of object dependence on the remaining objects. Object cohesion, defined as the ratio between the actual number of PAG edges within an object and the maximum number of edges that the object could contain without changing its attributes and methods, is an indicator of object complexity. Coupling among objects is defined as the ratio between the number of objects to which the object under analysis sends data or control, over the total number of remaining objects in the system. Coupling between objects reflects the strength of association established by a connection from one entity to another. By using it, we can estimate the influence of an object over the remaining objects within the system.

In order to decide about the quality of a given solution, based on the values obtained for autonomy, cohesion and coupling, criteria are required. In fact, as it is shown through the case study (section 5), there are no standard values that correspond to a "good" architecture. These values are bounded between two limits, (1) no clustering, leading to an elementary architecture (EA) having as many objects as tasks; and (2) full clustering, leading to a complex architecture (CA) having a single object containing all the tasks. For intermediate clustering, quality metrics are evaluated with `SysObj`, using the formal definition of the different metrics, as proposed in [18,19]. As an example of metric formulation, for an architecture with *n* objects, and discriminating between control and data attributes, *control autonomy metric*, CAt_{x_k}, for object x and index k, and *average control autonomy metric, ACAt,* are defined as:

$$CAt_{x\_k} = \frac{\sum_{i=1}^{n_{OA_{x\_k}}} \sum_{j=1}^{n_{OM_{x\_k}}} d_{o_T}(a_{i,j}) + \sum_{i=1}^{n_{OA_{x\_k}}} \sum_{j=1}^{n_{OM_{x\_k}}} d_{i_T}(a_{i,j}) + 2 \times \sum_{i=1}^{n_{OA_{x\_k}}} \sum_{j=1}^{n_{OM_{x\_k}}} d_T(a_{i,j})}{cce_{x\_k}} \tag{1}$$

$$ACAt = \frac{\sum_{k=1}^{n_{SO}} CAt_{x\_k}}{n_{SO}} \tag{2}$$

where $n_{OA_{x\_k}}$ ($n_{OM\,x\_k}$) is the number of attributes (methods) of object x_k; $a_{i,j}$ is the generic element of the Process and Attribute Matrix (PAM^2) describing the relationship among methods, j, and attributes i; cce_{x_k} represents the number of object x_k *control* edges that establish connection with other objects; $d_{o_C}(a_{i,j})$ { $d_{i_C}(a_{i,j})$ } represent the (-1) {(+1)} elements of the PAM. These edges diverge {converge} from vertice j (method) and converge {diverge} to vertice i (attribute). If $a_{i,j} = -1$ { $a_{i,j} = +1$ }, then $d_{o_C}(a_{i,j}) = 1$ { $d_{i_C}(a_{i,j}) = 1$ }; $d_C(a_{i,j})$ represent the (1) elements of the PAM. These edges identify eventual feedback in the graph. If $a_{i,j} = 1$, then $d_C(a_{i,j}) = 1$.

Using the metrics, formal criteria are required to guide the decision on what is the architectural solution that best fits system requirements. We propose the following criteria:

$$n_{SO} \ll n_{SP} \text{ (especially if } n_{SP} \gg 1) \tag{3}$$

$$n_{SO} \ni \quad ACl(n_{SO}) \leq 1 \tag{4}$$

$$n_{SO} \ni \quad ACoh(n_{SO}) = \overline{ACoh(n_{SO})} \tag{5}$$

$$n_L \; min \tag{6}$$

Here, ACl and ACoh are, respectively, the *average* autonomy and cohesion associated with each architecture, n_{SO} and n_{SP} are the number of system objects and system processes, respectively, and n_L is the number of loops among objects in the resulting architecture. The reasons for proposing these criteria are as follows: Condition (4), quantifying a experimentally verified heuristic, corresponds to the acceptance of objects with, at most, equal number of edges inside them than reaching/leaving them.

Condition (5) guarantees, in principle, that i) object complexity is not too high, not to low and ii) if it is necessary to include new functionality, this can be done without unmanageable increase of complexity. Condition (6) guarantees low and easily controllable coupling among objects. In fact, object loops should be avoided, to avoid time conflicts and to increase testability. Condition (1) gives a first estimate on n_{SO}. Experimental results show that these criteria usually lead to the high-quality architectures.

Another relevant feature of the quality of a given architecture is its testability. Hence, a set of testability oriented metrics and criteria are proposed. These metrics assess object controllability and observability, which are characteristics that quantifies the ability to reach object inputs and outputs. A formal definition of some of these metrics is [18,19]

Object Controllability

$$OCtr_{x\_k} = \frac{piafp}{iafp} \tag{7}$$

Object Observability

$$OObs_{x\_k} = \frac{poafp}{oapf} \tag{8}$$

Average System Controllability

$$ASCtr = \frac{\sum_{k=1}^{n_{SO}} OCtr_{x\_k}}{n_{SO}} \tag{9}$$

Average System Observability

$$ASObs = \frac{\sum_{k=1}^{n_{SO}} OObs_{x\_k}}{n_{SO}} \tag{10}$$

where, *piafp* is the number of primary input attributes; *iafp* is the number of input attributes; *poafp* is the number of primary output attribute *and oapf* is the number of output attributes; n_{SO} is the number of system objects. In the case study described below it is shown how these metrics can be used in order to guide the choice of the most adequate architecture.

5. Case Study

In order to ascertain the features of the proposed methodology, a generic system constituted by 8 processes and 8 actors is considered. The corresponding DFD is depicted in fig 3. Based on this DFD, different architectures can be obtained with the proposed methodology, as a result of different partitions carried out by `SysObj` and `Chaco`. In order to decide which is the architecture that best fits a given set of constraints, metrics and criteria are used as decision parameters, according to the procedure described in the previous section.

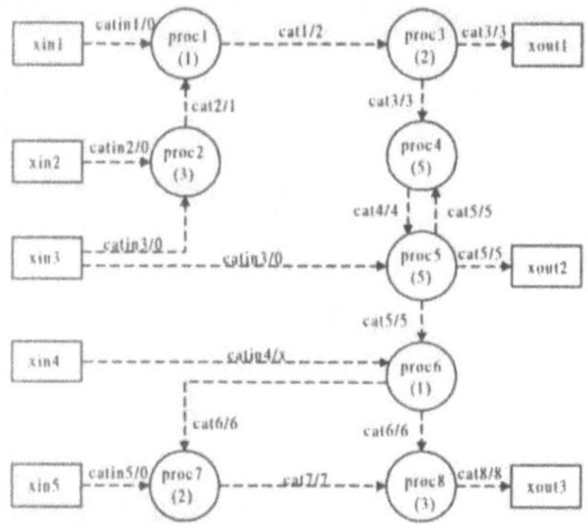

Fig 3 Data flow diagram of the generic system under study.

5.1 Decision parameters

For the DFD of Fig. 3, four different architectures are generated, corresponding to different n_{SO}. As referred, main decision parameters are average cohesion, system coupling, average autonomy and number of loops among objects (see Fig. 4).

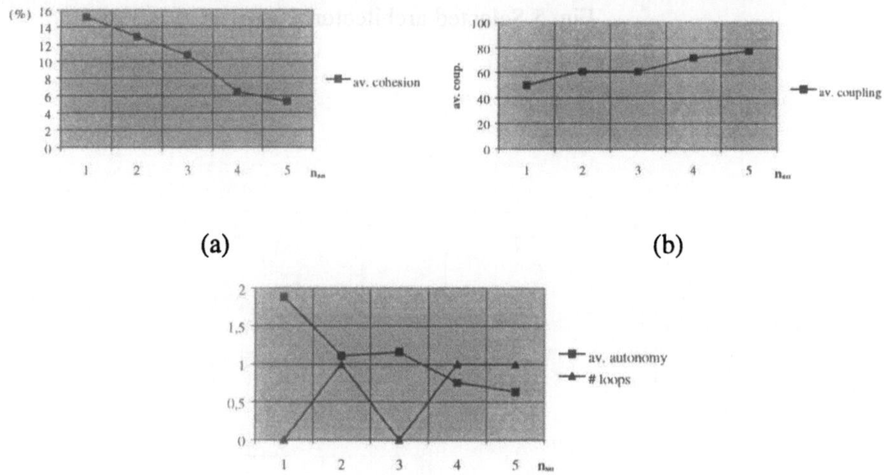

(a) (b)

(c)

Fig. 4 (a) Average cohesion (b) System coupling
(c) Average autonomy and number of loops among objects

As it can be observed, the 3-object architecture presents several advantages over the others solutions. In fact, it presents moderate coupling and cohesion, which is indicated by the equidistance among each of these values and the extreme values of the corresponding curve. Moreover it satisfies criterion (4) for the autonomy metric, and presents no loops among objects. In Fig. 5, process clustering for 3-object architecture solution is shown. The correspondent instance diagram is depicted in Fig 6.

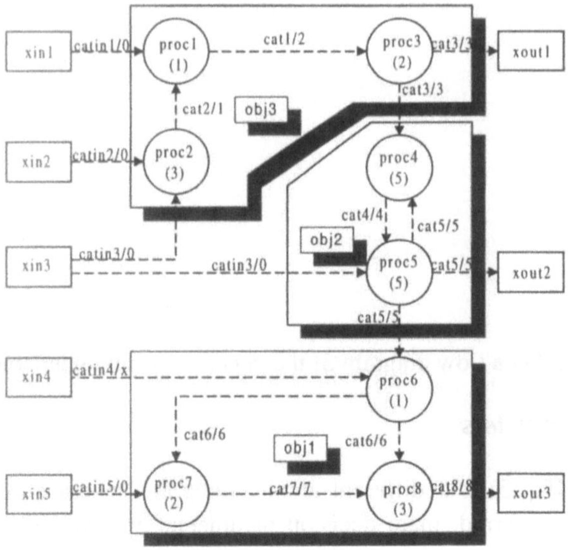

Fig. 5 Selected architecture;

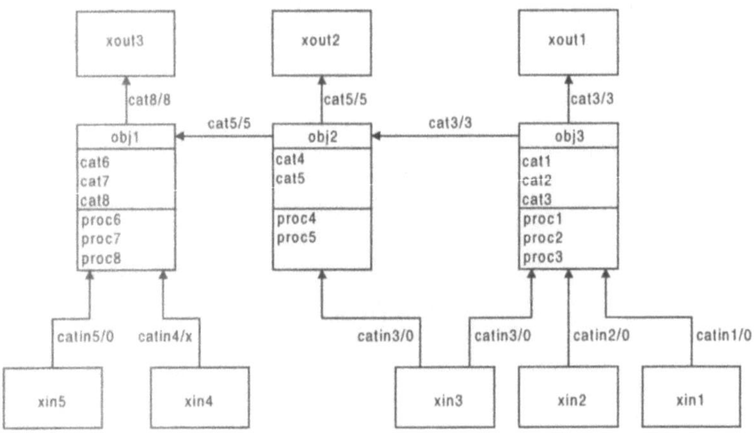

Fig. 6 Instance Diagram

5.2 Testability issues

As referred, testability issues should be taken into consideration in the choice of the best fitted architecture. In table 1, values for the different metrics are represented for the architecture solutions generated by `SysObj`. From a performance point of view, the key metrics for choosing a "good" architecture are autonomy and number of loops, whose values (Fig. 4) are repeated in this table to higlitght their correlation with testability oriented metrics, controlability and observability.

As can be observed in Table 1, the 3-object architecture solution may be chosen also as a result of using testability criteria. In fact, it does not correspond to maximum average values of controllability and observability; however, it presents the best trade-off between average and standard deviation (SD) values, and autonomy and number of loops. As a matter of fact, slightly better values for object controllability and observability are obtained with the 2-object architecture solution. However, it presents 1 loop among objects, while the 3-object solution presents no loops. Moreover, the 2-object solution may lead to objects which may be too complex to test.

nso	av. control.	SD contr.	av. observ.	SD obser.	av. auton.	SD auton.	# loops
2	37.5%	12.5%	41.6%	8.3%	1.1	0.1	1
3	41.6%	14.3%	38.8%	7.9%	1.2	0.2	0
4	37.5%	22.7%	41.6%	36.3%	0.8	0.5	1
5	33%	29.3%	46.6%	45.2%	0.6	0.5	1

Table 1- Object Controllability and Observability: average values and standard deviations (SD).

6. Conclusions

In conclusion, a methodology for the generation of real-time hw/sw system architectures has been proposed. The time dimension is introduced in the DFD corresponding to a use-case functional description, through task weighting. As a consequence, the time variable constrains the final architecture solution. The `SysObj` tool automatically generates a limited subset of possible architectures, and quality metrics and criteria are introduced for architecture quality evaluation. Both design and test features of the proposed architectures are taken into account. The design team is, hence, supported in the decision process, leading to a target 'best-fitted' architecture. A case study has been presented, that shows the usefulness of the proposed methodology.

Endnotes

[1]It is well known that a DFD doesn't convey information about process hierarchy or time sequence. In fact, it is, merely, a planar (at a given level of detail) representation of data and data transformation through processes.

[2] PAM is the description of the directed graph (representing the DFD), in which vertices are processes and/or attributes and edges represent either attribute update through a process, or a necessary input of an attribute to a process.
[3]These concepts are defined on section 4.

References

[1] D.D.Gajski et. al. "Specification and Design of Embedded Systems", Prentice Hall, 1994.

[2] L. Lavagno, A. Sangiovanni-Vincentelli, H. Hsieh, "Embedded System Codesign", Nato ASI-Series, Kluwer Academic Publishers, 1996.

[3] J.Rumbaugh, "OMT papers", 94/95, http://www.rational.com/support/techpapers/omt/.

[4] "System Design Technology Roadmap", Europe's Road to the Future, Version Final, Jan., 1998.

[5] M. Calha, J.P. Teixeira, I.C. Teixeira, "HW/SW Specification Using OOM Techniques", Proc. of the 7th IEEE Int. Workshop on Rapid Systems Prototyping, pp. 96-101, 1996.

[6] O.P. Dias, I.C. Teixeira, J.P. Teixeira, "Architectural Quality Evaluation for High-Level DFT", Proc. Int. IFIP Workshop on Logic and Architectural Synthesis (IWLAS), pp. 185 – 193, Grenoble, December, 1997.

[7] B. Selic, B, G. Gullekson, P. Ward, " Real-Time Object-Oriented Modeling", John Wiley & Sons, Inc., ISBN 0-471-59917-4, 1994.

[8] M. Awad, J. Kuusela, J. Ziegler, "Object-Oriented Technology for Real-Time Systems: A Practical Approach using OMT and Fusion", Prentice Hall, 1996.

[9] J. Gwinn, "Object-Oriented Programs in Real-time", ACM SIGPLAN Notices, Vol. 27, No. 2, Feb 1992, 1992.

[10] R.S. Pressman, "Software Engineering. A Practitioner's Approach" Fourth Edition, MacGrawHill, 1997.

[11] J. Rumbaugh, M. Blaha, W. Premerlani, F. Eddy and W. Lorensen, "Object-Oriented Modeling and Design", Prentice Hall, 1991.

[12] "UML - Unified Modeling Language", version 1.0, Rational Software Corporation, January, 1997, .http://www.rational.com.

[13] G. Booch, "Object-Oriented Design with Applications", The Benjamin/Cummings Publishing Company, Inc., 1994.

[14] C. Pereira, A. Frigeri, P. Darscht, W. Halang. "Object-Oriented Development of Real-Time Industrial Automation Systems", IFAC Triennial World Congress, San Francisco USA, pp. 321-326. ISBN:0-08042923-8, July 1996.

[15] O. P. Dias, I. C. Teixeira J. P. Teixeira, C.E. Pereira,"Design and Quality Assessment of Real-Time Hw/Sw Systems Architectures", accepted for presentation at the Design of Integrated Circuits and Systems Conference (DCIS), Madrid, Nov. 1998.

[16] B. Hendrickson, R. Leland, "The Chaco User's Guide – Version 2.0", Technical Report SAND95-2344, Sandia National Laboratories, Albuquerque, NM 87185-1110, July 1995.

[17] "Complexity Measurements", http://www.mccabe.com/appnote/complex.html.

[18] O. P. Dias, I. C. Teixeira J. P. Teixeira, C.E. Pereira,"Performance and Test Oriented Metrics and Criteria for Hw/Sw Design at System Level", Proceedings of Design and Diagnostics of Electronic Circuits and Systems Workshop (DDECS), pp. 219-225, 1998.

[19] O. P. Dias, I. C. Teixeira, J. P. Teixeira,"Metrics and Criteria for Quality Assessment of Testable Hw/Sw Systems Arquitectures", accepted for inclusion in the special issue of the Journal of Electronic Testing : Theory and Applications (JETTA), to appear at the end of 1998.

MODELING DISTRIBUTED STATE AS AN ABSTRACT OBJECT

Pertti Kellomäki and Tommi Mikkonen
Tampere University of Technology
P.O.Box 553, Fin-33101 Tampere, Finland
{pk, tjm}@cs.tut.fi

1. Introduction

Object-oriented software development emphasizes the use of abstractions. Inheritance is used for factoring common structure and functionality to abstract classes, providing abstract interfaces to objects. This helps in avoiding premature implementation bias.

Current methods of software engineering, such as OMT (Rumbaugh *et al.*, 1991), focus on the behavior of implementation level objects. In distributed systems, however, we can also identify abstractions that arise from the cooperation of several objects. These abstractions help in explaining the collective behavior of objects in more high level terms. An example of such abstractions is the way various components of a telephone network cooperate in order to provide a phone call.

Formal approaches to object-oriented development like Z++ (Lano, 1991) or VDM++ (Durr *et al.*, 1992) also usually focus on the behavior of single objects. In this paper, we use the DisCo specification method (Järvinen, 1992), (Järvinen *et al.*, 1991), which has been explicitly designed for expressing collective behavior in terms of synchronous actions. The DisCo language has a formal basis in the joint action theory (Back *et al.*, 1988), (Järvinen *et al.*, 1990) and Temporal Logic of Actions (Lamport, 1994), which gives DisCo specifications an unambiguous meaning. We can thus reason informally or formally about the behavior described by a DisCo specification. Moreover, a DisCo specification can be used as a precise reference to answer questions about the intended behavior of the system.

We see the possibility of early validation and verification of behavioral properties as the main advantage of our approach. When abstractions are expressed using a precise notation, we can use them for more than just conveying informal intuition. Animation can be used when specifications are validated by experts of the application domain, and informal or formal reasoning may be used for verifying temporal properties of the specification.

The rest of this paper is structured as follows. Section 2 introduces the basics of the DisCo method. Section 3 discusses abstractions and their temporal behaviors, and gives an example of such an abstraction. Section 4 discusses validation and verification using explicit abstractions of cooperation. We focus on effects on early stages of development. Related work is presented in Section 5, and Section 6 lists the main conclusions.

2. The DisCo method

In this section we give a short overview of DisCo, a specification method and language for the specification of reactive systems. For the purposes of this paper, the most important issues are the closed world principle, superposition, and preservation of properties in a refinement.

The approach adopted in DisCo is to begin the development by identifying variables and interactions whose role is fundamental to the behavior. The variables at this level may represent implementation-level entities such as phones, or abstractions such as phone calls. Details are then added in a modular manner, allowing implementation of the high-level abstractions by using more concrete objects.

In DisCo, variables are defined in terms of classes that are patterns for objects. Each object can be understood as a structured variable. Objects may contain local variables, references to other objects, and nested statemachines similarly to Statecharts (Harel, 1997). In addition, objects can be associated with each other by using relations.

The underlying computational model is based on *joint actions*, where a number of *objects* may exchange information. An action may be executed whenever suitable objects for which the action *guard* evaluates to true exist. Action execution is atomic, and nondeterministic choice is used for modeling concurrent activities. Actions are given in the format:

name(participants):
when guard
-> body,

where *participants* is a list of formal names for the participating objects, *guard* is a boolean-valued expression, and *body* is a sequence of statements.

At a high level of abstraction, it is not always clear who initiates operations, especially if several objects are involved. The joint action approach considers this to be an implementation detail that can be deferred, and therefore does not indicate which component initiates the execution of an action. Adopting this simplification liberates us from programming-level abstractions, making the approach suitable for high level specification where only the information exchanged and the commitment of the communicating parties is of interest (Kurki-Suonio *et al.*, 1997).

2.1. Closed-World Principle

The closed-world principle is the philosophical backbone of the DisCo methodology. Each DisCo specification is a complete description of a system in the sense that it describes all the possible changes to the variables introduced in the specification. The closed world principle implies that every DisCo specification models both a system and its environment, thus facilitating reasoning about their collective behavior.

Any introduction of new properties, referred to as a refinement, reveals more properties of the system, but cannot allow behaviors that the more abstract level does not allow. Thus, refinements can be understood analogous to dimensions of vectors. The analogy extends to the possibility to project the behavior of the system into a certain set of refinement steps.

2.2 Superposition and Preservation of Properties

DisCo specifications may be nondeterministic. Refinement steps may be used to superimpose stronger constraints on nondeterminism, by introducing new variables and operations on them. Operations may only assign to variables introduced in the same refinement step. Thus, a DisCo refinement can be understood as a system-wide layer, that applies advantages of program slices (Weiser, 1992) to specification. The method enforces that *safety properties* ('Something bad will never happen') introduced in one specification layer cannot be invalidated in subsequent layers. As guards of actions can be made stronger, preservation of *liveness properties* ('Something good will eventually happen') are not guaranteed by construction.

With such refinements, a specification can be "broadened" by providing new aspects as well as "deepened" by introducing new details on how some operations are implemented. The former allows incremental specification when the specification is still incomplete, whereas the latter enables implementation of an operation by using a more concrete representation. In practice, there may not always be clear distinction between the two.

3. Cooperation as an object

In a distributed system, the state of a high level abstraction, such as a phone call, may be distributed in the local states of several objects. We make the state of the abstraction explicit by representing the abstraction as an object. This helps in focusing on the collective behavior instead of the details of a distributed implementation. The explicit object describes the state of several distributed objects in a centralized fashion.

The use of a specification language with precise semantics enables us to use the abstractions for more than informal sketching. Behaviors can be expressed and validated with abstractions, with the assurance that the high level properties are not invalidated in later refinement steps.

In the following, we give an example of an abstraction of cooperation, and discuss its distributed implementation. Consider a mobile phone system that consists of phones and base stations. Each phone can be linked to a base station via a radio link, and base stations can establish links among themselves to route calls. We impose the rather unrealistic restriction that only one phone at a time may be connected to a base station.

When a phone moves about, it may disconnect from one base station and connect to another. If the phone is involved in a call, the connections between base stations are modified accordingly. Thus, a handover is possible, where a phone disconnects from one base station and connects to another during a call. A phone call consists of three connections: one connection between the base stations, and connections between the phones and the base stations. Over the duration of a call, any one of these connections may be changed.

3.1 Abstract Level

Even though a phone call is clearly a central notion in explaining how the system works, it is not part of the class hierarchy of the specification of the mobile phone network. It would not make much sense to inherit a phone call class in either phones or base stations. Nor is a phone call a subsystem composed of the connections, since the connections may be changed on the fly. Rather, a phone call is the result of cooperation between the phones and base stations.

By making this cooperation explicit, we can create a simpler model that can be used for verification and validation of high level properties of the system. We next give a specification of the mobile phone system where the call abstraction is represented as an explicit object. In this specification, a phone may be on or off, indicated by boolean variable *on*. In addition, each phone call contains a data field *parties*, a set of phones. The actions of the specification can be given as follows:

```
connect(p1, p2 : phone; c : call):
when c.parties = { }
   and p1.on
   and p2.on
   and forall c2 : call: (p1 in c2.parties or p2 in c2.parties) = false
   -> c.parties := {p1, p2},

disconnect(c : call):
   when not c.parties = { }
   -> c.parties := { },

on(p : phone):
   when not p.on
   -> p.on := true,

off(p : phone):
   when p.on
   -> p.on := false.
```

The model given by the specification is highly nondeterministic. Two phones that are in state *on* and not involved in a phone call may arbitrarily be connected, and a phone call may be disconnected at any time. However, the model can already be used to give exact answers to questions about the behavior of the system. For example, we can ask whether it is possible for more than two phones to be involved in a call, or whether "zombie" calls where one of the phones is in state *off* are possible. Validation and verification of such issues are discussed separately in Section 4.

The abstract phone call serves as a convenient place for storing various attributes a call might have: who is paying for the call, what is the duration of the call, etc.

3.2 Distributed Level

Once we are satisfied that the abstract specification captures our informal requirements, we use DisCo refinements to derive a less abstract specification of the system. For instance, the abstract call discussed earlier can be implemented by three connections: two between phones and base stations, and one between two base stations. We omit the specification here for brevity.

Due to the use of superposition, the specification of the distributed level formally contains the call objects introduced at the abstract level. However, we can justify an implementation where calls do not exist as implementation level objects if we can show how the state of each call can be computed. This also implies that the properties expressed in terms of abstract calls hold in such an implementation. The following invariant shows how the state of a call is computed (*connected* is the obvious relation). This may be established either informally of formally, as discussed in Section 4. The invariant is:

forall c **in** call, p1, p2 **in** phone:
    c.parties ={p1, p2} **implies**
        exists b1, b2 **in** basestation:
                connected(b1, b2)
            and connected(p1, b1)
            and connected(p2, b2).

4. Validation and verification

Verification and validation take place at all levels of design. At the highest level of abstraction, we validate the behavior of the abstract model against the requirements. We can also assert properties that a valid specification should possess, and attempt to verify these with informal reasoning or formal proofs. At lower levels, we may additionally verify invariants that show how higher-level abstractions are correctly implemented using objects that are closer to the implementation level.

4.1 Validation

Abstractions are particularly useful when the development involves people with no computing background. High-level operations performed by abstract objects enable such participants to use familiar concepts in validation, instead of using concepts arising from available implementation techniques.

If we only use implementation-level entities in validation, the essence of behavior is obscured behind implementation details. On the other hand, validating high-level abstractions whose behavior is not well defined is of little use. A combination of suitable abstractions and a well defined language for expressing them are thus needed.

The DisCo language has an operational interpretation, so an instance of the specification may be animated with the DisCo animation tool (Systä, 1991). Animation is particularly useful for embedded systems, where the behavior of the system as a whole is essential. Industrial experience also supports the use of animations (Isojärvi, 1997).

4.2 Verification

In addition to validating the behavior of a high level specification, we may also formulate properties that should hold if the specification correctly reflects our requirements. For example, we might want each phone to be involved in at most one call at a time, formulated as

forall c1, c2 **in** call, p **in** phone:
  p **in** c1.parties **and** p **in** c2.parties
    implies c1 = c2.

If this assertion is included in the specification, the animation tool evaluates the assertion after each step, and informs the user in case of a violation. This helps in catching errors when a specification is being developed.

Since the language has a precise semantics, we can also verify properties either informally or formally. In simple cases informal reasoning may be sufficient, but if more assurance is desired, the specification may be mechanically mapped to the logic of the PVS (Owre *et al.*, 1992) theorem prover, where mechanical formal verification may be carried out (Kellomäki, 1997). The assertions presented in this paper have been verified in this manner.

The DisCo specification methodology encourages the use of abstractions that are later implemented with lower level entities. This incurs an obligation to show that the abstractions are correctly implemented. These proof obligations are invariants linking abstract and concrete variables, and they can be verified with the desired level of formality.

5. Related work

In (Awad *et al.*, 1997), Awad and Ziegler recognize the need for representing collective behavior explicitly. They propose using Statecharts of a 'floating nature' to capture aspects of the behavior that cuts across objects and classes. This is very close to our approach. However, unlike them, we use a language with a formal basis which makes it possible to use the abstraction for early validation and verification.

Increasing use of design patterns (Gamma et al., 1995), (Buschmann et al., 1996) can be interpreted to bear goals similar to the discussed approach. The development is initiated by using abstractions of inter-object cooperation, referred to by using the name of the pattern. However, unlike in pattern-oriented development, we have a well-defined state for the abstractions as well, providing enhanced validation and verification facilities.

6. Conclusions

We presented an approach for modeling distributed state as an object. Despite being an abstraction, such an object can bear significant information for early validation and formal verification. Thus, use of high-level abstractions results in an increased confidence that the resulting system will be satisfying.

Acknowledgments

This research has been partly supported by the Academy of Finland (project 40500).

References

Awad, M. and Ziegler, J. (1997). A pracatical approach to object-oriented state modeling. *Software - Practice and Experience*, 27(3):311-328, Mar. 1997.

Back, R.J.R and Kurki-Suonio, R. (1988). Distributed cooperation with action systems. *ACM Transactions on Programming Languages and Systems*, (10):513-445.

Buschmann, F., Meunier, R., Rohneert, H., Sommerlad, P., and Stal, M. (1996) *A System of Patterns.* John Wiley & Sons.

Durr, E.H. and van Katwijk, J. (1992). VDM++ - A formal specification language for object-oriented designs. In *Technology of Object-oriented Languages and Systems*, Prentice-Hall International, pages 63-78. Proceedings of Tools Europe '92.

Gamma, E., Helm, R., Johnson, R., and Vlissides, J. (1995). *Design Patterns: Elements of Reusable Object-Oriented Software.* Addison-Wesley.

Harel, D. (1987). Statecharts: A visual formalism for complex systems. *Science of Computer Programming*, 8(3):231-274, June 1987.

Isojärvi, S. (1997). DisCo and Nokia: Experiences of DisCo with modeling real-time system in multiprocessor environment. FMEIndSem'97, Otaniemi, Finland, February 20, 1997.

Järvinen, H.-M. and Kurki-Suonio, R. (1991). DisCo specification language: marriage of actions and objects. In *Proceedings of the 11th International Conference on Distributed Computing Systems*, IEEE Computer Society Press, pages 142-151.

Järvinen, H.-M., Kurki-Suonio, R., Sakkinen, M., and Systä, K. (1990). Object-oriented specification of reactive systems. *In Proceedings of the 12th International Conference on Software Engineering*, IEEE Computer Society Press, pages 63-71.

Kellomäki, P. (1997). Verification of reactive systems using DisCo and PVS. In J. Fitzgerald, C.B. Jones, and P. Lucas, editors, *FME'97: Industrial Applications and Strengthened*

Foundations of Formal Methods, number 1313 in Lecture Notes in Computer Science, Springer-Verlag, pages 589-604.

Kurki-Suonio, R. and Mikkonen, T. (1997). Liberating object-oriented modeling from programming-level abstractions. In J. Bosch and S. Mitchell, editors, *Object-Oriented Technology: ECOOP'97 Workshop Reader*, number 1357 in Lecture Notes in Computer Science, Springer-Verlag, pages 195-199.

Lamport, L. (1994). The temporal logic of actions. *ACM Transactions on Programming Languages and Systems*, 16(3):872-923, May 1994.

Lano, K.C. (1991). Z++, an object-orientated extension to Z. In J.E. Nicholls, editor, Z User Workshop, Oxford 1990, Workshops in Computing, Springer-Verlag, pages 151-172.

Owre, S., Rushby, J.M., and Shankar, N. (1992). PVS: A prototype verification system. In D. Kapur, editor, 11th International Conference on Automated Deduction, number 607 in Lecture Notes in Artificial Intelligence, Springer-Verlag, pages 748-752.

Rumbaugh, J., Blaha, M., Premerlani, W., Eddy, F., and Lorensen, W. (1991). *Object-Oriented Modeling and Design.* Prentice Hall.

Systä, K. (1991). A graphical tool for specification of reactive systems. In *Proceedings of the Euromicro'91 Workshop on Real-Time Systems*, IEEE Computer Society Press, pages 12-19.

Weiser, M. (1982). Programmers use slices when debugging. *Communication of the ACM*, 25(7):446-452, July 1982.

DESIGN RATIONALE OF THE PURE OBJECT-ORIENTED EMBEDDED OPERATING SYSTEM[1]

Friedrich Schön*,
Wolfgang Schröder-Preikschat,
Olaf Spinczyk,
Ute Spinczyk

University of Magdeburg
Universitätsplatz 2
D-39106 Magdeburg, Germany
{olaf,ute,wosch}@cs.uni-magdeburg.de

** GMD FIRST*
Rudower Chaussee 5
D-12489 Berlin, Germany
fs@first.gmd.de

The PURE project aims at providing a portable, universal runtime executive for deeply embedded parallel/distributed systems. The phrase "deeply embedded" refers to systems forced to operate under extreme resource constraints in terms of memory, CPU, and power consumption. The notion "parallel/distributed" relates to the fact that embedded systems are becoming more and more complex in terms of architectural viewpoints. This paper discusses design issues of a family-based, object-oriented operating system targeting the area of deeply embedded systems in the above-mentioned sense. It is shown that a modular system consisting of a large number of reusable abstractions can be compiled to a fairly small and compact entity.

1. Introduction

Embedded systems are becoming more and more important --- and they are becoming more and more complex. Getting through daily life without being faced with electronically controlled devices is almost unthinkable. This holds not only for the general consumer market regarding cameras, HIFI, kitchen aids, washing machines etc., but also for other markets such as aircraft or automotive industries. Today's limousines, for example, can be considered (large scale) distributed systems on

[1] This work has been supported by the Deutsche Forschungsgemeinschaft (DFG), grant no. SCHR 603/1-1.

wheels. There are cars in daily operation consisting of over 60 networked processors (i.e. μ-controllers). Although these systems are quite large with respect to the number of μ-controllers, they are still small with respect to memory size. In the above mentioned case, 1-2 MB of global memory (for the entire embedded distributed system) is not uncommon --- and this would already be more than luxurious. Typically, a single μ-controller-based *electronic control unit* (ECU) will be equipped with less than 4 KB of memory.

The complexity of these "decentralized computer architectures" can be managed no longer by the application alone. Dedicated embedded operating systems are required to ensure manageability, adaptability, portability, and yet efficiency of the software. In addition, the resulting software structure must promote, and neither hinder nor prevent, the application of formal methods to gain clear statements on correctness and safety of the resulting system complex.

This paper describes the design concepts of the PURE embedded (distributed/parallel) operating system and discusses first implementation results. PURE is targeting deeply embedded systems, as e.g. automotive systems, and aims at providing a *portable, universal runtime executive* for resource-sparing (real-time) applications.

2. Design Approach

The approach followed by PURE is to understand an operating system as a *program family* (Parnas, 1979) and to use *object orientation* (Wegner, 1986) as the fundamental implementation discipline. The former concept (program families) helps prevent the design of a monolithic system organization, while object orientation enables the efficient implementation of a highly modular system structure.

2.1 Incremental System Design

The program family concept does not dictate any particular implementation technique. A so called "minimal subset of system functions" defines a platform of fundamental abstractions serving to implement "minimal system extensions". These extensions, then, are made on the basis of an *incremental system design* (Habermann, 1976), with each new level being a new minimal basis (i.e., *abstract machine*) for additional higher-level system extensions. A true application-oriented system evolves, since extensions are only made on demand, namely, when needed to implement a specific system feature that supports a specific application. Design decisions are postponed as long as possible. In this process, system construction takes place bottom-up but is controlled in a top-down (application-driven) fashion. In its last consequence, applications become the final system extensions. The traditional boundary between application and operating system disappears. The operating system extends into the application, and vice versa.

Inheritance is the appropriate technique to either introduce new system extensions or replace existing ones by alternate implementations. Either case, the system extensions are customized with respect to specific user demands and will be present at runtime only in coexistance with the corresponding application. Thus, applications are not forced to pay for (operating system) resources that will never be used.

2.2 Revival of Program Families

Applying the family concept in the software design process leads to a highly modular structure. Because of the strong analogy between the notions of "program family" and "object orientation" (Figure 1), it is almost natural to construct program families by using an object-oriented framework (Cordsen, 1991).

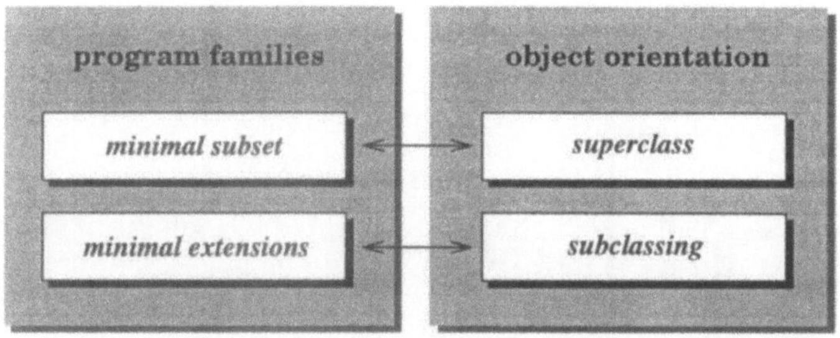

Figure 1. Program families vs. object orientation

Both approaches are, in a certain sense, dual to each other. The minimal subset of system functions in the program family concept has its counterpart in the superclass of the object-oriented approach. Minimal system extensions are thus introduced by means of subclassing. Inheritance and polymorphism are the proper mechanisms to allow different implementations of the same interface to coexist. Code reuse is significantly enhanced, increasing the commonalities of different family members.

In the realm of embedded distributed/parallel systems, inheritance must be applicable even in the case of crossing address space, node, and network boundaries (Nolte, 1998). This aspect is significant for the PURE development. The program family concept is the fundamental design principle. Object orientation is primarily being used as an implementation, not a design instrument.

2.3 Operating-System Construction Set

PURE is an open operating system. All its abstractions are revealed to system designers or even application programmers. The entire system is represented as a library, or a set of libraries, of small and "handy" object modules. These modules are small with respect to the number of exported references to functions or variables. This helps, e.g., state-of-the-art binders creating slim-line operating systems that contain only those components used (i.e. referenced) by a given application. Prerequisite however is a highly modular system architecture --- and this is achieved by a family-based design and an object-oriented implementation.

PURE has much in common with OSKit (Ford, 1997). Instead of inventing a new system architecture, as e.g. done with the Exokernel approach (Engler, 1995), PURE provides abstractions that allows one to construct many of those architectures. An operating-system architecture is not prescribed by PURE. Rather, a construction set for the development of operating systems is established. Whether an operating system is monolithic or based, e.g., on micro-kernel technology, is up to the actual "mechanic" who uses PURE elements to create a product according to some blueprint. In order to create a tailor-made operating system, the blueprint comes from the application itself.

3. System Architecture

The coarse structure of PURE in addition to the correlation to some (maybe automotive control) application is depicted in Figure 2.

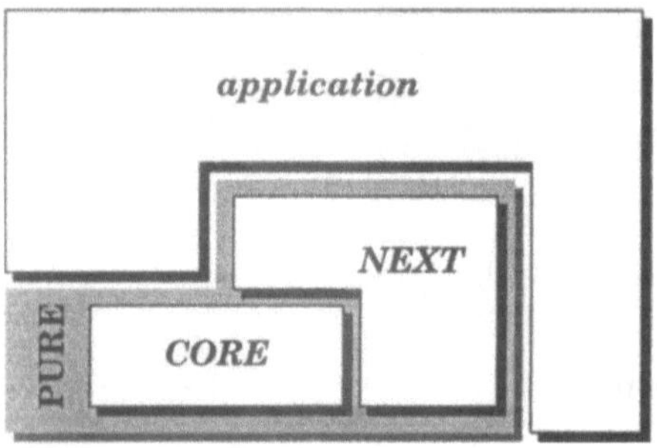

Figure 2. System architecture

PURE is made of a nucleus and nucleus extensions. The nucleus implements a *concurrent runtime executive*, i.e. CORE, for passive and active objects. By means of minimal *nucleus extensions*, NEXT, features such as application-oriented process and address space models, blocking (thread) synchronization, and problem-oriented (remote) message passing are added to the system. These extensions are present only if demanded by the application. They transform the nucleus into a distributed abstract thread processor.

3.1 The Nucleus

CORE implements a *minimal subset of system functions* for the scheduling of events and/or actions. Events are implemented by (hardware) interrupts, while actions are implemented by (featherweight) threads. The functions are provided by four building blocks:

1. the *flange*, i.e. abstractions for the attachment of objects to trap/interrupt vectors and propagation of exceptional events to higher levels,
2. the *sluice*, i.e. abstractions for the synchronization of interrupt-driven activities in an interrupt-transparent manner (i.e. without disabling of hardware interrupts),

3. the *signal-box*, i.e. abstractions for the non-blocking synchronization of active objects (i.e. threads), and
4. the *threads reel*, i.e. abstractions for the construction, scheduling, and destruction of active objects.

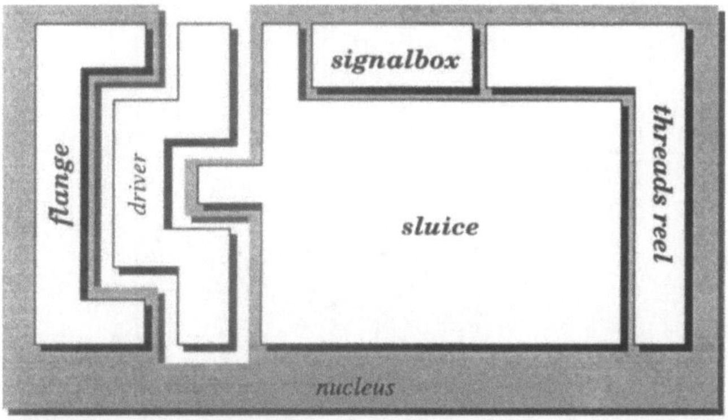

Figure 3. Nucleus building blocks

Figure 3 shows a fifth building block, the (device) *driver*, which is to be taken into account in a complete system design. However, in PURE, device drivers are not really part of the nucleus, but of NEXT or even the application. Solely, CORE provides mechanisms for a smooth integration of driver modules. In addition to enabling the attachment/detachment of driver abstractions to/from CPU exception vector entries (supported by *flange*), functions are provided (by *sluice*) for the synchronization of interrupt-driven code. Drivers are considered a glue between non-synchronized and synchronized parts of a PURE-based system.

3.2 The Nucleus Family

Depending on the actual application requirements, the nucleus building blocks appear in different configurations. Each of these configurations represent a member of the nucleus family. An excerpt from the nucleus family tree is shown in Figure 4.

The picture indicates six family members, each of which implements a specific operating mode. Each member is built by one or more function blocks and described by a functional hierarchy of these blocks. The function blocks can be reused in various configurations. In order not to restrict the family, design decisions have been postponed as far as possible and encapsulated by higher-level abstractions. As a consequence, PURE can be customized, for example, with respect to the following scenarios:

1. One way of operating the CPU is to let PURE run *interruptedly*. This family member merely supports low-level trap/interrupt handling. The nucleus is free of any thread abstraction. It only provides means for attaching/detaching exception handlers to/from CPU exception vectors (*interruption*).

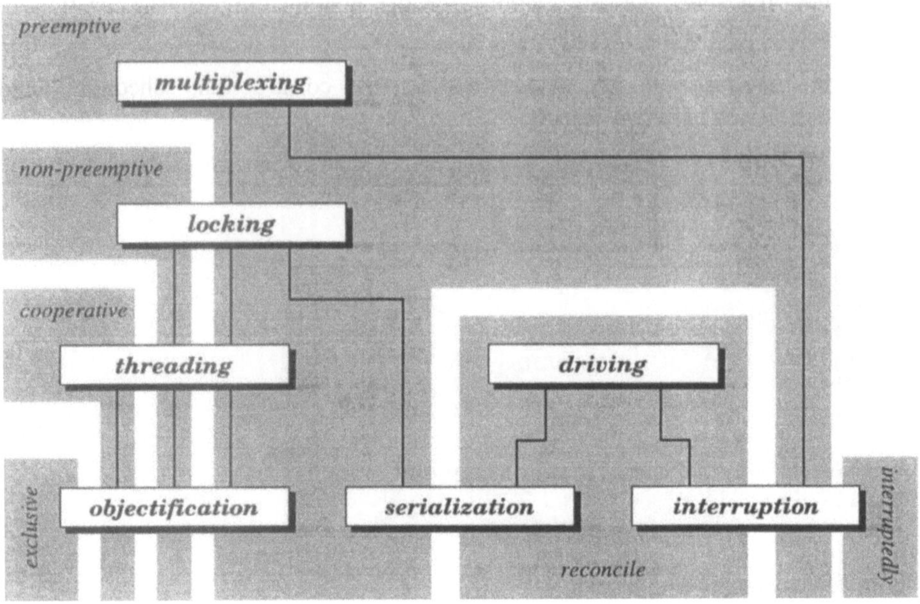

Figure 4. Nucleus family tree

2. In order to *reconcile* the asynchronously initiated actions of an *interrupt service routine* (ISR) with the synchronous execution of the interrupted program, a minimal extension to 1. was made. The originating family member ensures a synchronous operation of event handlers (*driving*) in an interrupt-transparent manner (*serialization*).

3. The second basic mode of operating the CPU means *exclusive* execution of a single active object. In this situation, the nucleus provides only means for *objectification* of a single thread. The entire system is under application control, whereby the application is assumed to appear as a specialized active object. There is only a single active object run by the system.

4. A minimal extension to 3. leads to *cooperative* thread scheduling. No other design decisions are made except that threads are implemented as active objects and scheduled entirely on behalf of the application (*threading*). There may be many active objects run by the system.

5. Adding support for the serialized execution of thread scheduling functions (*locking*) enables the *non-preemptive* processing of active objects in an interrupt-driven context. Thread scheduling still happens cooperatively, however the nucleus is prepared to schedule threads on behalf of application-level interrupt handlers. Actions of global significance, and enabled by interrupt handlers, are assumed to be synchronized properly (*serialization*).

6. Multiplexing the CPU between threads in an interrupt-driven manner establishes the autonomous, *preemptive* execution of active objects. In this

case, NEXT extends the nucleus by a device driver module (*multiplexing*) taking care of timed thread scheduling.

Comparing Figure 4 to Figures 2 and 3, the flange takes care of interruption, sluice is responsible for serialization, the threads reel implements locking, threading, and objectification, and NEXT covers (device) driving and (CPU) multiplexing.

3.3 Interrupt Transparency

A crucial aspect in the design of (embedded) operating systems concerns interrupt handling, in particular the synchronization of asynchronously initiated execution of code fractions. The underlying model has to be efficient and should also reduce the periods of times during which interrupts are physically disabled to an absolute minimum. Ideally, at software level, interrupts should never be disabled at all. The PURE concept follows this ideal pattern and, thus, ensures *interrupt transparency*: at no time, PURE disables (hardware) interrupts, or exploits special CPU instructions, for synchronization purposes.

In order to safely execute interrupt-driven concurrent code, a PURE-based interrupt handling subsystem, such as a device driver, is to be structured into two parts. The first part, the *prologue*, is attached to some CPU exception vector and will be immediately started upon signaling a hardware interrupt to the CPU. The second part, the *epilogue*, is considered a prologue continuation and will be started only if critical sections are inactive. Prologues always execute with the actual hardware priority. Except in the case of non-maskable interrupts (NMI), a high-priority prologue thus may prevent the invocation of a lower (or same) priority prologue. In contrast, epilogues always execute with all interrupts enabled, similar to the NMI case.

Prologues and epilogues are (logically) loosely coupled by a *guard* who takes care of the invocation of pending epilogues at the right moment. When a prologue wishes to start a continuation, it hands over to the guard the epilogue object to be synchronized/serialized. If the guard is free, the epilogue is called without any further delay. Otherwise, the epilogue is made pending and will be scheduled when the guard becomes free again.

A guard behaves like a *semaphore*, except that the delayed objects are not active (i.e. processes) but passive. The currently running, but interrupted, thread will never block when epilogues are to be made pending. The guard maintains a queue of epilogue objects. Since the guard operates in an interrupt-driven context, its queue operations need to be synchronized. This happens in an interrupt-transparent manner. A queuing strategy has been implemented that enables the dequeue operation, in order to run delayed epilogues upon leaving a guarded section, to be overlapped by enqueue operations issued by an interrupt handler (i.e. prologue). In addition, enqueue operations are allowed to overlap themselves, e.g. when a high-priority interrupt handler preempts a low-priority interrupt handler. In contrast to the PURE predecessor PEACE (Schröder-Preikschat, 1994), all necessary synchronization measures run with interrupts enabled. In PURE, the actual interrupt priority of a running process will never be defined by software, but only by the hardware.

4. Analysis

The PURE system is implemented in C++ and runs (as guest level and in native mode) on i80x86-, i860-, sparc-, and ppc60x-based platforms. A port to C 167-based, "CANned" μ-controllers is in progress. At the time being, the nucleus consists of over 100 classes exporting over 600 methods. Every class implements an abstract data type. Inheritance is employed extensively to build complex abstract data types. For example, the thread control block is made of about 45 classes arranged in a 14-level class hierarchy. Thus, PURE is of really high modular structure. This rises the question of costs in terms of memory consumption and performance.

4.1 Memory Consumption

As Table 1 shows, the highly modular nucleus structure still results in a small and compact implementation. Basis are the members of the nucleus family tree described along with Figure 4. The numbers were produced using GNU g++ 2.7.2.3 for the i586 running Linux Red Hat 5.0.

family member	size (in bytes)			
	text	data	bss	total
interruptedly	812	64	392	1268
serialize	1882	8	416	2306
exclusive	434	0	0	434
cooperative	1620	0	28	1648
non-preemptive	1671	0	28	1699
preemptive	3642	8	428	4062

Table 1. PURE memory consumption

A PURE implementation is represented in two different ways. In the development phase, a procedure-based system representation founds the basis. In this case, every class serves as compilation/binding unit. In the prototyping phase, a macro-based system representation is used. In this case, class methods are the compilation/binding units. Compared to a PURE development system, memory consumption of a PURE prototype is about 3-7 times smaller, but system generation time can be the 23-fold.

4.2 Performance

Figure 6 shows the number of (i586) CPU clock cycles spent during interrupt processing. The clock frequency in this experiment was 166 MHz and the measurement was made reading the i586 (on-chip) counter register. Again, the above-mentioned C++ compiler was used.

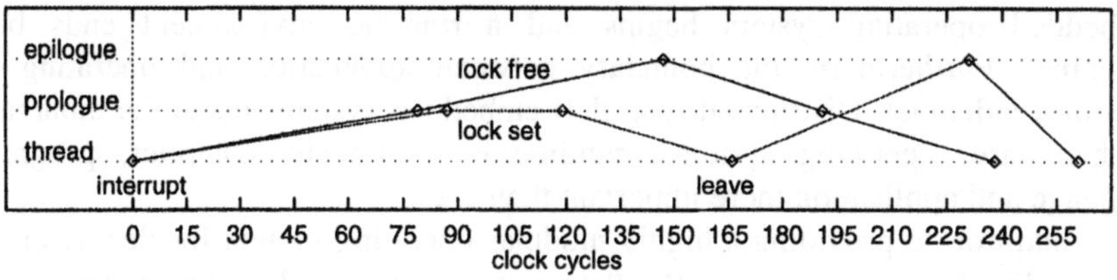

Figure 6. Interrupt latency

At clock 0, a thread will be interrupted. The numbers show that, depending on whether a guard is free (*lock free*) or locked (*lock set*), normal thread execution will be suspended for about 238 resp. 261 clock cycles. Prologue execution starts with clock tick 79 resp. 87. The minor difference is due to the different program instrumentations for the lock-free and lock-set cases. Epilogue execution starts with clock cycle 147 resp. 231. The difference of 84 cycles indicates the best-case delay of an epilogue when the guard is locked. Further delays depend on two factors: (1) the time to *leave* the guarded section[2] and (2) the number of preceding epilogues in the queue. Delaying an epilogue takes 32 clock cycles and propagating a delayed epilogue takes 65 clock cycles. Both phases pass through the interrupt-transparent queue synchronization. Resuming an interrupted thread when a prologue terminates costs 47 clock cycles. This is independent of whether the thread was interrupted inside or outside a guarded section. Leaving an epilogue takes 44 resp. 30 clock cycles. The difference is due to the different actions to be taken when returning from a lock-free or a lock-set case.

The numbers for thread scheduling depend on the employed nucleus family member (refer to Figure 4). They range from 49 clock cycles (*cooperative*) to 300 clock cycles (*preemptive*). All these performance figures demonstrate the still "featherweight" structure of PURE, although quite a large amount of abstractions (classes, modules, functions) are involved in all the occurrences. But: "*It is the system design which is hierarchical, not its implementation*" (Habermann, 1976).

5. Conclusion

Deeply embedded operating systems have their own raison d'être. They are designed to specifically support the execution of (control) applications under extremely limited resource constraints. In consideration of the specific demands of these applications, it becomes extremely difficult, if not impossible, successfully adopting existing operating systems.

In the realm of embedded systems consisting of several tens of interconnected (autonomous) μ-controllers, the operating-system design is crucial to meeting the application demands. A lightweight system structure is required, meaning to advance into traditional frontier districts of operating systems. The boundary where an

[2] The worst-case execution path of a guarded section has not yet been determined. However, it will be in the order of 300 cycles, which relates to the overhead of timer-driven thread rescheduling.

embedded operating system begins and a runtime environment ends becomes indistinct. Furthermore, the boundary between application and operating system becomes indistinct. Distributed (parallel) embedded systems make the amalgamation of hardware, operating systems, runtime environments, compiler, programming language and application more important than ever.

In addition to providing a highly modular operating system for deeply embedded parallel/distributed systems, the PURE project can be seen also as an experiment in the exploitation of object orientation for the implementation of resource-sparing system software. The "old-fashioned" program-family concept has been applied consequently to create featherweight system abstractions. In addition, "standard" development tools have been used for system generation. The results are quite promising --- but not yet totally satisfactory.

Future work concentrates on the development of an operating-system workbench. The idea is to offer to system and even application programmers a set of tools that enable the construction, static/dynamic configuration, and (automatic) generation of application-oriented operating systems. The workbench will be evaluated using an object-oriented "workpiece" of the OSEK operating system (OSEK, 1997), i.e. creating a "PURE-ly slim" but yet extensible family member for automotive systems.

References

OSEK/VDX Steering Committee (1997). OSEK/VDX Operating System, October 1997. Version 2.0 revision 1.

Cordsen, J. and Schröder-Preikschat, W. (1991). "Object-Oriented Operating System Design and the Revival of Program Families." In *Proceedings of the Second International Workshop on Object Orientation in Operating Systems (I-WOOOS '91)*, pages 24-28, Palo Alto, CA, October 17-18.

Engler, D. R. and Kaashoek, M. F. and O'Toole Jr., J. (1995) "Exokernel: An Operating System Architecture for Application-Level Resource Management." In *Proceedings of the Fifteenth ACM Symposium on Operating System Principles*, pages 251-266, Copper Mountain Resort, Colorado.

Ford, B. and Back, G. and Benson, G. and Lepreau, J. and Lin, A. and Shivers, O. (1997). "The Flux OSKit: A Substrate for Kernel and Language Research." In *Proceedings of the Sixteenth ACM Symposium on Operating System Principles*, pages 38-51, Saint-Malo, France.

Habermann, A. N. and Flon, L. and Cooprider, L. (1976). "Modularization and Hierarchy in a Family of Operating Systems." *Communications of the ACM*, 19(5):266-272.

Nolte, J. and Schröder-Preikschat, W. (1998). "Dual Objects -- An Object Model for Distributed System Programming." In *Proceedings of the Eighth ACM SIGOPS European Workshop, Support for Composing Distributed Applications*, http://www.acm.org/sigops/EW98/papers.html.

Parnas, D. L. (1979). "Designing Software for Ease of Extension and Contraction." *Transaction on Software Engineering*, SE-5(2).

Schröder-Preikschat, W. (1994). "The Logical Design of Parallel Operating Systems." *Prentice Hall International*, ISBN 0-13-183369-3.

Wegner, P. (1986). "Classification in Object-Oriented Systems." *SIGPLAN Notices*, 21(10),:173-182.

MIX
Papier aus verantwortungsvollen Quellen
Paper from responsible sources
FSC® C105338

If you have any concerns about our products,
you can contact us on
ProductSafety@springernature.com

In case Publisher is established outside the EU,
the EU authorized representative is:
Springer Nature Customer Service Center GmbH
Europaplatz 3, 69115 Heidelberg, Germany

Printed by Libri Plureos GmbH
in Hamburg, Germany